International Human Resource Management:
Managing People in a Multinational Context

Peter J. Dowling
University of Tasmania, Australia

Denice E. Welch
Norwegian School of Management

Randall S. Schuler
New York University

South-Western College Publishing
an International Thomson Publishing company I(T)P®

Cincinnati • Albany • Boston • Detroit • Johannesburg • London • Madrid • Melbourne • Mexico City
New York • Pacific Grove • San Francisco • Scottsdale • Singapore • Tokyo • Toronto

Publisher/Team Director: Dave Shaut
Executive Editor: John Szilagyi
Marketing Manager: Joe Sabatino
Developmental Editor: Alice Denny
Production Editor: Sally Nieman
Production House: Cover to Cover Publishing
Cover Designer: Jennifer Lynne Martin
Cover Photograph: image Copyright © 1998 PhotoDisc, Inc.
Internal Designer: Joe Devine

Library of Congress Cataloging-in-Publication Data

Dowling, Peter.
    International human resource management : managing people in a
    multinational context / Peter J. Dowling, Denice E. Welch, Randall
    S. Schuler.
        p.   cm.
    Includes bibliographical references and index.
    ISBN 0-538-86137-1
    1. International business enterprises--Personnel management.
    I. Welch, Denice E.   II. Schuler, Randall S.   III. Title.
    HF5549.5E45D69   1998
    658.3--dc21   98-28947
                                                                 CIP

    3 4 5 6 7 8 WE 5 4 3 2 1 0

Printed in Canada

I(T)P ®
International Thomson Publishing
South-Western College Publishing is an ITP Company.
The ITP trademark is used under license.

P R E F A C E

The globalization of business is having a significant impact on human resource management. The integration of European markets and of North American markets, along with developments in the Asia-Pacific region, is heightening this impact tremendously. It is more imperative than ever for firms to engage in human resource management on an international scale. This involves decisions concerning:

- the numbers and proportions of host-country nationals, third-country nationals, and parent-country nationals in staffing plants and offices all over the world;
- where and how to recruit these individuals, how to compensate them, and manage their performance; and
- whether human resource practices will be uniform across all locations or will be tailored to each location.

While sometimes these decisions are partially answered by the firm's international strategy and the countries in which it operates, there still remains a great deal of latitude in the design of the final package of international human resource management practices.

This third edition of *International Human Resource Management: Managing People in a Multinational Context* touches on human resource practices in many of the countries of the world. The primary focus of the book, however, is on the choices of international human resource management practices that confront multinational enterprises and some factors to consider in making those choices.

The book has been organized into nine chapters and one appendix containing a number of resources in international HRM. Chapter 1 begins with a description of international human resource management and what differentiates it from domestic human resource management.

Chapter 2 examines the organizational context of international HRM, including the impact of international growth on the firm's structure and internal control processes. It also looks briefly at the way in which mode of operation affects HR decisions. Recruitment and selection of international employees is the focus of Chapter 3, and Chapter 4 identifies the issues and choices in international performance management.

Chapter 5 discusses the dimensions of international training and development while Chapter 6 covers the many issues pertaining to international compensation and benefits. Chapter 7 is a new chapter that examines in some detail the important topic of repatriation. Chapter 8 examines the complexities and differences in labor relations when operating as a multinational firm and Chapter 9 examines issues and trends in managing a global workforce.

The appendix raises a number of challenging research issues in international human resource management and covers some resources (such as Web sites) available to students interested in this evolving field. We have included, where relevant, minicases to illustrate key points, along with new exhibits. The improvement in text presentation and coverage is a result of our own teaching, and the feedback provided by colleagues and students.

The contents of this edition reflect the overall development of the field. The past decade has seen a dramatic rise in the level of interest in the various aspects of international human resource management—from academics and practitioners alike. This is reflected in the movement away from the predominance of research on more practical expatriate management issues to looking at broader strategic IHRM issues and subsidiary concerns, and to theoretical development. As such, one could suggest that IHRM is no longer a field of scientific inquiry in its infancy. This trend is also recognition of the critical importance of managing people in a multinational context.

AACSB and Course Design

This book can be used in a variety of ways:

- It may be used as the main text in a course in international HRM. We would recommend the latest edition of *Readings and Cases in International Human Resource Management* by Mark Mendenhall and Gary Oddou as an excellent supplement.
- Or, it may be used as one of several texts in a comparative management or international management course, in combination, for example, with *International Dimensions of Organizational Behavior*, 3e, by Nancy Adler and/or *International Management: Concepts and Cases* by Arvind Phatak.

- A third use may be as a supplement to a traditional introductory HRM course to bring an international dimension into the course and satisfy AACSB requirements.

Acknowledgments

Consistent with the previous editions, our intent was to produce a book that is useful for students and practitioners alike. We have sought the input of both managers practicing international human resource management and academics teaching and researching international human resource management. Various colleagues around the world have assisted us also in the preparation of this edition. Their feedback provided insight in adding, deleting, and refining sections and chapters of the book. We send our appreciation to the following colleagues:

Sharif N As-Saber, Massey University
John Boudreau, Cornell University
Chris Brewster, Cranfield School of Management
Lorraine Carey, University of Tasmania
Helen De Cieri, University of Melbourne
Marilyn Fenwick, Monash University
Marion Festing, University of Paderborn
Cathy Fisher, University of Tasmania
Rebecca Marschan, Copenhagen Business School
Michael Poole, Cardiff Business School
Marja Tahvanainen, Helsinki School of Economics
Wolfgang Weber, University of Paderborn
Lawrence Welch, Norwegian School of Management
Patrick Wright, Cornell University
Cherrie Zhu, Monash University

We thank John Szilagyi, acquisitions editor; Alice Denny, developmental editor; Sally Nieman, production editor; and Joe Sabatino, our marketing manager at South-Western College Publishing for working with us and getting the book into its final form. Finally, we wish to thank Fiona Dowling and our families for their help and encouragement throughout this project.

Peter J. Dowling
Denice E. Welch
Randall S. Schuler

A B O U T T H E
A U T H O R S

P**eter J. Dowling** (Ph.D., The Flinders University of South Australia) is Professor of Management and Dean of the Faculty of Commerce & Law at the University of Tasmania, Australia. Previous teaching appointments include Monash University, the University of Melbourne, and California State University–Chico. He has also held visiting appointments at Cornell University, Michigan State University, and the University of Paderborn, Germany. His current research interests are concerned with international HRM, the cross-national transferability of HRM practices and strategic HRM. Professor Dowling has co-authored two books (*Human Resource Management in Australia*, with Randall Schuler, John Smart, and Vandra Huber, and *People in Organizations: An Introduction to Organizational Behavior in Australia*, with Terence Mitchell, Boris Kabanoff, and James Larson). He has also written or co-authored over forty journal articles and book chapters, and serves on the editorial boards of *Asia Pacific Journal of Human Resources*, *Human Resource Planning*, *International Journal of Human Resource Management*, and *Thunderbird International Business Review*. He is a former national vice president of the Australian Human Resources Institute, past editor of *Asia Pacific Journal of Human Resources* (1987–1996), and a Life Fellow of the Australian Human Resources Institute. His management development and consulting work includes the retail, mining, telecommunications, and finance industries in Australia, and a management development program for the nonferrous metals industry in the People's Republic of China.

Denice E. Welch (Ph.D., Monash University) is Associate Professor of International Management at the Norwegian School of Management in

Oslo, Norway, and Adjunct Professor, University of Western Sydney-Nepean, Australia. Previously, she was a senior member of the teaching staff at the Graduate School of Management, Monash University, Australia; and has held visiting positions at the Helsinki School of Economics and Business Administration, Finland; and the Copenhagen Business School, Denmark. Her research interests include international HRM, multinational management and internationalization. She has published extensively in international referenced journals (such as the *Journal of Management Studies*, *International Business Review*, *International Journal of Human Resource Management*, and *Human Resource Planning*) and conference proceedings. She has been on the Program Committee for many European International Business Academy meetings and was the Australian representative on the Board for this professional body (1993–94). She was Co-Organizer and Co-Chair of the European Institute for Advanced Studies in Management Conference on "Managing in Different Cultures" in Paris, France, 1992; Co-Chair of the 3rd Workshop in International Business in Vaasa, Finland, 1996; and Co-Chair of the 1998 Nordic Workshop in International Business, in Oslo, Norway. She is a member of the Academy of International Business, the European International Business Academy, and the Academy of Management.

Randall S. Schuler is Professor, Stern School of Business, New York University. His interests are international human resource management, strategic human resource management, the human resource management function in organizations, and the interface of business objectives and human resource objectives. He has authored or edited over thirty books including *Managing Quality*, *Human Resource Management: Positioning for the 21st Century*, 6e, *Case Problems in Management and Organizational Behavior*, 4e, *Human Resource Management in the Information Age*, *Managing Human Resources*, 5e, and *Managing Job Stress*. In addition, he has contributed over thirty chapters to reading books and has published over one hundred articles in professional journals and academic proceedings. Presently, he is Associate Editor of the *Journal of Business and Economic Studies* and is on the Editorial Boards of *European Management Journal*, *Academy of Management Review*, *Organizational Dynamics*, *Human Resource Planning*, *Human Resource Management*, *The International Journal of Human Resource Management*, *Asia Pacific Journal of Human Resources*, *Journal of Occupational Behavior*, *Journal of Occupational Health Psychology*, and *Journal of High Technology*

Management Research. He is a Fellow of the American Psychological Association, and is past editor of the *Human Resource Planning* journal. In addition to his academic work, he has conducted numerous executive and management development workshops in the United States, Europe, and Australia. His current consulting work focuses on aligning human resource activities with the needs of the business, realigning the structure of human resource departments to better serve the needs of the business, and developing HR vision statements and action strategies for human resource departments to pursue into the 21st century.

C O N T E N T S

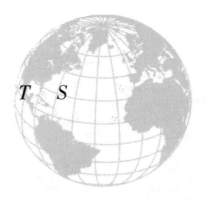

Chapter 1

Introduction and Overview   1

Chapter 2

The Organizational Context   29

Chapter 3

International Recruitment and Selection   69

Chapter 8
Labor Relations   231

Chapter 9
Issues, Challenges, and Theoretical Developments in IHRM   261

Appendix   307

Index   315

C H A P T E R   *1*
Introduction and Overview

As more firms move outside their domestic borders into the dynamic world of international business, the globalization of world markets appears to be gaining momentum. The last two decades, in particular, have seen dramatic changes in international trade and business. Once-safe markets are now fierce battlegrounds where firms aggressively fight for market share against foreign and domestic competitors. It is, therefore, not surprising to find that a large proportion of the workforce in an increasing number of firms, regardless of their national origin, is located in other countries. These trends are likely to continue well into the 21st century.

This globalization of business is forcing managers to grapple with complex issues as they seek to gain or sustain a competitive advantage. Faced with unprecedented levels of foreign competition at home and abroad, firms are beginning to recognize not only that international business is high on top management's list of priorities but that finding and nurturing the human resources required to implement an international or global strategy is of critical importance. Effective human resource management (HRM) is essential, especially for small and medium firms where international expansion places additional stress on limited resources, particularly people. As Duerr[1] points out:

> Virtually any type of international problem, in the final analysis, is either created by people or must be solved by people. Hence, having the right people in the right place at the right time emerges as the key to a company's

1

international growth. If we are successful in solving that problem, I am confident we can cope with all others.

APPROACHES TO INTERNATIONAL HRM: THE SCOPE OF THIS BOOK

The field of international HRM is characterized by three broad approaches.[2] Early work in this field[3] emphasized a crosscultural management approach and examined human behavior within organizations from an international perspective. A second approach developed from the comparative industrial relations and HRM literature[4] seeks to describe, compare, and analyze HRM systems in various countries. A third approach seeks to focus on aspects of HRM in multinational firms.[5] The approach taken in this book reflects the third approach, and our objective is to explore the implications that the process of internationalization has for the activities and policies of HRM. In particular, we are interested in how HRM is practiced in multinationals—hence, the subtitle of this book *Managing People in a Multinational Context*. While the focus of much of this book is on the established, multinational firm that owns or controls business activities in more than one foreign country (the term *multinational enterprise*, or *MNE* is also used in the literature), we recognize that small and internationalizing firms, which have yet to reach multinational firm status, also face international HRM issues (discussed in more detail in Chapter 2). In this first chapter, we define international HRM and examine in some detail the similarities and differences between domestic and international HRM.

Defining International HRM

Before we offer a definition of international HRM, we will first define the general field of HRM. Typically, HRM refers to those activities undertaken by an organization to utilize its human resources effectively. These activities would include at least the following:

- Human resource planning
- Staffing
- Performance management
- Training and development
- Compensation and benefits
- Labor relations

We now consider which activities change when HRM goes international. An article by Morgan[6] on the development of international HRM presents a model of international HRM (shown in Exhibit 1–1) that consists of three dimensions:

1. The three broad human resource activities: procurement, allocation, and utilization. (These three broad activities can be easily expanded into the six HR activities listed above.)
2. The three national or country categories involved in international HRM activities: the host country where a subsidiary may be located, the home country where the firm is headquartered, and "other" countries that may be the source of labor or finance.
3. The three types of employees of an international firm: host-country nationals (HCNs), parent-country nationals (PCNs), and third-country nationals (TCNs).[7] Thus, for example, IBM employs Australian citizens (HCNs) in its Australian operations, often sends U.S. citizens (PCNs) to Asia-Pacific countries on assignment, and may send some of its Singaporean employees on an assignment to its Japanese operations (as TCNs).

EXHIBIT 1–1   *Model of International HRM*

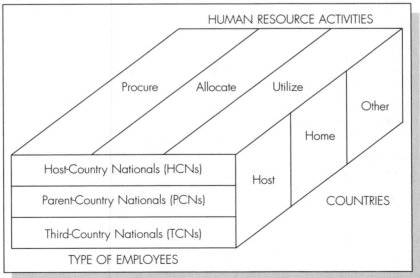

Source: Adapted from P.V. Morgan, 1986. International human resource management: Fact or fiction, *Personnel Administrator*, vol. 31, no. 9, p. 44.

Morgan defines international HRM as the interplay among these three dimensions—human resource activities, types of employees, and countries of operation. We can see that in broad terms international HRM involves the same activities as domestic HRM (e.g., procurement refers to HR planning and staffing); however, domestic HRM is involved with employees within only *one national boundary*.

In our view, the *complexities of operating in different countries and employing different national categories of workers* is a key variable that differentiates domestic and international HRM, rather than any major differences between the HRM activities performed. Many firms underestimate the complexities involved in international operations, and there is some evidence to suggest that business failures in the international arena may often be linked to poor management of human resources. For example, Desatnick and Bennett[8] conducted a detailed case study of a large U.S. multinational firm and concluded:

> The primary causes of failure in multinational ventures stem from a lack of understanding of the essential differences in managing human resources, at all levels, in foreign environments. Certain management philosophies and techniques have proved successful in the domestic environment: their application in a foreign environment too often leads to frustration, failure and underachievement. These "human" considerations are as important as the financial and marketing criteria upon which so many decisions to undertake multinational ventures depend.

Increasingly, domestic HRM is taking on some of the flavor of international HRM as it deals more and more with a multicultural workforce. Thus, some of the current focus of domestic HRM on issues of managing workforce diversity may prove to be beneficial to the practice of international HRM. It must be remembered, however, that management of diversity within a single national context may not necessarily transfer to a multinational context without some modification.

It is worthwhile examining in greater detail what is meant by the statement that international HRM is more complex than domestic HRM. Dowling[9] has summarized the literature on similarities and differences between international and domestic HRM and argues that the complexity of international HR can be attributed to six factors that differentiate international from domestic HRM. These factors are as follows:

1. More HR activities;
2. The need for a broader perspective;

3. More involvement in employees' personal lives;
4. Changes in emphasis as the workforce mix of expatriates and locals varies;
5. Risk exposure; and
6. More external influences.

Each of these factors is discussed in detail on the following pages to illustrate its characteristics.

More HR Activities

To operate in an international environment, a human resources department must engage in a number of activities that would not be necessary in a domestic environment such as: *international taxation, international relocation and orientation, administrative services for expatriates, host-government relations*, and *language translation services.*

Expatriates are subject to *international taxation*, and often have both domestic (i.e., home-country) and host-country tax liabilities. Therefore, tax equalization policies must be designed to ensure that there is no tax incentive or disincentive associated with any particular international assignment.[10] The administration of tax equalization policies is complicated by the wide variations in tax laws across host countries and by the possible time lag between the completion of an expatriate assignment and the settlement of domestic and international tax liabilities. In recognition of these difficulties, many multinational firms retain the services of a major accounting firm for international taxation advice.

International relocation and orientation involves arranging for predeparture training; providing immigration and travel details; providing housing, shopping, medical care, recreation, and schooling information; and finalizing compensation details such as delivery of salary abroad, determination of various international allowances, and taxation treatment. (The issue of expatriates returning to their home country [repatriation] is covered in detail in Chapter 7.) Many of these factors may be a source of anxiety for the expatriate and require considerable time and attention to resolve potential problems successfully—certainly much more time than would be involved in a domestic transfer/relocation such as New York to Dallas, Sydney to Melbourne, London to Cardiff, or Frankfurt to Munich.

A multinational firm also needs to provide *administrative services* for expatriates in the host countries in which it operates. Commenting on the need for these services for expatriates, a consultant in the area of international HRM has noted that:

> Anyone who has ever been responsible for an administrative service such as company-provided housing knows the importance of this activity, where both employees and spouses often 'help' the human resource manager by clarifying a policy and procedure.[11]

Providing administrative services can often be a time-consuming and complex activity because policies and procedures are not always clear cut and may conflict with local conditions. Ethical questions can arise when a practice that is legal and accepted in the host country may be at best unethical and at worst illegal in the home country. For example, a situation may arise in which a host-country requires an AIDS test for a work permit for an employee whose parent firm is headquartered in the United States, where employment-related AIDS testing remains a controversial issue. How does the corporate HR manager deal with the potential expatriate employee who refuses to meet this requirement for an AIDS test and the foreign affiliate which needs the services of a specialist expatriate from headquarters? These issues add to the complexity of providing administrative services to expatriates.

Host-government relations represent an important activity for an HR department, particularly in developing countries where work permits and other important certificates often are obtained more easily when a personal relationship exists between the relevant government officials and multinational managers. Maintaining such relationships helps resolve potential problems that can be caused by ambiguous eligibility and/or compliance criteria for documentation such as work permits. United States-based multinationals, however, must be careful in how they deal with relevant government officials, as payment or payment-in-kind such as dinners and gifts may violate the U.S. Foreign Corrupt Practices Act. (We cover international business ethics in more detail in Chapter 9.)

Provision of *language translation services* for internal and external correspondence is an additional international activity for the HR department. Morgan[12] notes that if the HR department is the major user of language translation services, the role of this translation group is often expanded to provide translation services to all foreign operation departments within the multinational.

The Need for a Broader Perspective

HR managers working in a domestic environment generally administer programs for a single national group of employees who are covered by a uniform compensation policy and taxed by one national government. Because HR managers working in an international environment face the problem of designing and administering programs for more than one national group of employees (e.g., PCN, HCN, and TCN employees who may work together in Zurich at the European regional headquarters of a U.S.-based multinational), they need to take a broader view of issues. For example, a broader, more international perspective on expatriate benefits would endorse the view that all expatriate employees, regardless of nationality, should receive a foreign service or expatriate premium when working in a foreign location. Yet some multinationals, which routinely pay such premiums to their PCN employees on international assignment (even if the assignments are to desirable locations), are reluctant to pay premiums to foreign nationals assigned to the home-country of the firm. Firms following such a policy often use the term *inpatriate* to describe foreign nationals assigned to the home-country of the firm.[13] (The utility of this term is unclear and is avoided in this book.) Such a policy confirms the common perception of many HCN and TCN employees that PCN employees are given preferential treatment.[14] Complex equity issues arise when employees of various nationalities work together, and the resolution of these issues remains one of the major challenges in the international HRM field. (Equity issues with regard to compensation are discussed in Chapter 6.)

More Involvement in Employees' Personal Lives

A greater degree of involvement in employees' personal lives is necessary for the selection, training, and effective management of both PCN and TCN employees. The HR department or professional needs to ensure that the expatriate employee understands housing arrangements, health care, and all aspects of the compensation package provided for the assignment (cost-of-living allowances, premiums, taxes, etc.). Many multinationals have an "International HR Services" section that coordinates administration of the above programs and provides services for PCNs and TCNs such as handling their banking, investments, home rental while on assignment, coordinating home visits, and final repatriation.

In the domestic setting, the HR department's involvement with an employee's family is limited. The firm may, for example, provide employee insurance programs or, if a domestic transfer is involved, the HR department may provide some assistance in relocating the employee and family. In the international setting, however, the HR department must be much more involved and needs to know more about the employee's personal life in order to provide the level of support required. For example, some governments require the presentation of a marriage certificate before granting a visa to an accompanying spouse. Thus, marital status could become an aspect of the selection process, regardless of the best intentions of the firm to avoid using a potentially discriminatory selection criterion. In such a situation, the HR department should advise all candidates being considered for the position of the host-country's visa requirements with regard to marital status and allow each candidate to decide whether he or she wishes to remain in the selection process. Apart from providing suitable housing and schooling in the assignment location, the HR department may also need to assist children left behind at boarding schools in the home country.[15] In more remote or less hospitable assignment locations, the HR department may be required to develop, and even run, recreational programs. For a domestic assignment, most of these matters either would not arise or would be primarily the responsibility of the employee rather than the HR department.

Changes in Emphasis as the Workforce Mix of PCNs and HCNs Varies

As foreign operations mature, the emphases put on various human resource activities change. For example, as the need for PCNs and TCNs declines and more trained locals become available, resources previously allocated to areas such as expatriate taxation, relocation, and orientation are transferred to activities such as local staff selection, training, and management development. The latter activity may require establishment of a program to bring high-potential local staff to corporate headquarters for developmental assignments. The need to change emphasis in HR operations as a foreign subsidiary matures is clearly a factor that broadens the responsibilities of local HR activities.

Risk Exposure

Frequently, the human and financial consequences of failure in the international arena are more severe than in domestic business. For example, expatriate failure (the premature return of an expatriate from an international assignment) is a potentially high-cost problem for international companies.[16] Direct costs (salary, training costs, and travel and relocation expenses) per failure to the parent firm may be as high as three times the domestic salary plus relocation expenses, depending on currency exchange rates and location of assignments.[17] Indirect costs such as loss of market share and damage to international customer relationships may be considerable.[18] (The topic of expatriate failure is discussed in more detail in Chapter 3.)

Terrorism is another aspect of risk exposure relevant to international HRM. Most major multinationals must now consider this factor when planning international meetings and assignments; it is estimated that firms spend 1 to 2 percent of their revenues on protection against terrorism. Clearly, terrorism has also had an effect on the way in which employees assess potential international assignment locations.[19] The HR department also may need to devise emergency evacuation procedures for highly volatile assignment locations. The invasion of Kuwait and the ensuing Gulf War in 1991 is an example of a situation in which employees unexpectedly and very rapidly became at risk.

More External Influences

Major external factors that influence international HRM are the type of government, the state of the economy, and the generally accepted practices of doing business in each of the various host countries in which the multinational operates. A host government can, for example, dictate hiring procedures, as is the case in Malaysia. During the 1970s the Malaysia government introduced a requirement that foreign firms comply with an extensive set of affirmative action rules designed to provide additional employment opportunities for the indigenous Malays who constitute the majority of the population but tend to be underrepresented in business and professional employment groups relative to Chinese Malays and Indian Malays. Various statistics showing employment levels of indigenous Malays throughout the firm must be forwarded to the relevant government department.

In developed countries, labor is more expensive and better organized than in less-developed countries, and governments require compliance with guidelines on issues such as labor relations, taxation, and health and safety. These factors shape the activities of the subsidiary HR manager considerably. In less-developed countries, labor tends to be cheaper and less organized, and government regulation is less pervasive—factors that are less time-consuming. The subsidiary HR manager also must spend time learning and interpreting the local ways of doing business and the general code of conduct regarding activities such as gift giving. It is also likely that the subsidiary HR manager will become more involved in administering benefits either provided or financed by the multinational such as housing, education, and other facilities not readily available in the local economy.

VARIABLES THAT MODERATE DIFFERENCES BETWEEN DOMESTIC AND INTERNATIONAL HRM

In our discussion so far, we have argued that the *complexity involved in operating in different countries and employing different national categories of employees*, rather than any major differences between the HRM activities performed, is a key variable that differentiates domestic and international HRM. In addition to complexity, there are four other variables that moderate (i.e., either diminish or accentuate) differences between domestic and international HRM. These variables (shown in Exhibit 1–2) are the *cultural environment*, the *industry* (or *industries*) *with which the multinational is primarily involved*, the *extent of reliance of the multinational on its home-country domestic market*, and the *attitudes of senior management*. These four additional variables are discussed in turn in the next section.

The Cultural Environment

There are many definitions of *culture*, but the term is usually used to describe a shaping process; that is, members of a group or society share a distinct way of life with common values, attitudes, and behaviors that are transmitted over time in a gradual, yet dynamic, process. As Phatak[20] explains:

> A person is not born with a given culture: rather she or he acquires it through the socialization process that begins at birth: an American is not born with a liking for hot dogs, or a German with a natural preference for beer: these behavioral attributes are culturally transmitted.

An important characteristic of culture is that it is so subtle a process that one is not always conscious of its effect on values, attitudes, and

EXHIBIT 1-2 *Variables That Moderate Differences Between International and Domestic Activities of the HRM Function*

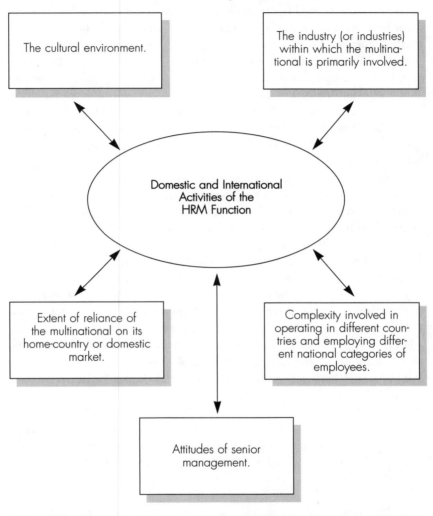

The cultural environment.

The industry (or industries) within which the multinational is primarily involved.

Domestic and International Activities of the HRM Function

Extent of reliance of the multinational on its home-country or domestic market.

Complexity involved in operating in different countries and employing different national categories of employees.

Attitudes of senior management.

Source: Peter J. Dowling, University of Tasmania.

behaviors. One usually has to be confronted with a different culture in order to fully appreciate this effect. Anyone traveling abroad, either as a tourist or businessperson, experiences situations that demonstrate cultural differences in language, food, dress, hygiene, and attitude to time. While the traveler can perceive these differences as novel, even enjoyable, for people required to live and work in a new country, such differences can prove difficult. They experience *culture shock*—a phenomenon experienced by people who move across cultures. The new environment requires many adjustments in a relatively short period of time, challenging people's frames of reference to such an extent that their sense of self, especially in terms of nationality, comes into question. People, in effect, experience a shock reaction to new cultural experiences that cause psychological disorientation because they misunderstand or do not recognize important cues. Culture shock can lead to negative feelings about the host country and its people and a longing to return home.[21] We cover the issue of adjusting to a new environment in Chapters 3, 4, and 7.

Because international business involves the interaction and movement of people across national boundaries, an appreciation of cultural differences and when these differences are important is essential. Research into these aspects helps to further our understanding of the cultural environment as an important variable that moderates differences between domestic and international HRM. However, while crosscultural and comparative research attempts to explore and explain similarities and differences, there are problems associated with such research. A major problem is that there is little agreement on either an exact definition of culture or on the operationalization of this concept. For many researchers, culture has become an omnibus variable, representing a range of social, historic, economic, and political factors that are invoked *post hoc* to explain similarity or dissimilarity in the results of a study. As Bhagat and McQuaid[22] have noted,

> *Culture* has often served simply as a synonym for *nation* without any further conceptual grounding. In effect, national differences found in the characteristics of organizations or their members have been interpreted as cultural differences.

To reduce these difficulties, researchers must specify their definition of culture *a priori* rather than *post hoc* and be careful not to assume that national differences necessarily represent cultural differences.

Another issue in crosscultural research concerns the *emic–etic* distinction.[23] *Emic* refers to *culture-specific aspects of concepts or behavior*, and *etic* refers to *culture-common aspects*. These terms have been borrowed from linguistics: A phon*emic* system documents meaningful sounds specific to a given language, and a phon*etic* system organizes all sounds that have meaning in any language.[24] Both the emic and etic approaches are legitimate research orientations. A major problem may arise, however, if a researcher imposes an etic approach (i.e., assumes universality across cultures) when there is little or no evidence for doing so. A well-known example of an imposed etic approach is the *convergence hypothesis* that dominated much of U.S. and European management research in the 1950s and 1960s. This approach was based on two key assumptions.[25] The first assumption was that there were principles of sound management that held regardless of national environments; thus, the existence of local or national practices that deviated from these principles simply indicated a need to change these local practices. The second assumption was that the universality of sound management practices would lead to societies becoming more and more alike in the future; given that the United States was the leading industrial economy, the point of convergence would be toward the U.S. model. Adoption of the convergence hypothesis has led to some rather poor predictions of future performance. For example, writing in the late 1950s, Harbison[26] concluded the following with regard to the Japanese managerial system:

> Unless basic rather than trivial or technical changes in the broad philosophy of organization building are forthcoming, Japan is destined to fall behind in the ranks of modern industrialized nations.

To use Kuhn's[27] terminology, the convergence hypothesis became an established paradigm that many researchers found difficult to give up, despite a growing body of evidence supporting a *divergence hypothesis*. In an important article reviewing the convergence/divergence debate, Child[28] made the point that there is evidence for both convergence and divergence. The majority of the convergence studies, however, focus on macrolevel variables (e.g., structure and technology used by firms across cultures), and the majority of the divergence studies focus on microlevel variables (e.g., the behavior of people within firms). His conclusion was that although firms in different countries are becoming more alike (an etic or convergence approach), the behavior of individuals within these firms is maintaining its cultural specificity (an emic or divergence approach). As noted above, both emic and etic approaches are legitimate research orientations, but methodological difficulties may arise if the distinction between these two approaches is ignored or if unwarranted universality assumptions are made.[29] The debate on assumptions of universality is not limited to the literature in international management.

Recently, this issue has become a topic of debate in the field of international relations and strategic studies where research from international management is cited.[30]

The Importance of Cultural Awareness

Despite the methodological concerns about crosscultural research, it is now generally recognized that culturally insensitive attitudes and behaviors stemming from ignorance or from misguided beliefs ("my way is best," or "what works at home will work here") not only are inappropriate but often cause international business failure. Therefore, an awareness of cultural differences is essential for the HR manager at corporate headquarters as well as in the host location.[31] Activities such as hiring, promoting, rewarding, and dismissal will be determined by the practices of the host country and often are based on a value system peculiar to that country's culture. A firm may decide to head up a new international operation with an expatriate general manager but appoint as the HR department manager a local—a person who is familiar with the host-country's HR practices. This practice can cause problems, though, for the expatriate general manager, as happened to an Australian who was in charge of a new mining venture in Indonesia. The local manager responsible for recruitment could not understand why the Australian was upset to find that he had hired most of his extended family rather than staff with the required technical competence. The Indonesian was simply ensuring that his duty to his family was fulfilled—since he was in a position to employ most of them, he was obligated to do so. The Australian, however, interpreted the Indonesian's actions as nepotism, a negative practice according to his own value system.[32]

Wyatt[33] recounts a good example of the fallacy of assuming "what works at home will work here" when dealing with work situations in another culture. The HR department staff of a large firm in Papua, New Guinea, were concerned over a number of accidents involving operators of very large, expensive, earth-moving vehicles. The expatriate managers investigating the accidents found that local drivers involved in the accidents were chewing betel nut, a common habit for most of the coastal peoples of Papua, New Guinea, and other Pacific islands. Associating the betel nut with depressants such as alcohol, the expatriate managers banned the chewing of betel nut during work hours. In another move to reduce the number of accidents, free coffee was provided at loading points, and drivers were required to alight from their vehicles at these locations. What the managers did not realize was that betel nut, like their culturally acceptable coffee, is, in fact, a stimulant, though some of the drivers were chewing it to cover up the fact that they drank beer before commencing work. As Wyatt points out, many indigenous workers used betel nut as a pick-me-up in much the same way as the expatriates used coffee.

As will be further discussed in Chapters 3 and 4, adjusting to a new cultural environment can cause problems for both the expatriate employee and the accompanying spouse and family members. Coping with cultural differences, and recognizing how and when these differences are relevant, is a constant challenge for the expatriate employee. Helping to prepare expatriates and their families for the cultural environment has now become a key activity for HR departments in those multinationals that appreciate (or have been forced, through experience, to appreciate) the impact that the cultural environment can have on staff performance and well-being.

Industry Type

Porter[34] suggests that the industry (or industries if the firm is a conglomerate) in which a multinational firm is involved is of considerable importance because patterns of international competition vary widely from one industry to another. At one end of the continuum of international competition is the *multidomestic industry*, one in which competition in each country is essentially independent of competition in other countries; traditional examples include retailing, distribution, and insurance. At the other end of the continuum is the *global industry*, one in which a firm's competitive position in one country is significantly influenced by its position in other countries; examples include commercial aircraft, semiconductors, and copiers. The key distinction between a multidomestic industry and a global industry is described by Porter as follows:

> The global industry is not merely a collection of domestic industries but a series of linked domestic industries in which the rivals compete against each other on a truly worldwide basis.... In a multidomestic industry, then, international strategy collapses to a series of domestic strategies. The issues that are uniquely international revolve around how to do business abroad, how to select good countries in which to compete (or assess country risk), and mechanisms to achieve the one-time transfer of know-how. These are questions that are relatively well developed in the literature. In a global industry,

however, managing international activities like a portfolio will undermine the possibility of achieving competitive advantage. In a global industry, a firm must in some way integrate its activities on a worldwide basis to capture the linkages among countries.

The role of the HRM function in multidomestic and global industries can be analyzed using Porter's value-chain model.[35] In Porter's model, HRM is seen as one of four support activities for the five primary activities of the firm. Since human resources are involved in each of the primary and support activities, the HRM function is seen as cutting across the entire value chain of a firm. If the firm is in a multidomestic industry, the role of the HR department will most likely be more domestic in structure and orientation. At times there may be considerable demand for international services from the HRM function (e.g., when a new plant or office is established in a foreign location and the need for expatriate employees arises), but these activities would not be pivotal. Indeed, many of these services may be provided via consultants and/or temporary employees. The main role for the HRM function would be to support the primary activities of the firm in each domestic market to achieve a competitive advantage through either cost/efficiency or product/service differentiation.[36] If the multinational is in a global industry, however, the "imperative for coordination" described by Porter would require a HRM function structured to deliver the international support required by the primary activities of the multinational.

The need to develop coordination raises complex problems for any multinational. As Laurent[37] has noted:

> In order to build, maintain, and develop their corporate identity, multinational organizations need to strive for consistency in their ways of managing people on a worldwide basis. Yet, and in order to be effective locally, they also need to adapt those ways to the specific cultural requirements of different societies. While the global nature of the business may call for increased consistency, the variety of cultural environments may be calling for differentiation.

Laurent proposes that a truly international conception of human resource management would require the following steps:

1. An explicit recognition by the parent organization that its own peculiar ways of managing human resources reflect some assumptions and values of its home culture.

2. An explicit recognition by the parent organization that its peculiar ways are neither universally better nor worse than others but are different and likely to exhibit strengths and weaknesses, particularly abroad.
3. An explicit recognition by the parent organization that its foreign subsidiaries may have other preferred ways of managing people that are neither intrinsically better nor worse, but could possibly be more effective locally.
4. A willingness from headquarters to not only acknowledge cultural differences, but also to take active steps in order to make them discussable and therefore usable.
5. The building of a genuine belief by all parties involved that more creative and effective ways of managing people could be developed as a result of crosscultural learning.

In offering this proposal, Laurent acknowledges that these are difficult steps that few firms have taken:

> They have more to do with states of mind and mindsets than with behaviors. As such, these processes can only be facilitated and this may represent a primary mission for executives in charge of international human resource management.[38]

Implicit in Laurent's analysis is the idea that by taking the steps he describes, a multinational attempting to implement a global strategy via coordination of activities would be better able to work through the difficulties and complex trade-offs inherent in such a strategy. Increasingly, multinationals are taking a more strategic approach to the role of HRM and are using staff transfers and training programs to assist in coordination of activities. We discuss these issues in more detail later in this chapter and in subsequent chapters in the book.

Reliance of the Multinational on Its Home-Country Domestic Market

A pervasive but often ignored factor that influences the behavior of multinationals and resultant HR practices is the extent of reliance of the multinational on its home-country domestic market. When, for example, we look through lists of very large firms (such as those that appear in *Fortune* and other business magazines), it is frequently assumed that a global market perspective would be dominant in the firm's culture and thinking. However, size is not the only key variable when looking at a multinational—the extent of reliance of the multinational on its home-country domestic market is also very important. In fact, for many firms, a small home market is one of the major motives for "going international."

The United Nations Conference on Trade and Development (UNCTAD) in its annual survey of foreign direct investment calculates what it refers to as an "index of transnationality," which is an average of ratios of foreign assets to total assets, foreign sales to total sales, and foreign employment to total employment.[39] Based on this index of transnationality, the most foreign-oriented multinational is Nestlé, with 87 percent of assets, 98 percent of sales, and 97 percent of employees located outside of Switzerland. The top ten multinationals are as follows:

1. Nestlé (Switzerland)
2. Thomson (Canada)
3. Holderbank Finacière (Switzerland)
4. Seagram (Canada)
5. Solvay (Belgium)
6. Asea Brown Boveri (Sweden/Switzerland)
7. Electrolux (Sweden)
8. Unilever (Britain/Netherlands)
9. Philips (Netherlands)
10. Roche (Switzerland)

There is not one U.S. firm in the top fifteen multinationals listed—Coca-Cola and McDonald's are ranked 31st and 42nd, respectively. The reason is as obvious as it is important—*the size of the domestic market for U.S. firms*. A very large domestic market influences all aspects of how a multinational organizes its activities. For example, a multinational will be more likely to use an international division as the way it organizes its international activities (see Chapter 2) and, even if it uses a global product structure, the importance of the domestic market will be pervasive. A large domestic market will also influence the attitudes of senior managers (discussed in more detail in the next section) and will generate a large number of managers with an experience base of predominantly, or even exclusively, domestic market experience. Thus, multinationals from small advanced economies like Switzerland (population 7 million), Belgium (10 million), Sweden (9 million), and The Netherlands (15 million) are in a quite different position to U.S. multinationals based in the largest single national market in the world with over 250 million people. The demands of a large domestic market present a challenge to the globalization efforts of many U.S. firms. As Cavusgil[40] has noted in an important book on internationalizing business education, the task of internationalizing business education in the United States is a large one. So, too, is the task facing many U.S. firms in terms of developing global managers.

Attitudes of Senior Management to International Operations

The point made by Laurent that some of the changes required to truly internationalize the HR function "have more to do with states of mind and mindsets than with behaviors" illustrates the importance of a final variable that may moderate differences between international and domestic HRM: the attitudes of senior management to international operations.

It is likely that if senior management does not have a strong international orientation, the importance of international operations may be underemphasized (or possibly even ignored) in terms of corporate goals and objectives. In such situations, managers may tend to focus on domestic issues and minimize differences between international and domestic environments. They may assume that there is a great deal of transferability between domestic and international HRM practices. This failure to recognize differences in managing human resources in foreign environments, regardless of whether it is because of ethnocentrism, inadequate information, or a lack of international perspective, frequently results in major difficulties in international operations.[41] The challenge for the corporate HR manager is to work with top management in fostering the desired "global mindset." This goal requires, of course, an HR manager who is able to think globally and to formulate and implement HR policies that facilitate the development of globally oriented staff.[42] In this book we attempt to demonstrate some ways in which an appreciation of the international dimensions of HRM can assist in this process.

EXPANDING THE ROLE OF HRM IN INTERNATIONAL FIRMS

It would appear that, despite the impact that international growth has on a firm's HR activities, the precise nature and extent of that impact on corporate performance is not well understood by many senior managers. Possible explanations are:

- HR managers only become involved in strategic decisions when there is a critical mass of expatriates to be managed;
- Senior management is more likely to recognize HR issues when staff transfers become of significant strategic value to achieving international business objectives, and therefore are more likely to leverage the resources required to more effectively manage this process; and
- There is often a considerable time lag before HR constraints on international expansion come to the attention of senior corporate management.

Some support for the above list comes from the strategic management literature. For example, Bhatt et. al.[43] examined the role of HR staff and managers in the strategic planning of multinational firms. The study assessed whether and how the HR department and staff were involved in planning at the corporate and strategic business unit (SBU) levels. The study concluded that HR involvement at the corporate level tended to be informal, limited in scope, and heavily dependent upon the competence and personal characteristics of the senior HR manager. The HR manager played a major role separate from the department or functional area. Staffing was the main area in which the HR manager was involved in strategy formulation; other traditional HR areas (e.g., compensation and evaluation of manager performance) were viewed as general management concerns and not primarily HR related. At the SBU level, the HR department was more involved in strategic planning; its role was more established and the emphasis was on how HR staff could help implement a strategy. As Doz and Prahalad[44] point out, an HR system can be strong only if it receives extensive support and involvement from senior management. We will take up the strategic role of HRM in multinationals in our concluding chapter.

A related issue is the need for HR staff to become internationally, some say globally, oriented.[45] It is difficult to advocate international HRM policies if one is not fully appreciative of the importance of the firm's international operations to its overall profitability and competitiveness, and aware as well of the special demands placed on the HR function by the complex global environment. A global perspective, through a broader view of issues, enables the development of more effective corporate policies.[46] The need for a global perspective applies to both the individual HR manager and the HR department. To accomplish this goal, Reynolds[47] suggests that HR managers be transferred from headquarters to international operations, not into subsidiary HR departments but into other line positions that will broaden their perspectives. Moving HR staff from the subsidiaries into headquarters is another way of encouraging headquarters HR staff to appreciate the international operations of the firm and to develop the policies and activities to support staff throughout the entire global network.

However, as Brandt[48] points out, "How fast and how far an individual HR manager can move toward globalizing his or her function often depends on a firm's size, the nature of its operations, and its degree of centralization or decentralization." Smaller firms with limited resources may find it impossible to finance staff transfers for development purposes, but they may be able to identify other ways to globally orientate HR staff, such as an annual visit to key foreign subsidiaries. Larger multinationals schedule frequent meetings of corporate and subsidiary HR managers as a way to foster corporate identity and to ensure greater consistency in global HR practices.[49]

Despite these practices, Reynold's[50] survey of thirty-five major U.S. multinationals showed that internationalizing the HR function has some way to go. He found that HR professionals with international experience were typically narrowly focused on expatriate compensation. By examining the time allocation of HR staff in the firms surveyed, Reynolds determined that 54 percent of their time was devoted to expatriate compensation and only 10 percent to international HR strategy. As we shall discuss in Chapter 6, compensation is a complex issue for multinationals, and as Reynolds rightly points out, the focus should not be denigrated. However, it is clear that in order to support its international growth strategies, the multinational requires staff whose perspective of the international dimensions of HRM takes in more than expatriate compensation; an expanded view of the role of HRM in international operations is required.

SUMMARY

The purpose of this chapter has been to provide an overview of the field of international HRM. We did this by discussing a model and definition of international HRM and examining in some detail how this differed from domestic HRM. We concluded that the *complexity involved in operating in different countries and employing different national cate-gories of employees,* rather than any major differences between the HR activities performed, is a key variable differentiating domestic and international HRM. We also discussed four other variables that moderate differences between domestic and international HRM: the *cultural environment,* the *industry (or industries) with which the multinational is primarily involved,* the *extent of reliance of the multinational on its home-country domestic market,* and the *attitudes of senior management.* We also discussed the need for an expanded view of the role of HRM in international operations.

In our discussion of the international dimensions of HRM, we will draw on HRM literature. Subsequent chapters will examine the international dimensions of the major activities of HRM—HR planning and business operations, recruitment and selection, performance management, training and development, repatriation, compensation, and labor relations. We will provide comparative data on HRM practices in different countries, but our major emphasis is on the international dimensions of HRM confronting firms, whether large or small, that face the challenge of managing people in a multinational context.

QUESTIONS

1. What are the main similarities and differences between domestic and international HRM?
2. Define these terms: *PCN, HCN,* and *TCN.*
3. Discuss two HR activities in which a multinational firm must engage that would not be required in a domestic environment.
4. Why is a greater degree of involvement in employees' personal lives inevitable in many international HRM activities?
5. Discuss the variables that moderate differences between domestic and international HR practices.

FURTHER READING

1. Dowling, P.J., 1986. Human resource issues in international business, *Syracuse Journal of International Law and Commerce,* vol. 13, no. 2, pp. 255–271.
2. Dowling, P.J., 1988. International HRM, *Human Resource Management: Evolving Roles and Responsibilities,* vol. 1. L. Dyer, ed.

ASPA/BNA Handbook of Human Resource Management Series. Washington DC: BNA.
3. Gannon, M.J., 1994. *Understanding Global Cultures: Metaphorical Journeys Through 17 Countries.* Thousand Oaks, CA: Sage.
4. Kamoche, K., 1996. The integration-differentiation puzzle: A resource-capability perspective in international human resource management, *International Journal of Human Resource Management*, vol. 7, no. 1, pp. 230–244.
5. Kobrin, S.J., 1994. Is there a relationship between a geocentric mind-set and multinational strategy?, *Journal of International Business Studies*, vol. 25, no. 3, pp. 493–511.
6. Wolf J. (Guest editor), 1997. International human resource and cross-cultural management, *Management International Review*, vol. 37, Special issue, January.

ENDNOTES

1. M.G. Duerr, 1986. International business management: Its four tasks, *Conference Board Record*, October, p. 43.
2. This section is based on various presentations by the first author and the following paper: H. De Cieri, and P.J. Dowling, (forthcoming). Strategic human resource management in multinational enterprises: Theoretical and empirical developments, in *Research and Theory in SHRM: An Agenda for the 21st Century*, P. Wright et. al., eds. Greenwich, CT: JAI Press.
3. For recent examples of this approach, see N. Adler, 1997. *International Dimensions of Organizational Behavior*, 3rd ed. Cincinnati, OH: South-Western; and A. Phatak, 1997. *International Management: Concepts & Cases*, Cincinnati, OH: South-Western.
4. See, for example, C. Brewster, and A. Hegewisch, 1994. *Policy and Practice in European Human Resource Management—The Price Waterhouse Cranfield Survey*, London: Routledge.
5. See, for example, P. Dowling, and R. Schuler, 1990. *International Dimensions of Human Resource Management*, 1st ed. Boston, MA: PWS-Kent; and P. Dowling, R. Schuler, and D. Welch, 1994. *International Dimensions of Human Resource Management*, 2d ed. Belmont, CA: Wadsworth.
6. P. Morgan, 1986. International human resource management: Fact or fiction, *Personnel Administrator*, vol. 31, no. 9, pp. 43–47.

7. While it is clear in the literature that PCNs are always expatriates, it is often overlooked that TCNs are also expatriates. See H. De Cieri, S.L. McGaughey, and P.J. Dowling, 1996. Relocation, *International Encyclopedia of Business and Management*, M. Warner, ed. vol. 5, London: Routledge, pp. 4300–4310, for further discussion of this point.

8. R.L. Desatnick, and M.L. Bennett, 1978. *Human Resource Management in the Multinational Company*, New York: Nichols.

9. P.J. Dowling, 1988. International and domestic personnel/human resource management: Similarities and differences, *Readings in Personnel and Human Resource Management*, 3rd ed. R.S. Schuler, S.A. Youngblood, and V.L. Huber, eds. St. Paul, MN: West Publishing.

10. See D.L. Pinney, 1982. Structuring an expatriate tax reimbursement program, *Personnel Administrator*, vol. 27, no. 7, pp. 19–25; and M. Gajek, and M.M. Sabo, 1986. The bottom line: What HR managers need to know about the new expatriate regulations, *Personnel Administrator*, vol. 31, no. 2, pp. 87–92.

11. F. Acuff, 1984. International and domestic human resources functions, Organization Resources Counselors, *Innovations in International Compensation*, New York.

12. P. Morgan, International human resource management.

13. The *International Human Resource Management Reference Guide 1997–1998*, which is published by the Institute for International Human Resources (a division of the Society for Human Resource Management, Alexandria: VA), defines an *inpatriate* as a "Foreign manager in the United States" (p. V-4). A "Foreign manager in the United States" is defined (on the same page) as "an **expatriate** in the United States where the United States is the host-country and the manager's home-country is outside of the United States." Curiously, the *Reference Guide* also states that the word *inpatriate* "can also be used for U.S. expatriates returning to an assignment in the United States." This is a contradiction of the first part of the definition of an inpatriate being a "Foreign manager in the United States" and is illogical. U.S. expatriates returning to the United States are PCNs and cannot also be classed as "Foreign managers in the United States"—perhaps they are "repatriates," but they are not inpatriates. As defined, this term is only of use in the United States. Given the substantial amount of jargon in international HRM, it is

questionable as to whether the term *inpatriate* adds enough value to justify its use.

14. R.D. Robinson, 1978. *International Business Management: A Guide to Decision Making*, 2d. ed. Hinsdale, IL: Dryden.

15. Although less common in the United States, the use of private boarding schools is common in countries (particularly European countries) that have a colonial tradition where both colonial administrators and business people would often undertake long foreign assignments and expect to leave their children at a boarding school in their home-country. This is especially true of Great Britain, which also has a strong cultural tradition of the middle and upper classes sending their children to private boarding schools (curiously described by the British as "public" schools, even though they are all private institutions that charge fees) even if the parents were working in Britain.

16. R.L. Tung, 1981. Selection and training of personnel for overseas assignments, *Columbia Journal of World Business*, vol. 16, no. 1, pp. 68–78.

17. M. Mendenhall, and G. Oddou, 1985. The dimensions of expatriate acculturation: A review, *Academy of Management Review*, vol. 10, pp. 39–47; M.G. Harvey, 1983. The multinational corporation's expatriate problem: An application of Murphy's Law, *Business Horizons*, vol. 26, no. 1, pp. 71–78.

18. Y. Zeira, and M. Banai, 1984. Present and desired methods of selecting expatriate managers for international assignments, *Personnel Review*, vol. 13, no. 3, pp. 29–35.

19. See "Terrorism," Chapter 4 in T.M. Gladwin, and I. Walter, 1980. *Multinationals Under Fire: Lessons in the Management of Conflict.* New York: John Wiley. M. Harvey, 1993. A survey of corporate programs for managing terrorist threats, *Journal of International Business Studies*, vol. 24, no. 3, pp. 465–478.

20. A.V. Phatak, 1995. *International Dimensions of Management*, 4th ed. Cincinnati: South-Western.

21. J.E. Harris, and R.T. Moran, 1979. *Managing Cultural Differences*, Houston: Gulf.

22. R.S. Bhagat, and S.J. McQuaid, 1982. Role of subjective culture in organizations: A review and directions for future research, *Journal of Applied Psychology*, vol. 67, pp. 653–685.

23. See J.W. Berry, 1980. Introduction to methodology, in *Handbook of Cross-Cultural Psychology, Vol. 2: Methodology*, H.C. Triandis, and

J.W. Berry, eds. Boston: Allyn & Bacon; H. De Cieri, and P.J. Dowling, 1995. Cross-cultural issues in organizational behavior, *Trends in Organizational Behavior*, vol. 2, C.L. Cooper, and D.M. Rousseau, eds. Chicester, U.K.: John Wiley & Sons, pp. 127–145; and M.B. Teagarden, and M.A. Von Glinow, 1997. Human resource management in cross-cultural contexts: Emic practices versus etic philosophies, *Management International Review*, 37 (1 - Special Issue), pp. 7–20.

24. See H. Triandis, and R. Brislin, 1984. Cross-cultural psychology, *American Psychologist*, vol. 39, pp. 1006–1016.

25. See G. Hofstede, 1983. The cultural relativity of organizational practices and theories, *Journal of International Business Studies*, vol. 14, no. 2, pp. 75–89.

26. F. Harbison, 1959. Management in Japan, in *Management in the Industrial World: An International Analysis*, F. Harbison, and C.A. Myers, eds. New York: McGraw-Hill.

27. T.S. Kuhn, 1962. *The Structure of Scientific Revolution*, 2d ed. Chicago, IL: University of Chicago Press.

28. J.D. Child, 1981. Culture, contingency and capitalism in the cross-national study of organizations, in *Research in Organizational Behavior*, vol. 3, L.L. Cummings, and B.M. Staw, eds. Greenwich, CT: JAI Publishers.

29. See D.A. Ricks, 1993. *Blunders in International Business*. Cambridge, MA: Blackwell, for a comprehensive collection of mistakes made by multinational firms that paid insufficient attention to their cultural environment in their international business operations. For further literature on this topic see the following: P.S. Kirkbride, and S.F.Y. Tang, 1994. From Kyoto to Kowloon: Cultural barriers to the transference of quality circles from Japan to Hong Kong, *Asia Pacific Journal of Human Resources*, 32, no. 2, pp. 100–111; M. Tayeb, 1994. Organizations and national culture: Methodology considered, *Organization Studies*, 15, no. 3, pp. 429–446; and P. Sparrow, R.S. Schuler, and S.E. Jackson, 1994. Convergence or divergence: Human resource practices and policies for competitive advantage worldwide, *International Journal of Human Resource Management*, 5, no. 2, pp. 267–299; M. Morishima, 1995. Embedding HRM in a social context, *British Journal of Industrial Relations*, 33, no. 4, pp. 617–643; and J.E. Delery, and D.H. Doty, 1996. Modes of theorizing in strategic human resource management: Tests

of universalistic, contingency, and configurational performance predictions, *Academy of Management Journal*, 39, pp. 802–835.

30. S.P. Huntington, 1996. The West: Unique, not universal, *Foreign Affairs*, November/December, pp. 28–46.

31. R.L. Tung, 1993. Managing cross-national and intra-national diversity, *Human Resource Management*, 32, no. 4, pp. 461–477.

32. P.J Dowling, D.E. Welch, and H. De Cieri, 1989. International joint ventures: A new challenge for human resource management, in *Proceedings of the Fifteenth Conference of the European International Business Association*, R. Luostarinen, ed. Helsinki, December.

33. T. Wyatt, 1989. Understanding unfamiliar personnel problems in cross-cultural work encounters, *Asia Pacific HRM*, vol. 27, no. 4, p. 5.

34. M.E. Porter, 1986. Changing patterns of international competition, *California Management Review*, vol. 28, no. 2, pp. 9–40.

35. M.E. Porter, 1985. *Competitive Advantage: Creating and Sustaining Superior Performance*, New York: The Free Press.

36. See R.S. Schuler, and I.C. MacMillan, 1984. Gaining competitive advantage through human resource management practices, *Human Resource Management*, vol. 23, no. 3, pp. 241–255, for a discussion of these strategies.

37. A. Laurent, 1986. The cross-cultural puzzle of international human resource management, *Human Resource Management*, vol. 25, pp. 91–102.

38. Ibid., p. 100.

39. This section is based on a short article on multinationals, which appeared in *The Economist*, September 27, 1997, p. 119. The UNCTAD index uses 1995 data.

40. S. Tamer Cavusgil, 1993. *Internationalizing Business Education: Meeting the Challenge*, East Lansing, MI: Michigan State University Press.

41. Desatnick, and Bennett, *Human Resource Management in the Multinational Company*.

42. See C. Bartlett, and S. Ghoshal, 1992. *Transnational Management: Text, Cases, and Readings in Cross-Border Management*, Boston, MA: Irwin; and V. Pucik, 1992. Human resources in the future: An obstacle or a champion of globalization?, *Human Resource Management*, 36, pp. 163–167.

43. B. Bhatt et. al., 1988. The relationship between the global strategic planning process and the human resource management function, in *Readings in Human Resource Management*, 3rd ed. R.S. Schuler, S.A. Youngblood, and V.L. Huber, eds. St. Paul, MN: West Publishing Co., pp. 427–435; see also G. Oddou, and M. Mendenhall, 1991. Succession-planning for global managers: How well are we preparing our future decision makers?, *Business Horizons*, vol. 34, no. 1, pp. 26–34; and L.K. Stroh, and P.M. Caligiuri, 1998. Strategic human resources: A new source for competitive advantage in the global arena, *International Journal of Human Resource Management*, vol. 9, no. 1, pp. 1–17.

44. Y.L. Doz, and C.K. Prahalad, 1986. Controlled variety: A challenge for human resource management in the MNC, *Human Resource Management*, vol. 25, no. 1, pp. 55–71.

45. It should be noted that the concept of "global" (and "globalization") has been the subject of some debate in the literature. A good coverage of this debate and various definitions of "global" can be found in B. Parker, 1996. Evolution and revolution: From international business to globalization, in S.R. Clegg, C. Hardy, and W.R. Nord, eds. *Handbook of Organization Studies*, London: Sage.

46. P.J. Dowling, International and domestic personnel/human resource management: Similarities and differences.

47. C. Reynolds, 1992. Are you ready to make IHR a global function?, *HR News*, February.

48. E. Brandt, 1991. Global HR, *Personnel Journal*, March, p. 38.

49. Ibid.

50. Reynolds, Are you ready to make IHR a global function?

CHAPTER 2
The Organizational Context

The human resource (HR) function does not operate in a vacuum. As with other areas of the organization, the shift from a domestic to a global focus affects the HR activities described in Chapter 1. As a consequence, HR activities are determined by, and influence, various organizational factors, such as:

- Stage of internationalization;
- Mode of operation used in the various foreign markets;
- Method of control and coordination; and
- Strategic importance of the overseas operations to total corporate profitability.

To a certain extent, how the internationalizing firm copes with the HR demands of its various foreign operations determines its ability to execute its chosen expansion strategies. Indeed, Finnish research suggests that personnel policies should lead rather than follow international operation decisions,[1] yet one could argue that most companies take the opposite approach—that is, follow market-driven strategies. For example, after reading the cases in Exhibit 2–1, one could ask whether GE's top managers fully anticipated the HR investment that the Tungsram acquisition would entail prior to its decision to purchase the Hungarian firm. GE is a large multinational with experience and resources to draw on. For smaller, newly internationalizing firms, lack of suitable staff may be a major constraint, as the experience of the Australian firm in Exhibit 2–1 demonstrates.

EXHIBIT 2-1

GE's Acquisition in Hungary

In January 1990, the U.S. multinational, General Electric (GE), invested in Tungsram, a Hungarian lighting company, as part of its European market expansion strategy. By 1994, its equity had risen to 99.6 percent. The Hungarian operation had 13 existing factories employing 17,600 workers. GE initially appointed a Hungarian-born U.S. expatriate as its top manager, though he was later replaced when Tungsram was brought under the direct control of GE Lighting Europe in 1993. Staff transfers played an important role in training and developing the Hungarian staff. Key executives were brought over from the United States for varying lengths of time (three to six months) to assist in knowledge and skills transfer. Management training also involved sending Tungsram staff to the United States, giving selected Hungarians exposure to GE's working environment, and American life in general. In order to improve Tungsram's competitiveness, GE reduced staff levels by almost half and closed five plants, despite the unionized environment; it also invested heavily in training (quality programs) to improve production workers' output. During this period, its European market share increased from 5 percent in 1989 to 15 percent in 1994.[2]

Australian Systems Limited

Australian Systems Limited (ASL) is a subsidiary of a UK project firm, operating in the highly competitive construction industry. In 1994, ASL was one of nine companies, out of 200 applicants, judged prequalified to bid for work connected with the extension and modernization of a major airport in South-East Asia. ASL's managing director was pleased that his small company was internationally competitive, but commented that there were always two constraints in international project operations: finance and people. He explained:

> "Finance is always an issue in terms of how much you can put into it. And the other thing is available resources—people. Finding good people is always difficult. We used to think it was our specialized part of the industry, but most of the business people I talk to bemoan the fact of getting good people—good marketing, good engineering, whatever." He added: "When we started to look at resources, the bottom line is that if we had won [the South-East Asian airport project], plus what [work] we had already, we would have had to close the order books for twelve months because we would not find the people to handle more work."[3]

The demands placed by international growth on the HRM department and its responses are the focus of this chapter. By way of introduction, we outline various approaches to staffing foreign operations. We then follow the path a domestic firm may take as it evolves into a global entity with a focus on how this development is reflected in its form of structure, the approach to control and coordination, and the mode of operation used. The purpose is to draw out the international dimension of human resource management to provide a meaningful context for the remainder of the book.

INTERNATIONAL HUMAN RESOURCE MANAGEMENT APPROACHES

In Chapter 1 we discussed the IHRM implications of Porter's multidomestic and global industry classifications to illustrate how multinational strategies have HR consequences. Here, we are concerned with perhaps a more fundamental aspect—the allocation of human resources to the various international operations to ensure effective strategic outcomes. The IHRM literature uses four terms to describe MNE approaches to managing and staffing their subsidiaries: ethnocentric, polycentric, regiocentric, and geocentric. These terms are taken from the seminal work of Perlmutter,[4] who claimed that it was possible to identify among international executives three primary attitudes—ethnocentric, polycentric, and geocentric—toward building a multinational enterprise, based on top management assumptions upon which key product, functional, and geographical decisions were made. To demonstrate these three attitudes, Perlmutter used aspects of organizational design, such as decision-making, evaluation and control, information flows, and complexity of organization. He also included "perpetuation," which he defined as "recruiting, staffing, development." A fourth attitude—regiocentric—was added later.[5]

Although the HR implications of the approaches identified by Perlmutter will be examined in detail in Chapter 3, it is important to briefly outline them here, since they have a bearing on our discussion of the organizational structure and control mechanisms that typically are adopted by firms as their internationalization progresses. The four approaches are:

1. *Ethnocentric:* Few foreign subsidiaries have any autonomy; strategic decisions are made at headquarters. Key positions at the domestic and foreign operations are held by headquarters' management personnel. In other words, subsidiaries are managed by expatriates from the home country (PCNs).

2. *Polycentric:* The MNE treats each subsidiary as a distinct national entity with some decision-making autonomy. Subsidiaries are usually managed by local nationals (HCNs) who are seldom promoted to positions at headquarters. Likewise, PCNs are rarely transferred to foreign subsidiary operations.
3. *Geocentric:* Here, the MNE is taking a worldwide approach to its operations, recognizing that each part (subsidiaries and headquarters) makes a unique contribution with its unique competence. It is accompanied by a worldwide integrated business, and nationality is ignored in favor of ability. For example, the chief executive officer of the Swedish multinational Electrolux claims that within this global company there is no tradition to hire managing directors from Sweden, or locally, but to find the person best suited for the job;[6] that is, the color of one's passport does not matter when it comes to rewards, promotion, and development. PCNs, HCNs, and TCNs can be found in key positions anywhere, including those at the senior management level at headquarters and on the board of directors.
4. *Regiocentric:* Reflects the geographic strategy and structure of the multinational. Like the geocentric approach, it utilizes a wider pool of managers but in a limited way. Personnel may move outside their countries but only within the particular geographic region. Regional managers may not be promoted to headquarter positions but enjoy a degree of regional autonomy in decision making. It may be seen as a precursory step towards geocentrism.

While these attitudes have been a useful way of demonstrating the various approaches to staffing foreign operations, it should be stressed that the above categories refer to managerial attitudes that reflect the socio-cultural environment in which the internationalizing firm is embedded, and are based on Perlmutter's study of U.S. firms.

These attitudes also may reflect a general top management attitude, however, the nature of international business often forces adaptation upon implementation. For instance, a firm may adopt an ethnocentric approach to all its foreign operations, but a particular host government may require the appointment of its own people in the key subsidiary positions; so, for that market, a polycentric approach is mandatory, making a uniform approach unachievable. Likewise, a recent Korn/Ferry International survey of 35 businesses active in Russia found that Western companies tended to maintain an ethnocentric approach to staffing despite attempts to "Russify" the local operations.[7] As well, the strategic importance of the foreign market, the maturity of the operation, and the degree of cultural distance between the parent and host country, influence the way in which the firm approaches a particular staffing decision.[8] In some cases an MNE may use a combination of approaches—for example, it may operate its European interests in a regiocentric manner and its Southeast Asian interests in an ethnocentric way until there is greater confidence in operating in that region of the world.

Because of these operating realities, it is sometimes difficult to equate precisely managerial attitudes towards international operations with the structural forms discussed in the next section. The environmental contingencies facing the particular internationalizing firm influence its strategic position, managerial mindset, organizational structure, and staffing approaches. The four typologies derived by Bartlett and Ghoshal[9]—international, global, multidomestic, and transnational—are useful illustrations of these linkages.

THE PATH TO GLOBAL STATUS

In addition to the strategic imperatives, mindsets, and staffing approaches outlined above, IHRM is affected by the way the internationalization process itself is managed. Most firms pass through several stages of organizational development as the nature and size of their international activities grow. As they go through these evolutionary stages, their organizational structures[10] change, typically due to the strain imposed by growth and geographical spread, the need for improved coordination and control across business units, and the constraints imposed by host-government regulations on ownership and equity. Multinationals are not born overnight; the evolution from a domestic to a truly global organization may involve a long and somewhat tortuous process with many and diverse steps, as illustrated in Exhibit 2–2. Although research into internationalization has revealed a common process, it must be stressed that this process is not exactly the same for all firms. As Exhibit 2–2 shows, some firms may use licensing, subcontracting, or other operation modes, instead of establishing their own foreign production or service facilities.

Some firms go through the various steps rapidly while others evolve slowly over many years, although recent studies have identified a speeding up of the process. For example, some firms are able to accelerate the process through acquisitions, thus leapfrogging over intermediate steps

EXHIBIT 2-2   *Stages of Internationalization[11]*

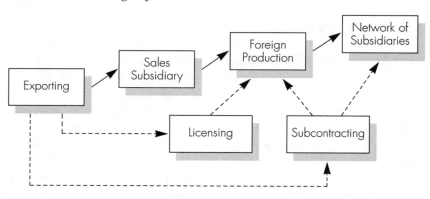

(i.e., move directly into foreign production through the purchase of a foreign firm rather than initial exporting, followed by sales subsidiary, as shown in Exhibit 2–2). Nor do all firms follow the same sequence of stages as they internationalize—some firms can be driven by external factors such as host-government action (e.g., forced into a joint venture) or an offer to buy a company. Others are formed expressly with the international market in mind.[12] In other words, the number of steps, or stages, along the path to multinational status varies from firm to firm, as does the time frame involved.[13] The concept of an evolutionary process, however, is useful in illustrating the organizational adjustments required of a firm moving along the path to multinational status. As we have said, linked to this evolutionary process are structural responses, control mechanisms, and HRM policies. The following section examines the typical path from domestic to global organization and draws out key HRM implications.

Export

Exporting is the typically initial stage for firms entering international operations. As such, it rarely involves much organizational response until the level of export sales reaches a critical point. Of course, simple exporting may be difficult for service companies (such as legal firms) so that they may be forced to make an early step into foreign direct investment operations (via a branch office, or joint venture).[14]

Exporting often tends to be handled by an intermediary (e.g., an export agent or foreign distributor—usually a HCN, as local market knowledge is deemed critical). As export sales increase, an export manager may be appointed to control foreign sales and actively seek new markets. This person is commonly from the domestic operations—that is, a PCN. Further growth in exporting may lead to the establishment of an export department at the same level as the domestic sales department as the firm becomes more committed to, or more dependent on, its foreign export sales as Exhibit 2–3 shows.

At this stage, exporting is controlled from the domestic-based home office, through a designated export manager. The role of the HR department is unclear, as indicated by the dotted arrow between these two functional areas in Exhibit 2–3. Welch and Welch[15] argue there is a paucity of empirical evidence about HR responses at this early internationalization stage, even though there are HR activities involved (such as the selection of export staff), and perhaps training of the foreign agency staff. They suggest that as these activities are handled by the marketing department, or exporting staff, the HR department has little, if any, involvement with the development of policies and procedures surrounding the HR aspects of the firm's early international activities.

EXHIBIT 2-3 *Export Department*[16]

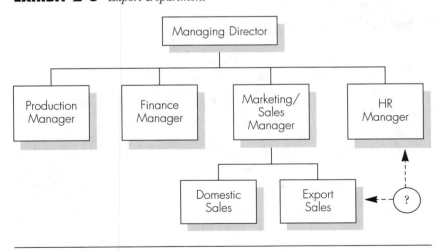

Sales Subsidiary

As the firm develops expertise in foreign markets, agents and distributors are often replaced by direct sales with the establishment of sales subsidiaries or branch offices in the foreign market countries. This stage may be prompted by problems with foreign agents, more confidence in the international sales activity, the desire to have greater control, and/or the decision to give greater support to the exporting activity, usually due to its increasing importance to the overall success of the organization. The export manager is given the same authority as other functional managers, as illustrated in Exhibit 2–4.

Exporting is still controlled at corporate headquarters, but the firm must make a decision regarding the coordination of the sales subsidiary, including staffing. If it wishes to maintain direct control, reflecting an ethnocentric attitude, it opts to staff the sales subsidiary from its headquarters through the use of parent-country nationals (PCNs). If it regards country-specific factors—such as knowledge of the foreign market, language, sensitivity to host-country needs—as important, it may staff the subsidiary with host-country nationals (HCNs). However, it would appear that many firms use PCNs in key sales subsidiary positions.

The decision to use PCNs leads into expatriation management issues and activities. It may be that, at this point, the HR department becomes actively involved in the personnel aspects of the firm's international operations, though there is little empirical evidence as to when, and how, HR-designated staff become involved (as indicated by the question mark in Exhibit 2–4).

EXHIBIT 2–4 *Sales Subsidiary*

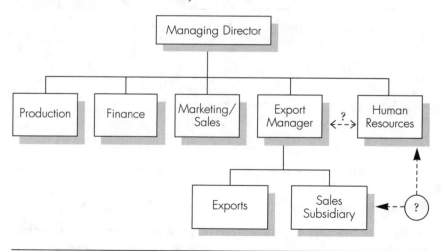

International Division

For some firms, it is a short step from the establishment of a sales subsidiary to foreign production or service facility. This step may be considered small if the firm already is assembling the product abroad to take advantage of cheap labor or to save shipping costs or tariffs, for example. Alternatively, the firm may have a well-established export and marketing program that enables it to take advantage of host-government incentives, or to counter host-government controls on foreign imports by establishing a foreign production facility. For some firms, though, the transition to foreign investment is a large, sometimes prohibitive, step. For example, an Australian firm that was successfully exporting mining equipment to Canada began to experience problems with after-sales servicing and delivery schedules. The establishment of its own production facility was considered too great a step, so the firm entered into a licensing agreement with a Canadian manufacturer.[17] According to Stopford and Wells,[18] in the 1960s, most U.S. manufacturing firms stumbled into manufacturing abroad without much design. Early investments in foreign production facilities were often defensive reactions against the threat of losing markets that had been acquired almost accidentally in the first place.

Having made the decision to produce overseas, the firm may establish its own foreign production facilities, or enter into a joint venture with a local firm, or buy a local firm. Regardless of the method of establishment, foreign production/service operations tend to trigger the creation of a separate international division in which all international activities are grouped, as Exhibit 2–5 illustrates.

With the spread of international activities, the firm establishes what has been referred to as "miniature replicas" (the foreign subsidiaries are structured to mirror that of the domestic organization). The subsidiary managers report to the head of the international division, and there may be some informal reporting directly to the various functional heads. For example, as shown in Exhibit 2–5, there may be contact regarding staffing issues between the HR managers in the two subsidiaries and the HR manager at corporate headquarters.

Many firms at this stage of internationalization are concerned about maintaining control of the newly established subsidiary, and will place PCNs in all key positions in the subsidiary. However, some firms decide that local employment conditions require local handling and place a HCN in charge of the subsidiary HR function, thus making an exception

EXHIBIT 2-5 *International Division*

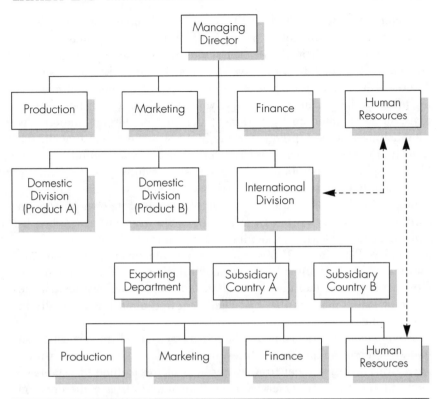

to the overall ethnocentric approach; others may place HCNs in several key positions, including HRM, to comply with host-government directives.

The role of corporate HR staff is primarily concerned with expatriate management though there will be some monitoring of the subsidiary HR function—formally through the head of the International Division. Pucik[19] suggests that, initially, corporate HR activities are confined to supervising the selection of staff for the new international division. Expatriate managers perform a major role: "identifying employees who can direct the daily operations of the foreign subsidiaries, supervising transfer of managerial and technical know-how, communicating corporate policies, and keeping corporate HQ informed."

As the firm expands its foreign production or service facilities into other countries, increasing the size of its foreign workforce, accompanied by a growth in the number of expatriates, more formal HR policies become necessary. Welch and Welch[20] argue that the capacity of corporate HR staff to design appropriate policies may depend on how institutionalized existing approaches to expatriate management concerns have become, especially policies for compensation and predeparture training, and that the more isolated the corporate HR function has been from the preceding international activities, the more difficult the task is likely to be. These authors add that "an additional difficulty for the HRM department, when attempting to play a more proactive role, is that it may well lack credibility and the competencies to handle international personnel demands may be seen as residing outside its current domain." In other words the export department (or its equivalent) may have been in charge of international staffing issues and instigated required personnel responses, and now considers it has the competence to manage expatriates.

Global Product/Area Division

Over time, the firm moves from the early foreign production stage into a phase of growth through production (or service), standardization, and diversification. Consequently, the strain of sheer size may create problems, and the international division becomes overstretched making effective communication and efficiency of operation difficult. In some cases, corporate top managers may become concerned that the international division has enjoyed too much autonomy, acting so independently from the domestic operations to the extent that it operates as a separate unit—a situation that cannot be tolerated as the firm's international activities become strategically more important.

Typically, tensions will emerge between the parent company (headquarters) and its subsidiaries, stemming from the need for national responsiveness at the subsidiary unit and global integration imperatives at the parent headquarters. The demand for national responsiveness at the subsidiary unit develops because of factors such as differences in market structures, distribution channels, customer needs, local culture, and pressure from the host government. The need for more centralized global integration by headquarters comes from having multinational customers, global competitors, and the increasingly rapid flow of information and technology—and from the quest for large volume for economies of scale.

As a result of these various forces for change, the multinational confronts two major issues of structure:

- The extent or degree to which key decisions are to be made at parent headquarters or at the subsidiary units (centralization vs. decentralization), and
- The type, or form, of control exerted by the parent over the subsidiary unit (bureaucratic control vs. normative).

The structural response, at this stage of internationalization, can be either a product- or service-based global structure (if the growth strategy is through product or service diversification) or an area-based structure (if the growth strategy is through geographical expansion). (See Exhibits 2–6a and 2–6b.)

As part of the process of accommodating subsidiary concerns through decentralization, the MNE strives to adapt its HRM activities to each host-country's specific requirements. This naturally impacts on the corporate HRM function. (The dotted arrows in both exhibits denote other functions than HRM and marketing.) As indicated by the dashed arrows, there is an increasing devolution of responsibility for local employee decisions to each subsidiary, with corporate HR staff performing a monitoring role, intervening in local affairs only in extreme circumstances. For example, in the late-1980s, Ford Australia had a ceiling on its HRM decisions, and any decision that involved an amount above that ceiling (such as promotions above a certain salary grade) had to be referred to its regional HQ for corporate approval. Expatriate management remained the responsibility of corporate HR staff.

This HRM monitoring role reflects management's desire for central control of strategic planning—formulating, implementing, and coordinating strategies for its worldwide markets. As well, the growth in foreign exposure combined with changes in the organizational structure of international operations results in an increase in the number of employees needed to oversee the activities between the parent firm and its foreign affiliates. Within the human resource function, the development of managers able to operate in international environments becomes a new imperative.[21]

As the multinational grows and the trend toward a global perspective accelerates, it increasingly confronts the "think global, act local" paradox.[22] The increasingly complex international environment—characterized by global competitors, global customers, universal

EXHIBIT 2-6A *Global Product Division*

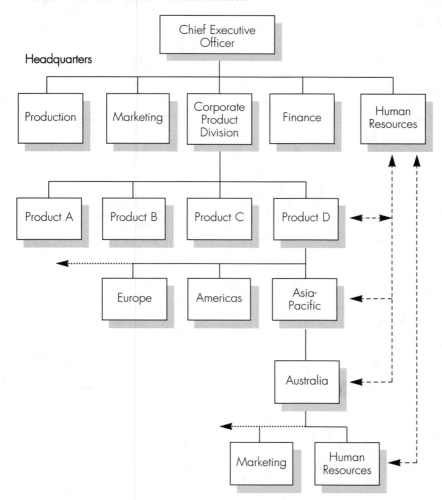

products, rapid technological change, and world-scale factories—
pushes the multinational toward global integration while, at the same
time, host governments and other stakeholders (customers, suppliers,
and employees) push for local responsiveness. To facilitate the challenge
of meeting these conflicting demands, the multinational typically needs
to consider a more appropriate structure, and the choice appears to be
either the matrix, the mixed structure, the heterarchy, the transnational,

EXHIBIT 2-6B *Global Area Division*

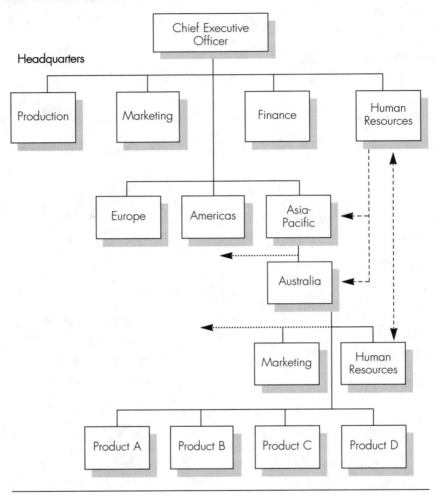

or the multinational network. These options are now described and discussed.

The Matrix

In the matrix structure, the multinational is attempting to integrate its operations across more than one dimension. As shown in Exhibit 2–7, the international or geographical division and the product division share

EXHIBIT 2-7   *The Matrix*

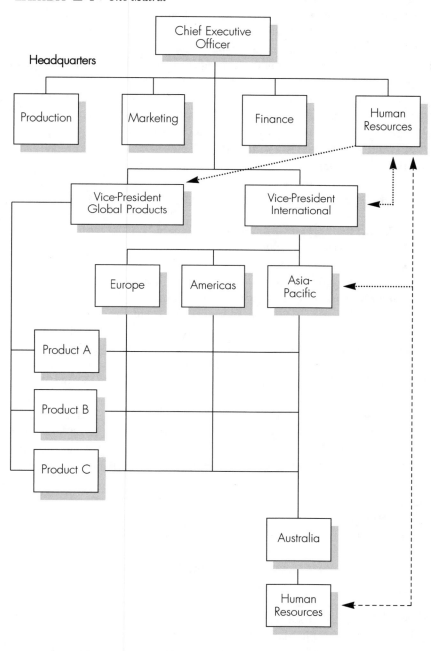

joint authority, thus violating Fayol's principle of unity of command. Advocates of this structural form see as its advantages that conflicts of interest are brought out into the open, and that each issue with priority in decision making has an executive champion to ensure it is not neglected. In other words, the matrix is considered to bring into the management system a philosophy of matching the structure to the decision-making process. Galbraith and Kazanjian[23] argued that the matrix "continues to be the only organizational form which fits the strategy of simultaneous pursuit of multiple business dimensions, with each given equal priority.... [The] structural form succeeds because it fits the situation." In practice, firms that have adopted the matrix structure have met with mixed success. One reason is that it is an expensive form that requires careful implementation and commitment on the part of top management to be successful.

In Exhibit 2–7, area managers are responsible for the performance of all three products within the various countries that comprise their regions, while product managers are responsible for sales of their specific product ranges across the areas. For example, Product A Manager would be concerned with sales of Product A in Europe, the Americas, and in the Asia-Pacific area. Product managers report to the Vice-President Global Products for matters pertaining to product, and to the Vice-President International for geographical matters. There is a similar dual reporting line for functional staff. This is illustrated in Exhibit 2–7 through the HR departments and the corporate level (dotted arrows), and to country managers and subsidiary HR managers (dashed arrows). The HR manager in the Australia subsidiary would report to the country manager (Australia) as well as to the Asia-Pacific Area Manager (and thus indirectly to the Vice-President International). Country HR managers may also be involved in staffing issues involving product division staff (reporting indirectly to Vice-President Global Products). There may be additional reporting requirements to corporate HR at headquarters.

One supporter of the matrix organization, Barnevik,[24] the former chief executive officer of Asea Brown Boveri (ABB), the European electrical systems and equipment manufacturer, discussing his organization's approach, explains:

ABB is an organization with three internal contradictions. We want to be global and local, big and small, radically decentralized with centralized reporting and control. If we resolve those contradictions, we create real organization advantage. That is where the matrix comes in. The matrix is the framework through which we organize our activities. It allows us to optimize our businesses globally *and* maximize performance in every country in which we operate. Some people resist it. They say that the matrix is too rigid, too simplistic. But what choice do you have? To say you don't like a matrix is like saying you don't like factories or you don't like breathing. It is a fact of life. If you deny the formal matrix, you wind up with an informal one—and that is much harder to reckon with. As we learn to master the matrix, we get a truly multidomestic organization.

It is in the attempt to master the matrix that many multinationals have floundered. Bartlett and Ghoshal[25] comment that, in practice, particularly in the international context, the matrix has proven to be all but unmanageable. They isolate four contributing factors:

1. Dual reporting, which leads to conflict and confusion;
2. Proliferation of communication channels, which creates informational logjams;
3. Overlapping responsibilities, which produce turf battles and a loss of accountability; and
4. Barriers of distance, language, time, and culture, which make it virtually impossible for managers to resolve conflicts and to clarify the confusion.

Bartlett and Ghoshal conclude that the most successful multinationals today focus less on searching for the ideal structure, and more on developing the abilities, behavior, and performance of individual managers. This assists in creating "a matrix in the minds of managers," where individual capabilities are captured and the entire firm is motivated to respond cooperatively to a complicated and dynamic environment.

If, however, the multinational opts for a matrix structure, particular care must be taken with staffing. As Ronen[26] notes:

It requires managers who know the business in general, who have good interpersonal skills, and who can deal with the ambiguities of responsibility and authority inherent in the matrix system. Training in such skills as planning procedures, the kinds of interpersonal skills necessary for the matrix, and the kind of analysis and orderly presentation of ideas essential to planning within a group is most important for supporting the matrix approach. Moreover, management development and human resource planning are even more necessary in the volatile environment of the matrix than in the traditional organizations.

Mixed Structure

In an attempt to manage the growth of diverse operations, or because attempts to implement a matrix structure have been unsuccessful, some firms have opted for what can only be described as a mixed form. In a survey conducted by Dowling,[27] more than one-third (35 percent) of respondents indicated that they had mixed forms, and around 18 percent had product or matrix structures. Galbraith and Kazanjian[28] also identify mixed structures that seem to have emerged in response to global pressures and trade-offs:

> For example, organizations that pursued area structures kept these geographical profit centers, but added worldwide product managers. Colgate-Palmolive has always had strong country managers. But, as they doubled the funding for product research, and as Colgate Dental Creme became a universal product, product managers were added at the corporate office to direct the R & D funding and coordinate marketing programs worldwide.
>
> Similarly, the product-divisionalized firms have been reintroducing the international division. At Motorola, the product groups had worldwide responsibility for their product lines. As they compete with the Japanese in Japan, an international group has been introduced to help coordinate across product lines.

Although all structural forms that result from the evolutionary development of international business are complex and difficult to manage effectively, given a firm's developing capabilities and experience at each new stage, mixed structures appear even more complex and harder to explain and implement, as well as control. Thus, as our discussion of the matrix structure emphasized, it is important that all employees understand the mixed framework and that attention is also given to supporting mechanisms, such as corporate identity, interpersonal relationships, management attitudes, and HR systems, particularly promotion and reward policies.

Beyond the Matrix

Some writers are identifying a new stage of development that builds on the product/area and matrix structures. Early studies of headquarters–subsidiary relationships tended to stress the resources, people, and information flows from headquarters to subsidiary, examining these relationships mainly in the context of control and coordination. However, in the large, mature multinational, these flows are multidirectional: from headquarters to subsidiary, from subsidiary to subsidiary, and between subsidiaries (see Exhibit 2–8). The result can be a complex network of interrelated activities and relationships.

It is possible to identify three main approaches from the multinational management literature—the heterarchy, the transnational, and the network firm. Although they have been given different terms, each form recognizes that, at this stage of internationalization, the concept of a superior structure that neatly fits the corporate strategy becomes inappropriate. The proponents of each of these three forms are in agreement that multinationals at this stage become less hierarchical. As Marschan[29] explains reconsidering the long-standing principle that "the parent knows best" requires a radical change in the way the entire multinational is managed, turning it from an organizational pyramid into an integrated network. These new forms and their IHRM implications are outlined below.

EXHIBIT 2–8   *Beyond the Matrix*

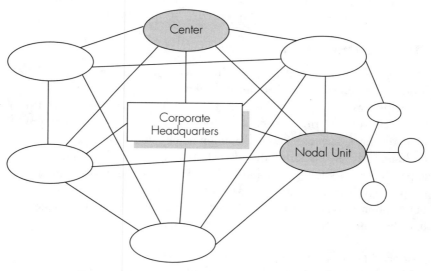

The Heterarchy

The heterarchy is a structural form proposed by Hedlund[30] that recognizes that a multinational may have a number of different kinds of centers apart from the traditional center referred to as "headquarters." Hedlund argued that competitive advantage does not necessarily reside in any one country (the parent country, for example). Rather, it may be found in many countries, so each subsidiary center may be simultaneously a center and a global coordinator of discrete activities, thus performing a strategic role not just for itself, but for the MNE as a whole (the subsidiary labeled "center" in Exhibit 2–8). For example, some multinationals may centralize research and development in a particular subsidiary. In a heterarchical MNE, control is less reliant on the top–bottom mechanisms of previous hierarchical modes and more reliant on normative mechanisms, such as the corporate culture and a widely shared awareness of central goals and strategies.

From a HRM perspective, the heterarchy is interesting in that its success appears to rest solely on the ability of the multinational to formulate, implement, and reinforce the required human resource elements. Hedlund recognizes that the heterarchy demands skillful and experienced personnel as well as sophisticated reward and punishment systems in order to develop the normative control mechanisms necessary for effective performance. The use of staff as an informal control mechanism is important, which we explore later in this chapter.

The Transnational

The term *transnational* has been coined to describe a new organizational form that is characterized by an interdependence of resources and responsibilities across all business units regardless of national boundaries. The transnational tries to cope with the large flows of components, products, resources, people, and information among its subsidiaries, while simultaneously recognizing the distributed specialized resources and capabilities. As such, it demands a complex process of coordination and cooperation involving strong cross-unit integrating devices, a strong corporate identity, and a well-developed worldwide management perspective. In their study, Bartlett and Ghoshal[31] noted:

> Among the companies we studied, there were several that were in the process of developing such organizational capabilities. They had surpassed the classic capabilities of the *multinational* company that operates as decentralized federations of units able to sense and respond to diverse international needs and opportunities; and they had evolved beyond the abilities of the global company with its facility for managing operations on a tightly controlled worldwide basis through its centralized hub structure. They had developed

what we termed *transnational* capabilities—the ability to manage across national boundaries, retaining local flexibility while achieving global integration. More than anything else this involved the ability to link local operations
to each other and to the center in a flexible way, and in so doing, to leverage
those local and central capabilities.

In fact, the matrix, the heterarchy, and the transnational share a common
theme regarding the human resource factor. Therefore, developing
transnational managers or global leaders who can think and act across
national and subsidiary boundaries emerges is an important task for top
management introducing these complex organizational forms. Staff
transfers play a critical role in integration and coordination.

The Multinational as a Network

Some scholars are advocating viewing certain large and mature internationalized firms as a network, in situations where:

- Subsidiaries have developed into significant centers for investments,
  activities, and influence, and can no longer be regarded as at the
  periphery;[32]
- Interaction between headquarters and each subsidiary is likely to be
  dyadic, taking place between various actors at many different organizational levels and covering different exchanges, the outcome of
  which will be important for effective global performance; and
- Such MNEs are loosely coupled political systems rather than tightly
  bonded, homogeneous, hierarchically controlled systems.[33] This runs
  counter to the traditional structure where linkages are described formally via the organization's structure and standardized procedures,
  and informally through interpersonal contact and socialization.[34]

Exhibit 2–8 attempts to depict such an intricate crisscrossing of relationships. One subsidiary may act as a nodal unit linking a cluster of
satellite organizations. Thus, one center can assume responsibility for
other units in its country or region.

The management of a multicentered networked organization is complex. Apart from the intraorganizational network (comprising of headquarters and the numerous subsidiaries), each subsidiary also has a
range of external relationships (involving local suppliers, customers,
competitors, host governments, and alliance partners). The management of both the intraorganizational and interorganizational spheres,

and of the total integrated network, is crucial to global corporate performance. It involves what has been termed a less-hierarchical structure, featuring five dimensions: delegation of decision-making authority to appropriate units and levels; geographical dispersal of key functions across units in different countries; de-layering of organizational levels; de-bureaucratization of formal procedures; and differentiation of work, responsibility, and authority across the networked subsidiaries.[35]

In line with this view, Ghoshal and Bartlett[36] have expanded their concept of the transnational to define the MNE as an interorganizational system which is comprised of a network of exchange relationships among different organizational units, including headquarters and national subsidiaries, as well as external organizations, such as host governments, customers, suppliers, and competitors, with which the different units of the multinational must interact. These authors argue a new way of structuring is not the issue—it is more the emerging management philosophy, with its focus on management processes: "The actual configuration of the processes themselves, and the structural shell within which they are embedded, can be very different depending on the businesses and the heritage of each company."[37] Ghoshal and Bartlett cite GE, ABB, and Toyota as prime examples of companies involved in developing such processes, with Intel and Corning, Philips and Alcatel, Matsushita and Toshiba regarded as companies embarking upon a network-type configuration. Likewise, the Ford Motor Company abandoned its regional structure in 1993, and adopted a multidisciplinary product team approach, networking plants across regions.[38]

Different Countries Take Different Paths

The above discussion takes a generalist view of the growth of the internationalizing firm through the various stages to multinational status, and the correspondent organizational structures. However, it is important to note a cultural element.

As can be seen from Exhibit 2–9, European firms have tended to take a different structural path than their U.S. counterparts. Franko's study of seventy European multinationals revealed that European firms moved directly from a functional "mother–daughter" structure to a divisionalized global structure (with worldwide product or area divisions) or matrix organization without the transitional stage of an international division.[39] Human resource management practices, changing to serve the needs of the new structure, adjusted accordingly. Swedish firms have traditionally

EXHIBIT 2-9 *U.S., European, and Japanese Structural Changes*

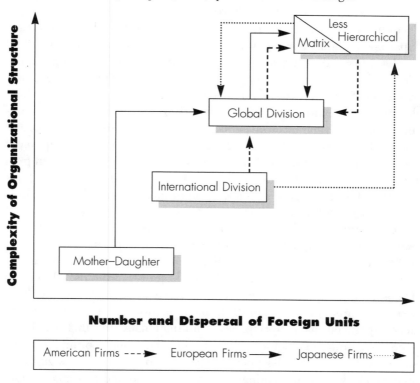

Source: R. Marschan, 1996. *New Structural Forms and Inter-unit Communication in Multinationals,* Helsinki: Helsinki School of Economics. Reproduced with permission.

adopted the mother–daughter structure, but Hedlund suggests that this is changing. The Swedish multinationals in his study tended to adopt a mixture of elements of the mother–daughter structure and elements of the product division at this stage of their internationalization process.[40] While there is little empirical data to substantiate this, it would appear that there is a preference for matrix-type structures within European firms, particularly Nordic multinationals. One could suggest that this structural form has better suited the more collaborative, group-oriented work organization found within these firms. Needless to say, as can be seen from the above exhibit, some European multinationals have also tried and abandoned the matrix, as the backward arrows in Exhibit 2–9 portray.

Japanese multinationals are evolving along lines similar to their U.S. counterparts. Export divisions have become international divisions but, according to Ronen,[41] the rate of change is slower. The characteristics of Japanese organizational culture (such as the control and reporting mechanisms and decision-making systems), the role of trading companies, and the systems of management appear to contribute to the slower evolution of the international division. In some cases, despite their high degree of internationalization, Japanese firms may not adapt their structure as they become more dispersed. As mentioned previously, Ghoshal and Bartlett were able to include Japanese firms in their description of the network multinational. A 1996 study[42] of 54 companies, taken from the *Fortune* 1991 list of the world's 500 largest industrial corporations revealed that the degree of internationalization differed between firms from the United States, Europe, and Japan. The study also reports that the U.S. multinationals in the sample gave more autonomy to their international operations than did their Japanese counterparts.

We should mention that internationalizing firms from other Asian nations may also vary in structural form and growth patterns. As will be discussed in Chapter 3, Korean conglomerates (*chaebols*) appear to have a stronger preference for growth-through-acquisitions than the "greenfield" approach taken by Japanese multinationals, and this will influence their structural responses in terms of control and coordination. The so-called Chinese bamboo network/family firms may face significant challenges as their international activities expand and it becomes more difficult to maintain the tight family control that characterizes overseas-Chinese firms. As the chairman of one Chinese multinational[43] commented with regard to the effects of international growth: "You have no choice but to trust foreigners and to delegate. You run out of family rather rapidly."

Fashion or Fit?

The above discussion has traced the evolution of the firm from a domestic-oriented into a global-oriented firm. A note of caution is added: Growth in the firm's international business activity does require structural responses, but the evolutionary process will differ across multinationals. Apart from the country of origin aspect, other variables—size of organization, pattern of internationalization, management policies, and so on—also play a part. Researchers have identified the pattern described here, but the danger is to treat the stages as normative rather than descriptive. To quote Bartlett:[44]

For some [MNEs] it seemed that organizational structure followed fashion as much as it related to strategy. Reorganizations from international divisions to global product or area organizations, or from global structures to matrix forms, became widespread. This, after all, was the classic organizational sequence described in the "stages theories." Yet many companies that had expected such changes to provide them with the strategy-structure "fit" to meet the new pressures were disappointed. Developing a multidimensional decision-making process that was able to balance the conflicting global and national needs was a subtle and time-consuming process not necessarily achieved by redrawing the lines on a chart. Examples of failed or abandoned multinational organizations abound.

The movement charted in Exhibit 2–9 demonstrates this. For example, as previously mentioned, arrows indicating a backward movement from the matrix/less-hierarchical box to the global division reflect how some firms have tried and abandoned such structural forms. The exhibit, therefore, is a useful reminder that the networked firm is *not* the ultimate end state, though one can often get the impression from some writers that all internationalizing firms aspire one day to be referred to as "transnational/networked."

Control and Coordination

Of the management processes that accompany less-hierarchical configurations, coordination appears to be a major cause of concern. Indeed, firms that classify themselves as global operators confront common coordination issues. As the chairman and chief executive officer of the French hotel and travel company, Accor, recently explained in a newspaper interview:[45]

Accor has to be a global company, in view of the revolution in the service sector which is taking place.... National [hotel chains] cannot optimize their operations. They cannot invest enough money.... Globalization brings considerable challenges which are often underestimated. The principal difficulty is getting our local management to adhere to the values of the group.... Every morning when I wake I think about the challenges of coordinating our operations in many different countries.

Human resource management plays a key role in control and coordination processes, particularly where less-hierarchical structures we discussed above are concerned:

- Ghoshal and Bartlett argue that the key means for vital knowledge generation and diffusion is through personal contact. This means that networked organizations need processes to facilitate contacts. Training and development programs, held in regional centers or at headquarters, become an important forum for the development of personal networks that foster informal communication channels, as well as for building corporate culture. However, recent research suggests that the ability to participate in such forums depends on fluency in the common corporate language.[46]
- Network relationships are built and maintained through personal contact. Therefore, staffing decisions are crucial to the effective management of the linkages that the various subsidiaries have established. Nevertheless, staffing decisions may be made, and often are, without regard to their effect on network relationships.[47]
- As with the heterarchy, the management processes in a networked multinational rely heavily on the ability of key staff to integrate operations to provide the internal company environment that fosters the required level of cooperation, commitment, and communication flows between functions and subsidiary units.
- Staff transfers are also an important part of the required management processes, particularly that of control. Despite the costs and challenges involved, which we shall discuss in the next chapter, multinationals continue to rely on the movement of key staff to assist in coordination and control. In fact, the literature suggests that staff transfers become an important element in the soft control mechanisms described above.[48] The case of GE in Hungary (Exhibit 2–1) is a good example of how staff transfers were an important part of GE's attempts to integrate its new acquisition into its "global family." Transfers of HCNs to headquarters were a useful way of exposing Hungarians from Tungsram to GE's corporate culture. Training and development programs played a role here, too.
- Expatriates are used to instill a sense of corporate identity in subsidiary operations, and to assist in the transfer of corporate norms and values as part of corporate cultural (or normative) control.

Thus, proponents of less-hierarchical configurations argue there is greater reliance on informal control mechanisms than on the formal, bureaucratic control mechanisms that accompanied the traditional hierarchy. As seen from the above list, the informal control mechanisms highlighted in Exhibit 2–10 are assisted by HR practices.

EXHIBIT 2-10   *Control Mechanisms in the Networked MNE*

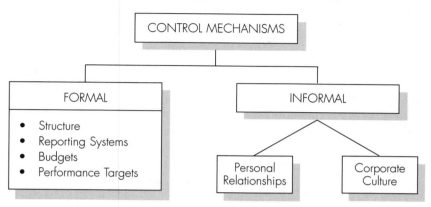

Source: Adapted from R. Marchan, D. Welch, and L. Welch, 1996. Control in less-hierarchical multinationals: The role of personal networks and informal communication, *International Business Review*, vol. 5, no. 2, pp. 137–150.

It is also important to remember that international growth affects the firm's approach to HRM. For this reason, we have attempted to draw out the HRM implications at each stage of internationalization. As mentioned at the beginning of this chapter, firms vary from one another as they go through the stages of international development, and react in different ways to the circumstances they encounter in the various foreign markets. Therefore, we find a wide variety of matches between IHRM approaches, organizational structure, and stage of internationalization. For example, almost half the U.S. firms surveyed by Dowling[49] reported that the operations of the human resource function were unrelated to the nature of the firm's international operations. A recent study by Monks[50] of nine subsidiaries of multinationals operating in Ireland found that the majority adopted a local approach to the HR function, with headquarters involvement often limited to monitoring the financial implications of HR decisions.

MODE OF OPERATION

The above discussion on structural adjustments has been based on the literature relating to the growth of the multinational enterprise. The organizational forms illustrated are primarily concerned with integrating wholly owned subsidiaries. However, as Welch and Welch argue,[51] internationalizing firms may also adopt contractual (such as, licensing, franchising, management contracts, and projects) and cooperative (such as joint ventures) modes in order to enter and develop foreign markets. Naturally, these modes are not mutually exclusive: A firm may have licensing arrangements with a foreign joint venture, or have a general strategy of growth through international franchising but combine this with a wholly owned subsidiary or a joint venture in some markets. These authors present a framework to illustrate how IHRM activities, such as staff placement, simultaneously link and influence the mode of operation utilized to support an internationalization strategy. This framework is reproduced in Exhibit 2–11. Welch and Welch explain:[52]

> The many forms of operation modes may demand different skills and place varying stresses on the resources of the company, particularly on its personnel. For example, licensing might involve only limited commitments of staff, whereas the availability of key people becomes particularly critical for the success of a management contract in which the company is required to transfer a number of experienced managerial and technical staff to run a foreign facility.

EXHIBIT 2-11   *Linking Operation Mode and HRM*

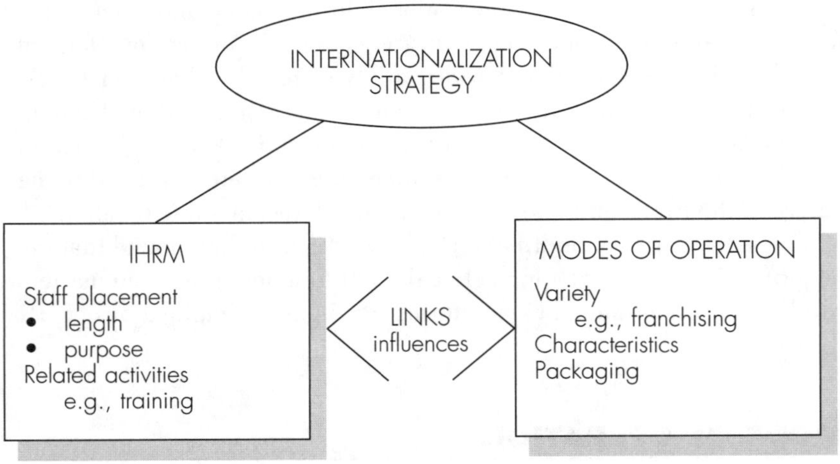

Source: D. Welch, and L. Welch, 1994. Linking operation mode diversity and IHRM, *The International Journal of Human Resource Management*, vol. 5, no. 4, p. 915. Reproduced with permission of the editor.

While decrying the paucity of empirical evidence regarding the IHRM demands of the contractual modes of operation, the authors suggest that HRM concerns affect, and may even govern, the choice of market entry mode. They use the entry of the U.S. hamburger chain, McDonald's, into Russia to illustrate the interconnection between mode of entry and IHRM. Expatriates were involved in assisting with the selection and training of local staff—each crew member received the standard McDonald's training (60 hours of training per crew member). Russians selected for managerial positions were sent to McDonald's Institute of Hamburgerology in Toronto, Canada, and to the Hamburger University in Oakbrook, Illinois, in the United States. When the first restaurant opened, they had a staff of 630 employees.[53]

Management contracts are also used as a way of operating in foreign markets. They involve a management role in the foreign company for a specified period of time and fee, and therefore require the posting of staff for extended periods of time. Walt Disney is an example of a firm that utilizes this mode of operation; the establishment of Euro-Disney (France) combined 49 percent equity with a management fee of 3 percent of gross revenue.[54] Management contracts are also used in the hotel and airline industries.

By its very nature, this form of contractual mode means that skilled, usually talented staff will be needed. Knowledge transfer is an important component, involving the training of HCN staff. However, there is little treatment of the HR demands of a successful management contract in the IHRM literature. In one of the few international business texts that covers this contractual mode of operation, the authors[55] comment:

> The overall success of the contract operation, including the training aspect, depends on the quality of staff transferred or appointed to the contract venture, and therefore overall international human resource management by the company. Because management contracts are normally not a mainstream operational method, when used they will often receive secondary consideration in staffing requirements. For this reason, companies tend not to be keen to commit large numbers of quality staff to contract operations. Likewise the client organization prefers not to have large numbers of expatriate staff as it makes eventual replacement more difficult. Thus, for both sides there is an incentive to keep down foreign staff numbers.

There is a similar paucity of information associated with the IHRM demands of international project management—for the project firm itself, as well as the range of contributing firms (i.e., subcontractors, joint-venture partners, etc.) that may be involved in the international project.

Interfirm Linkages

Another mode of operation is that of an alliance. A firm may enter into an alliance with an external party (or parties) such as a competitor, a key supplier, or an affiliated firm in order to compete more effectively in the global marketplace.[56] Since these partnerships come in all shapes and sizes,[57] the term *alliance* has come to mean different things to different people: strategic alliance, cooperative venture, collaborative agreement, or corporate linkage (of which one form may be a joint venture).[58] For the purpose of this discussion, we will use a broad definition: "A corporate alliance is a formal and mutually agreed commercial collaboration between companies. The partners pool, exchange, or integrate specified business resources for mutual gain. Yet the partners remain separate businesses."[59]

The key point is that an alliance is a form of business relationship that involves some measure of interfirm integration that goes beyond the traditional buyer–seller relationship, but stops short of a full merger or acquisition, though some alliances can develop into mergers or takeovers at a later date.[60] The particular type of venture that emerges is a function of the strategic importance of the venture to the parent company and the extent to which the parent seeks control over the resources allocated to the venture.

There was a marked growth in alliance formation in the 1980s.[61] Alliances can now be found in such diverse industries as telecommunications, aerospace, automobiles, electronics, and transportation equipment. Shared activities can include research and development, production, and marketing. An alliance can involve arrangements such as licensing agreements, marketing or distribution partnerships, and consortia.

Regardless of the motive for entering into such an arrangement, the resultant partnership adds another dimension to a firm's structure. In order to meet the objectives of the collaborative partnership within the context of broader corporate strategy, the firm needs to integrate or link the partnership venture to its own existing activities and functions and to devise a method of monitoring its performance. The way the partnership is interlinked naturally depends on the form that the collaboration takes.

As we have seen with other modes of operation, the various forms of interfirm linkages affect HRM in different ways, depending on the type of alliance involved. For example, in an international joint venture, when a new entity brings together managers from two or more firms, the managers must become accustomed to working with a foreign partner (or partners). "Staffing the joint venture with managers who are flexible in terms of different management styles and philosophies is probably the single most important task facing the human resource function at this critical time."[62] Indeed, Lorange[63] links success to a match between the form of cooperative venture and human resource components, maintaining that "the human resource function is particularly critical to successful implementation of such cooperative ventures." In their analysis of strategic alliances, Cascio and Serapio[64] classify these collaborative forms of business relationships according to the extent of interaction required among people from the collaborating companies; they point out, for example, that a joint venture involves more interaction than does a marketing or distribution partnership. While the specific nature of joint venture management issues and HR implications will be further explored in Chapter 9, it is important to note here that HR factors play a crucial role in this type of relationship.

LINKING HR TO INTERNATIONAL EXPANSION STRATEGIES

The preceding sections have explored the interrelationship between the HR function and the firm's involvement in international business operations. Clearly, it is important that the internationalizing firm considers the HR implications of its international strategies—recognizing that people are a critical component for the successful implementation and attainment of these expansion strategies. Using an inductive, grounded-theory approach from a study of four Australian firms, including the Australian subsidiary of the U.S.-based Ford Motor Company, Welch[65] has developed a theoretical model that links firm-specific variables (such as stage in internationalization, organizational structure, and organizational culture) and situation variables (such as staff availability, need for control) with IHRM approaches and activities. Contextual variables (such as cultural distance and host-country legal requirements) are also included. This model is adapted as Exhibit 2–12. Welch suggests these linkages may explain the various interrelationships between

EXHIBIT 2-12 *Determinants of IHRM Approaches and Activities*

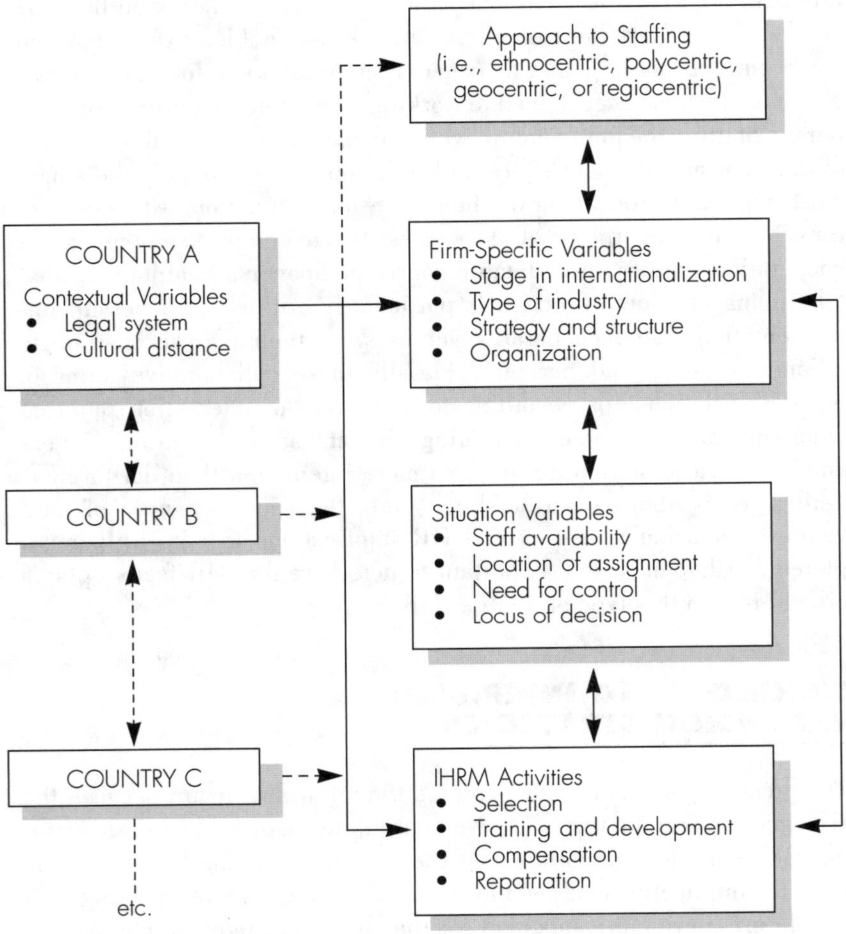

Source: Adapted from D. Welch, 1994. Determinants of international human resource management approaches and activities: A suggested framework, *Journal of Management Studies*, vol. 31, no. 2, p. 150.

organizational factors and IHRM activities that may determine a firm's approach to the staffing of overseas operations; that is, whether a multinational adopts an ethnocentric, polycentric, geocentric, or regiocentric approach to staff subsidiary operations.

The theoretical model may be helpful in drawing together the various organizational factors and HR issues discussed in this chapter. The

HRM staffing approaches do influence and are influenced by organizational factors as well as country factors. For instance, a firm that is maturing into a networked organization (firm-specific variable) will require IHRM approaches and activities that will assist its ability to develop a flexible global organization that is centrally integrated and coordinated yet locally responsive—a geocentric approach. However, a key assumption underlying the geocentric staffing philosophy is that the multinational has sufficient numbers of high-caliber staff (PCNs, TCNs, and HCNs) constantly available for transfer anywhere, whenever global management needs dictate.[66] In practice, it is not easy to find or nurture the required numbers of high-quality staff (firm-specific and situation variables), nor assign them to certain operations due to host-country requirements (country-specific variables). The IHRM activities—selection, training and development, compensation, and repatriation—discussed in the remainder of this textbook play an important role in the development of the effective policies required to sustain a preferred approach to staffing.

SUMMARY

This chapter focused on the organizational context in which IHRM activities take place. It has outlined the major approaches to staffing international operations before tracing the typical path taken by a domestic firm as it evolves into a global player. Different structural arrangements have been identified, along with control and coordination aspects associated with each form. The various modes used by multinationals for foreign market entry and expansion have also been included in this chapter to demonstrate IHRM implications. One should remember, though, that these stages of development and modes of operation are not to be taken as normative. Research suggests a pattern and a process of internationalization, but firms do vary in how they adapt to international operations—we use nationality of the parent firm to demonstrate this.

Nevertheless, the stages identified in this chapter have been a convenient method of highlighting the challenges and responses of international growth and expansion. The purpose has been to identify the HR implications of the various options and responses that international growth places on the firm. We have, through this discussion, been able to demonstrate that there is an interconnection between international

HRM approaches and activities and the organizational context, and that HR managers have a crucial role to play. In order to better perform this role, it would seem important that HR managers understand the various international structural options—along with the control and coordination demands imposed by international growth, and the HR implications that accompany the range of operation modes outlined in this chapter.

QUESTIONS

1. What are the stages a firm typically goes through as it grows internationally and how does each stage affect the HR function?
2. What are the specific HRM challenges in a networked firm?
3. What are some of the problems associated with a matrix structure?
4. The opening of McDonald's in Moscow demonstrates the HR demands associated with new market entry. What did the company do to handle these? What role did staff transfers play?
5. What can the HRM department/function do to assist in the firm's international growth strategy?

FURTHER READING

1. Buckley, P.J., and P. Ghauri, eds., 1993. *The Internationalization of the Firm: A Reader*, London: Academic Press.
2. Ghadar, F., and N.J. Adler, 1989. Management culture and the accelerated product life cycle, *Human Resource Planning*, vol. 12, no. 1, pp. 37–42.
3. Ghoshal, S., and C. Bartlett, 1995. Building the entrepreneurial corporation: New organizational processes, new managerial tasks, *European Management Journal*, vol. 13, no. 2, pp. 139–155.
4. Hedlund, G., 1994. A model of knowledge management and the N-Form Corporation, *Strategic Management Journal*, vol. 15, pp. 73–90.
5. Hendry, C., 1994. *Human Resource Strategies for International Growth*, London: Routledge.
6. Malnight, T.W., 1996. The transition from decentralized to network-based MNC structures: An evolutionary perspective, *Journal of International Business Studies*, vol. 27, no. 1, pp. 43–65.
7. Miller, S. Beechler, B. Bhatt, and R. Nath, 1986. The relationship between the global strategic planning process and the human

resource management function, *Human Resource Planning*, vol. 9, no. 1, pp. 9–25.

8. Oviatt, B.M., and P.P. McDougall, 1994. Towards a theory of international new ventures, *Journal of International Business Studies*, vol. 25, no. 1, pp. 45–64.

9. Serapio, M.G., and W.F. Cascio, 1996. End games in international alliances, *Academy of Management Executive*, vol. 10, no. 1, pp. 62–73.

10. Wolf, J., 1997. From 'starworks' to networks and heterarchies?, *Management International Review*, vol. 37, no. 1 (Special issue), pp. 145–169.

ENDNOTES

1. M. Svard, and R. Luostarinen, 1982. Personnel needs in the internationalizing firm, FIBO Publication No. 19, Helsinki: Helsinki School of Economics.

2. 1992. *International Management*, December, pp. 42–45; N. Dention, 1993. Tungsram fails to shine for GE, *Financial Times*, March 17, p. 18; 1994. *Business Central Europe*, Tungsram turns a corner, March, p. 25.

3. Interview with manager concerned, conducted as part of an evaluation study of an Australian Government Export Promotion Scheme, by D. Welch, L. Welch, I. Wilkinson, and L. Young. The company's name has been disguised to respect the anonymity of the study's participants.

4. H.V. Perlmutter, 1969. The tortuous evolution of the multinational corporation, *Columbia Journal of World Business*, vol. 4, no. 1, pp. 9–18.

5. D.A. Heenan, and H.V. Perlmutter, 1979. *Multinational Organization Development*, Reading, MA: Addison-Wesley.

6. Electrolux in-house magazine *Appliance*, E-26, 1995.

7. John Thornhill, 1996. Opportunities blossom in the Wild East, *Financial Times*, August 2, Recruitment Section, p. 1.

8. N. Boyacigiller, 1990. The role of expatriates in the management of interdependence, complexity and risk in multinational corporations, *Journal of International Business Studies*, vol. 21, no. 3, pp. 357–381; D.E. Welch, 1994. Determinants of international human resource management approaches and activities: A suggested

framework, *Journal of Management Studies*, vol. 31, no. 2, pp. 139–164.

9. C.A. Bartlett, and S. Ghoshal, 1988. Organizing for worldwide effectiveness: The transnational solution, *California Management Review*, Fall, pp. 54–74.

10. The organization's structure defines the tasks of individuals and business units within the firm and the processes that result from the intertwined tasks: identifying how the organization is divided up (differentiated) and how it is united (integrated).

11. The first two authors would like to acknowledge the contribution of Lawrence Welch in the development of this exhibit.

12. B.M. Oviatt, and P.P. McDougall, 1994. Towards a theory of international new ventures, *Journal of International Business Studies*, vol. 25, no. 1, pp. 45–64.

13. J. Johanson, and J.E. Vahlne, 1990. The mechanism of internationalisation, *International Marketing Review*, vol. 7, no. 4, pp. 11–24; L.S. Welch, and R. Luostarinen, 1988. Internationalization: Evolution of a concept, *Journal of General Management*, vol. 14, no. 2, pp. 34–55.

14. A study of U.S. service firms involved in international operations showed that wholly owned subsidiary/branch office was the most common method, though engineering and architecture firms used direct exports, and consumer services used licensing/franchising (K. Erramilli, 1991. The experience factor in foreign market entry behavior of service firms, *Journal of International Business Studies*, vol. 22, no. 3, pp. 479–501). Similar results were found in a study of Australian service firms (LEK Partnership, 1994. *Intelligent Exports and the Silent Revolution in Services*, Canberra: Australian Government Publishing Service).

15. D.E. Welch, and L.S. Welch, 1997. Pre-expatriation: The role of HR factors in the early stages of internationalization, *The International Journal of Human Resource Management*, vol. 8, no. 4, pp. 402–413.

16. The first two authors would like to acknowledge the contributions of Helen De Cieri, Rebecca Marschan, and Lawrence Welch in the development of the organizational charts used in this chapter.

17. 1975. Canadian licensing venture helps firm improve penetration, *Overseas Trading*, vol. 27, no. 16, p. 398.

18. J. Stopford, and L. Wells, 1972. *Managing the Multinational*, London: Longmans.

19. See V. Pucik, 1985. Strategic human resource management in a multinational firm, *Strategic Management of Multinational Corporations: The Essentials*, H.V. Wortzel, and L.H. Wortzel, eds. New York: John Wiley, p. 425.
20. Welch, and Welch, Pre-expatriation: The role of HR factors, p. 409.
21. Pucik, Strategic human resource management in a multinational firm.
22. Bartlett, and Ghoshal, Organizing for worldwide effectiveness.
23. J.R. Galbraith, and R.K. Kazanjian, 1986. Organizing to implement strategies of diversity and globalization: The role of matrix designs, *Human Resource Management*, vol. 25, no. 1, p. 50. See also T.T. Naylor, 1985. The international strategy mix, *Columbia Journal of World Business*, vol. 20, no. 2; and R.A. Pitts, and J.D. Daniels, 1984. Aftermath of the matrix mania, *Columbia Journal of World Business*, vol. 19, no. 2 for a discussion on the matrix structure.
24. W. Taylor, 1991. The logic of global business: An interview with ABB's Percy Barnevik, *Harvard Business Review*, March–April, pp. 95–96.
25. C.A. Bartlett, and S. Ghoshal, 1990. Matrix management: Not a structure, a frame of mind, *Harvard Business Review*, July–August, pp. 138–145.
26. S. Ronen, 1986. *Comparative and Multinational Management*, New York: John Wiley.
27. P.J. Dowling, 1988. International HRM, *Human Resource Management: Evolving Roles and Responsibilities*, vol. 1, L. Dyer, ed. ASPA/BNA Handbook of Human Resource Management Series, Washington: D.C.: BRA.
28. Galbraith, and Kazanjian, Organizing to implement strategies, p. 50.
29. R. Marschan, 1996. *New Structural Forms and Inter-Unit Communication in Multinationals*, Helsinki: Helsinki School of Economics.
30. G. Hedlund, 1986. The hypermodern MNC—A heterarchy?, *Human Resource Management*, vol. 25, no. 1, pp. 9–35.
31. Bartlett, and Ghoshal, Organizing for worldwide effectiveness, p. 66.
32. U. Anderson, M. Forsgren, C. Pahlberg, and P. Thilenius, 1990. Global firms in internationalized networks, in *Proceedings of the Sixteenth Annual Conference of the European International Business*

Association, J. Duran, ed. Madrid, December, p. 2. See also K. Roth, and A.J. Morrison, 1992. Implementing global strategy: Characteristics of global subsidiary mandates, *Journal of International Business Studies*, vol. 23, no. 4.

33. M. Forsgren, 1990. Managing the international multi-centre firm: Case studies from Sweden, *European Management Journal*, vol. 8, no. 2, pp. 261–267. Much of this work has been based on the concepts of social exchange theory and interaction between actors in a network.

34. J.I. Martinez, and J.C. Jarillo, 1989. The evolution of research on coordination mechanisms in multinational corporations, *Journal of International Business Studies*, Fall, pp. 489–514.

35. R. Marschan, 1997. Dimensions of less-hierarchical structures in multinationals, in *The Nature of the International Firm*, I. Björkman, and M. Forsgren, eds. Copenhagen: Copenhagen Business School Press.

36. S. Ghoshal, and C.A. Bartlett, 1990. The multinational corporation as an interorganizational network, *Academy of Management Review*, vol. 8, no. 2, pp. 603–625.

37. S. Ghoshal, and C. Bartlett, 1995. Building the entrepreneurial corporation: New organizational processes, new managerial tasks, *European Management Journal*, vol. 13, no. 2, p. 145.

38. *Financial Times* series on *The Global Company*, October 15, 1997, p. 14.

39. L. Leksell, 1981. *Headquarter-Subsidiary Relationships in Multinational Corporations*, Stockholm: Stockholm School of Economics.

40. G. Hedlund, 1984. Organization in-between: The evolution of the mother–daughter structure of managing foreign subsidiaries in Swedish MNCs, *Journal of International Business Studies*, Fall, pp. 109–123.

41. Ronen, *Comparative and Multinational Management*.

42. R.B. Peterson, J. Sargent, N.K. Napier, and W.S. Shim, 1996. Corporate expatriate HRM policies, internationalization and performance, *Management International Review*, vol. 36, no. 3, pp. 215–230.

43. Victor Fung, Chairman of Li Fung, one of Hong Kong's oldest and largest trading groups, 1997. A multinational trading group with Chinese characteristics, *Financial Times*, November 7, p. 12.

44. C.A. Bartlett, 1982. How multinational organizations evolve, *Journal of Business Strategy*, vol. 3, no. 1. See also T. Hout, M.E. Porter,

and E. Rudden, 1982. How global companies win out, *Harvard Business Review*, vol. 60, no. 5.

45. Interview by Andrew Jack, 1997. *Financial Times*, October 13, p. 14.

46. R. Marschan, D. Welch, and L. Welch, 1997. Language: The forgotten factor in multinational management, *European Management Journal*, vol. 15, no. 5, pp. 591–598.

47. D.E. Welch, and L.S. Welch, 1993. Using personnel to develop networks: An approach to subsidiary management, *International Business Review*, vol. 2, no. 2.

48. For a literature review and discussion on the use of staff transfers as a control mechanism, see D. Welch, M. Fenwick, and H. De Cieri, 1994. Staff transfers as a control strategy: An exploratory study of two Australian organizations, *International Journal of Human Resource Management*, vol. 5, no. 2, pp. 473–489.

49. P.J. Dowling, 1989. Hot issues overseas, *Personnel Administrator*, vol. 34, no. 1, pp. 66–72.

50. K. Monks, 1996. Global or local? HRM in the multinational company: The Irish experience, *International Journal of Human Resource Management*, vol. 7, no. 3, pp. 721–735.

51. D. Welch, and L. Welch, 1994. Linking operation mode diversity and IHRM, *The International Journal of Human Resource Management*, vol. 5, no. 4, pp. 911–926.

52. Ibid., p. 915.

53. O. Vikhanski, and S. Puffer, 1993. Management education and employee training at Moscow McDonald's, *European Management Journal*, vol. 11, no. 1, pp. 102–107.

54. 1992. *The Economist*, September 26.

55. R. Luostarinen, and L.S. Welch, 1990. *International Business Operations*, Helsinki: Export Consulting KY.

56. R.N. Osborn, and C.C. Baughn, 1990. Forms of interorganizational governance for multinational alliances, *Academy of Management Journal*, vol. 33, no. 3, pp. 503–519; J.C. Jarillo, and H.H. Stevenson, 1991. Co-operative strategies—The payoffs and the pitfalls, *Long-Range Planning*, vol. 24, no. 1, pp. 64–70.

57. D. Scott-Kemmis, T. Darling, R. Johnston, F. Collyer, and C. Cliff, 1990. *Strategic Alliances in the Internationalisation of Australian Industry*, Canberra, Australia: Australian Government Publishing Service.

58. Luostarinen, and Welch, *International Business Operations*.
59. Business International, 1990. *Making Alliances Work: Lessons from Companies' Successes and Mistakes*, London: Business International, Ltd., p. 27.
60. Ibid.
61. Scott-Kemmis et. al., *Strategic Alliances*.
62. Lei, and J.W. Slocum, Jr., 1991. Global strategic alliances: Payoffs and pitfalls, *Organizational Dynamics*, Winter, p. 57.
63. P. Lorange, 1986. Human resource management in multinational cooperative ventures, *Human Resource Management*, vol. 25, no. 1, p. 133.
64. W.F. Cascio, and M.G. Serapio, 1991. Human resources systems in an international alliance: The undoing of a done deal?, *Organizational Dynamics*, Winter, pp. 63–74. R.S. Schuler, and E. Van Slujis, 1992. Davidson Marley BV: Establishing and operating an international joint venture, *European Management Journal*, vol. 10, December, pp. 428–436.
65. Welch, Determinants of international human resource management approaches and activities.
66. D. Welch, 1994. HRM implications of globalization, *Journal of General Management*, vol. 19, no. 4, pp. 52–68.

International Recruitment and Selection

H iring and placing people in positions where they can perform effectively is a goal of most organizations, whether domestic or international. As you will appreciate from our discussion on IHRM in the preceding chapters, there are staffing issues that internationalizing firms confront that are either not present in a domestic environment, or are complicated by the international context in which these activities take place. Take, for example, this scenario: A U.S. multinational wishes to appoint a new finance director for its Indian subsidiary. It may decide to fill the position by selecting from finance staff available in its parent operations (i.e., a PCN), or to recruit locally (a HCN), or seek a suitable candidate from one of its other foreign subsidiaries (a TCN). How it responds is determined partly by factors such as:

- Its general staffing policy on key positions in headquarters and subsidiaries (i.e., ethnocentrism, polycentrism, geocentrism, and regiocentrism);
- Its ability to attract the right candidate; and
- The constraints placed by the host government on hiring policies.

The focus of this chapter, then, is on recruitment and selection activities in an international context. Recruitment is defined as searching for and obtaining potential job candidates in sufficient numbers and quality so that the organization can select the most appropriate people to fill its job needs. Selection is the process of gathering information for the purposes of evaluating and deciding whom should be employed in particular jobs.[1] We will explore the key issues surrounding international recruitment and selection, with a focus on selection criteria. As well, we will look at various factors—such as female managers, dual-career couples, equal opportunity legislation, and expatriate failure—that impact on the multinational's ability to recruit and select high-caliber staff. For convenience, we will use the term *multinational* throughout this chapter, but it is important to remember that the issues, howbeit variously, pertain to all internationalizing companies—regardless of size, industry, stage in internationalization, nationality of origin, and geographical diversity. We will begin with a more detailed look at the four staffing options outlined in Chapter 2.

EXECUTIVE NATIONALITY STAFFING POLICIES

The four approaches to multinational staffing decisions—ethnocentric, polycentric, geocentric, and regiocentric—tend to reflect the managerial philosophy towards international operations held by top management at headquarters. It is important that we explore each of these approaches further, as each has important implications for international recruitment and selection practices.

The Ethnocentric Approach

An ethnocentric approach to staffing results in all key positions in a multinational being filled by parent-country nationals (PCNs). While this approach may be common for firms at the early stages of internationalization, there are often sound business reasons for pursuing an ethnocentric staffing policy including:

- A perceived lack of qualified host-country nationals (HCNs), and
- The need to maintain good communication, coordination, and control links with corporate headquarters.

For instance, when a multinational acquires a firm in another country, it may wish to initially replace local managers with PCNs to ensure that the new subsidiary complies with overall corporate objectives and policies, or because local staff may not have the required level of competence. Thus, an ethnocentric approach to a particular foreign market situation could be perfectly valid for a very experienced multinational.

An ethnocentric policy, however, has a number of disadvantages. Zeira[2] has identified several major problems:

- An ethnocentric staffing policy limits the promotion opportunities of HCNs, which may lead to reduced productivity and increased turnover among that group.
- The adaptation of expatriate managers to host countries often takes a long time during which PCNs often make mistakes and make poor decisions.
- When PCN and HCN compensation packages are compared, the often-considerable income gap in favor of PCNs is viewed by HCNs as unjustified.
- For many expatriates a key international position means new status, authority, and an increase in standard of living. These changes may affect expatriates' sensitivity to the needs and expectations of their host-country subordinates.

Expatriates are also very expensive to maintain in international locations. A recent study[3] found that 50 percent of responding firms estimated that the average cost of expatriates was three to four times that of normal salary, and 18 percent indicated more than four times the salary.

The Polycentric Approach

A polycentric staffing policy is one in which HCNs are recruited to manage subsidiaries in their own country and PCNs occupy positions at corporate headquarters. The main advantages of a polycentric policy, some of which address shortcomings of the ethnocentric policy identified above, are:

- Employing HCNs eliminates language barriers, avoids the adjustment problems of expatriate managers and their families, and removes the need for expensive cultural awareness training programs.
- Employment of HCNs allows a multinational company to take a lower profile in sensitive political situations.
- Employment of HCNs is less expensive, even if a premium is paid to attract high-quality applicants.
- Employing HCNs gives continuity to the management of foreign subsidiaries. This approach avoids the turnover of key managers that, by its very nature, results from an ethnocentric approach.

A polycentric policy, however, has its own disadvantages. Perhaps the major difficulty is that of bridging the gap between HCN subsidiary managers and PCN managers at corporate headquarters. Language barriers, conflicting national loyalties, and a range of cultural differences (e.g., personal value differences and differences in attitudes to business) may isolate the corporate headquarters staff from the various foreign subsidiaries. The result may be that a multinational firm could become a "federation" of independent national units with nominal links to corporate headquarters.

A second major problem associated with a polycentric staffing policy concerns the career paths of HCN and PCN managers. Host-country managers have limited opportunities to gain experience outside their own country and cannot progress beyond the senior positions in their own subsidiary; parent-country managers also have limited opportunities to gain international experience. As headquarters positions are held only by PCNs, the senior corporate management group will have limited exposure to international operations and, over time, this will constrain strategic decision making and resource allocation.

Of course, in some cases the host government may dictate that key managerial positions be filled by its nationals. Alternatively, the multinational may wish to be perceived as a local company as part of a strategy of local responsiveness. Having HCNs in key, visible positions assists this.

The Geocentric Approach

The geocentric approach option utilizes the best people for the key jobs throughout the organization, regardless of nationality. There are two main advantages to this approach: it enables a multinational firm to develop an international executive team, and it overcomes the "federation" drawback of the polycentric approach. Phatak[4] believes the feasibility of implementing a geocentric policy is based on five related assumptions:

1. Highly competent employees are available not only at headquarters, but also in the subsidiaries;
2. International experience is a condition for success in top positions;
3. Managers with high potential and ambition for promotion are constantly ready to be transferred from one country to another;
4. Competent and mobile managers have an open disposition and high adaptability to different conditions in their various assignments; and

5. Those not blessed initially with an open disposition and high adaptability can acquire these qualities as their experience abroad accumulates.

As with the other staffing approaches, there are disadvantages associated with a geocentric policy. First, host governments want a high number of their citizens employed and will utilize immigration controls in order to force HCN employment if not enough people with adequate skills are available. In addition to this constraint on the implementation of a geocentric policy, most Western countries require companies to provide extensive documentation if they wish to hire a foreign national instead of a local national. Providing this documentation can be time-consuming, expensive, and at times futile. Of course, the same drawback applies to an ethnocentric policy. A related issue, that will be discussed later, is the difficulty of obtaining a work permit for the accompanying spouse or partner.

Another disadvantage is that a geocentric policy can be expensive to implement because of increased training and relocation costs. A related factor is the need to have a compensation structure with standardized international base pay, which may be higher than national levels in many countries. Finally, large numbers of PCNs, TCNs, and HCNs need to be sent abroad in order to build and maintain the international team required to support a geocentric staffing policy. To successfully implement a geocentric staffing policy, therefore, requires longer lead time and more centralized control of the staffing process. This necessarily reduces the independence of subsidiary management in these issues, and this loss of autonomy may be resisted by the subsidiary.

As shown in Exhibit 3–1, Welch[5] identifies IHRM barriers that may impede a multinational from building the staffing resources required to sustain the geocentric policy that is implicit in globalization literature. The barriers—staff availability, time and cost constraints, host-government requirements, and ineffective HRM policies—reflect the issues surrounding the geocentric approach listed in the literature reviewed above. Welch argues that top management commitment to a geocentric staffing policy is necessary to overcome these barriers. While there may be a genuine predisposition among top managers at headquarters regarding the staffing of its global operations, leveraging critical resources in order to build the necessary international team of managers may prove to be a major challenge.

EXHIBIT 3-1   *Geocentric Staffing Requirements*

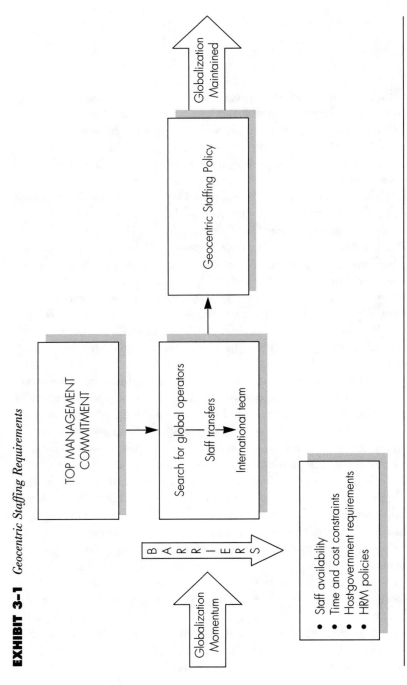

Source: D. Welch, 1994. HRM implications of globalization, *Journal of General Management*, vol. 19, no. 4, p. 57. Reproduced with permission.

The Regiocentric Approach

A fourth approach to international staffing is a regional approach. One illustration of this approach is a regiocentric policy, which Heenan and Perlmutter[6] define as functional rationalization on a more-than-one country basis. The specific mix will vary with the nature of a firm's business and product strategy, but for a multinational one way is to divide its operations into geographical regions and transfer staff within these regions. For example, a U.S.-based firm could create three regions: Europe, the Americas, and Asia-Pacific. European staff would be transferred throughout the European region (say a Briton to Germany, a French national to Belgium, and a German to Spain). Staff transfers to the Asia-Pacific region from Europe would be rare, as would transfers from the regions to headquarters in the United States.

One motive for using a regiocentric approach is that it allows interaction between executives transferred to regional headquarters from subsidiaries in the region and PCNs posted to the regional headquarters. This approach also reflects some sensitivity to local conditions, since local subsidiaries are staffed almost totally by HCNs. Another advantage is that a regiocentric approach can be a way for a multinational to gradually move from a purely ethnocentric or polycentric approach to a geocentric approach.[7] To a certain extent, that appears to be the path taken by some multinationals, such as the Ford Motor Company. However, there are some disadvantages in a regiocentric policy. It can produce federalism at a regional rather than a country basis and constrain the organization from taking a global stance. Another difficulty is that while this approach does improve career prospects at the national level, it only moves the barrier to the regional level. Staff may advance to regional headquarters but seldom to positions at the parent headquarters.

A Philosophy Toward Staffing

In summary, based on top-management attitudes, a multinational can pursue one of several approaches to international staffing. It may even proceed on an *ad hoc* basis, rather than systematically selecting one of the four approaches discussed above. A danger with this approach, according to Robinson[8] is that:

> the firm will opt for a policy of using parent-country nationals in foreign management positions by default, that is, simply as an automatic extension of domestic policy, rather than deliberately seeking optimum utilization of management skills.

This option is really a policy by default; there is no conscious decision or evaluation of appropriate policy. The "policy" is a result of corporate inertia, inexperience, or both. The major disadvantage here (apart from the obvious one of inefficient use of resources) is that the firm's responses are reactive rather than proactive, and a consistent human resources strategy that fits its overall business strategy is difficult to achieve.

As was discussed in Chapter 2, the approach of an appropriate policy on executive nationality tends to reflect organizational needs. For instance, if the multinational places a high priority on organizational control, then an ethnocentric policy will be adopted. However, there are difficulties in maintaining a uniform approach to international staffing. Therefore, strategies in different countries may require different staffing approaches. A U.S. multinational may take a geocentric approach toward its operations in Europe and Asia-Pacific but, say, an ethnocentric approach toward its operations in Africa.

ISSUES IN STAFF SELECTION

We have now established the rationale behind the various staffing approaches that have been identified. Based on this literature, Exhibit 3–2 summarizes the main advantages and disadvantages of utilizing the various nationality groups available to the multinational: parent-country nationals (PCNs), third-country nationals (TCNs), and host-country nationals (HCNs). We now will examine the selection issues surrounding the three categories of nationality, commencing with selection issues around the use of expatriates—a term which may include both PCNs and TCNs, though much of the literature on this topic deals with PCNs.

Expatriate Selection

Given the important role commonly assigned to expatriates, it is logical to assume that MNEs take great care in their selection process. However, it would appear from the now considerable literature on expatriate selection that this is an area fraught with complexity. Predicting future performance potential when hiring or promoting staff is challenging at the best of times, but operating in foreign environments certainly adds another level of uncertainty. For this reason, before we take a critical look at the literature on the criteria for expatriate selection, based on a range of predictors of successful performance, we will consider the current

EXHIBIT 3-2 *Selecting Managers—The Advantages and Disadvantages of Using PCNs, TCNs, and HCNs*

Parent-Country Nationals

Advantages
- Organizational control and coordination is maintained and facilitated.
- Promising managers are given international experience.
- PCNs may be the best people for the job because of special skills and experiences.
- There is assurance that subsidiary will comply with company objectives, policies, and so on.

Disadvantages
- The promotional opportunities of HCNs are limited.
- Adaptation to host country may take a long time.
- PCNs may impose an inappropriate HQ style.
- Compensation for PCNs and HCNs may differ.

Third-Country Nationals

Advantages
- Salary and benefit requirements may be lower than for PCNs.
- TCNs may be better informed than PCNs about host-country environment.

Disadvantages
- Transfers must consider possible national animosities (e.g., India and Pakistan).
- The host government may resent hiring TCNs.
- TCNs may not want to return to their own countries after assignment.

Host-Country Nationals

Advantages
- Language and other barriers are eliminated.
- Hiring costs are reduced, and no work permit is required.
- Continuity of management improves, since HCNs stay longer in positions.
- Government policy may dictate hiring of HCNs.
- Morale among HCNs may improve as they see career potential.

Disadvantages
- Control and coordination of HQ may be impeded.
- HCNs have limited career opportunity outside the subsidiary.
- Hiring HCNs limits opportunities for PCNs to gain foreign experience.
- Hiring HCNs could encourage a federation of national rather than global units.

debate surrounding **expatriate failure**. The term *expatriate failure* has been defined as the premature return of an expatriate (i.e., a return home before the period of assignment is completed). In such a case, an expatriate failure represents a selection error, often compounded by ineffective expatriate management policies. Lately, there has been some discussion in the literature about the usefulness of defining expatriate failure so narrowly. An expatriate may be ineffective and poorly adjusted yet, if not recalled, he or she will not be considered a failure. Because of an inability either to effectively handle the new responsibilities or to adjust to the country of assignment, performance levels may be diminished. These results will not be immediately apparent but can have long-term consequences in terms of subsidiary performance. However, if the expatriate remains for the duration of the assignment, for all intents and purposes, the assignment will have been considered a success. Thus, the premature return rate is not a perfect measure of success or failure, and may underestimate the problem.

Also, in a somewhat provocative article published in 1995, Harzing[9] has questioned the reported failure rates in the U.S. literature. She claims there is:

> almost no empirical foundation for the existence of high failure rates when measured as premature re-entry. Unfortunately, there has been no reliable large-scale empirical work on this subject for more than fifteen years.

As she rightly points out, the major work in this area was that of Tung[10] who surveyed a number of U.S., European, and Japanese multinationals. Her results indicated a higher rate of early recalls in the U.S. multinationals in her sample ($n = 80$) than did the European ($n = 29$) and Japanese ($n = 35$) firms. Twenty-four percent of the U.S. firms had recall rates below 10 percent; whereas 59 percent of the West European and 76 percent of the Japanese firms reported recall rates of less than 5 percent. Tung's results suggested that expatriate failure may be of more concern to U.S. firms.

Further studies appear to confirm Tung's European results. For example, Brewster[11] conducted a study of 25 MNEs across five industries from five European countries. He reports low rates of early recall, consistent with those reported by Tung. More recently, Forster[12] conducted a study of expatriate failure rates in 36 U.K.-based firms. Using the broadest definition of failure (i.e., including underperformance and retention upon completion of the assignment), he suggests that a high proportion of staff do struggle to cope with their international assignments. Forster concludes:

> if we accept that a broader definition of EFRs [expatriate failure rates] is warranted, then it can be argued that the actual figure of those who are 'failing' on IAs [international assignments] could be somewhere between 8 per cent and 28 per cent of U.K. expatriates and their partners.

Another study found that failure/performance problems/adjustment problems were the most frequently experienced problems listed by U.K. firms (27 percent).[13]

A 1997–98 Price Waterhouse[14] study of international assignment policy and practice among European multinationals (including U.S. subsidiaries) asked for data on expatriate failure rates. Seventeen percent of the 184 companies surveyed reported recall rates of over 5 percent with a further 65 percent reporting at least some failures, compared with the 1995 study results (15 percent and 63 percent, respectively). The report's author concludes: "One in twenty-five companies reported a failure rate in excess of 10%." What is significant is that the study added "under-performance" to its definition of assignment failure, and found:

> The rates for employees currently under-performing on assignment as a result of difficulties in adapting to their cultural surroundings are even higher. 29% of companies report a rate in excess of one in twenty, with 7% reporting a rate over one in ten.

What can we conclude from this debate? There are several points to be considered:

1. In the absence of more recent empirical studies, we are still left with the impression that expatriate failure is higher in U.S. multinationals. We should note that there has not been a follow-up study of Tung's early work. The European studies reported above were conducted at various intervals since Tung's original study, and do not include the same countries. Further, other non–U.S. researchers have been reporting from regional or single country perspectives. For example, in their study of Nordic firms, Björkman and Gertsen[15] report expatriate failure rates of less than 5 percent; and, in their study of international HRM policies of four MNEs operating internationally from Australia, Dowling and Welch[16] found that expatriate failure was not a major concern for these firms.

2. The above studies tend not to differentiate between types of expatriate assignments, the level of "international" maturity,[17] or firm size—factors that may influence failure in its broadest sense. Broadening out the definition of expatriate failure beyond that of premature return is warranted.

3. Regardless of the definition or precise amount of "failure," its very exposure as a problem has broadened the issue to demonstrate the complexity of international assignments. In fact, one could argue that the so-called persistent myth of high U.S. expatriate failure rates has been a positive element in terms of the attention that has subsequently been directed towards expatriation practices.

4. It may be that companies operating internationally have since become more aware of the problems associated with expatriate failure and have learned how to avoid them. That is, multinationals have become more sophisticated in their approach to IHRM activities.

The costs associated with expatriate failure need a brief mention. These can be both **direct** and **indirect**. Direct costs include airfares and associated relocation expenses, and salary and training. The precise amount varies according to:

- Level of the position concerned;
- Country of destination;
- Exchange rates; and
- Whether the "failed" manager is replaced by another PCN.

The "invisible" or indirect costs are harder to quantify in dollar terms but can prove to be more expensive for the company. Many expatriate positions involve contact with host-government officials and key clients. Failure at this level may result in loss of market share, difficulties with host-government officials, and demands that PCNs be replaced with HCNs (thus affecting the multinational's general staffing approach). The possible effect on local staff is also an indirect cost factor, since morale and productivity could suffer.[18] Zeira and Banai[19] argue that multinational corporations should consider these factors as the real cost of expatriate failure, rather than the direct costs for salary and repatriation. The two cases in Exhibit 3–3 illustrate the potential damages of expatriate failure.

Failure also, of course, has an effect on the expatriate concerned, who may lose self-esteem, self-confidence, and prestige among peers.[20]

EXHIBIT 3-3   *International Assignments Pose Challenges*

Case 1: What works at home does not necessarily work abroad[21]

A four-day strike and pay rises of ten to fifteen percent were part of the cost paid by a South Korean textile firm for an incident involving one of the expatriate managers in its Vietnamese factory. A Vietnamese worker was confronted by his South Korean boss. Speaking in Korean, the manager yelled at him for being in the wrong place in the factory. As he did not understand her, the Vietnamese did not respond. The South Korean manager kicked and slapped him—as "in South Korea it is common for employers to scold or even beat employees if they make a big mistake." Here, though, such behavior resulted in ten of the Vietnamese's co-workers retaliating in kind. The manager was rushed to the hospital and the workers went on strike. The South Korean manager was subsequently repatriated.

Case 2: Happy to be going home[22]

A U.S. family, from the Midwest, was posted to Melbourne, Australia. The expatriate's role was to assist the Australian subsidiary improve its quality control and supplier relationships. Chuck was placed in charge of the purchasing department. After twelve months, he had successfully established good links with the company's key component suppliers and was in the process of arranging joint company quality training programs with these suppliers to ensure the newly-instigated *just-in-time* inventory procedures were on a sound footing. Chuck was enjoying his new role. Meanwhile, his ten-year old daughter was finding it difficult to make friends in the expensive private school the company had arranged for her to attend. His wife was also finding life in Australia somewhat hard to cope with. "On the surface, it seems so much like home, but Australians are not at all the same as us Americans, and some people make disparaging remarks about us. They use terms such as 'Yanks.' I miss not being able to find familiar things, such as brownie mix, in the supermarket." Both wife and daughter were very happy when circumstances provided an acceptable reason for an early end to Chuck's assignment. His elderly mother suffered a bad fall, and there were no other family members to take care of her. The family was repatriated after 14 months into a three-year assignment. The expatriate was replaced by another PCN.

Future performance may be marked by decreased motivation, lack of promotional opportunities, or even increased productivity to compensate for the failure. Finally, the expatriate's family relationships may be threatened. These are additional costs to organizations that are often overlooked. As Guptara[23] argues: "A company that sends out people who may not be suitable for working cross-culturally is being grossly negligent."

Expatriates tend to have a higher profile, so reducing the incidence, and thereby the cost, is of some strategic importance. Naturally, the debate about the degree to which expatriate failure occurs has been accompanied by investigation and speculation about why failure occurs. We can get some idea from the two cases presented in Exhibit 3–3. Empirical and anecdotal evidence suggests, though, that the major contributing factor is **inability to adjust to the foreign culture**. As part of her study, Tung[24] asked respondents to indicate reasons for expatriate failure in their companies. There were national differences in the responses between the U.S. and Japanese firms, as can be quickly seen from Exhibit 3–4. For the European firms, "inability of the spouse to adjust" was the only consistent response provided.

It should be pointed out that the spouse (or accompanying partner) carries a heavy burden. Upon arrival in the country of assignment, the responsibility for settling the family into its new home falls on the spouse, who may have left behind a career, along with friends and social support networks (particularly relatives). Servants may be involved, for which the spouse is seldom prepared. It is often not possible for the spouse or partner to work in the country of assignment. The well-being and education of the children also concern the spouse. Though the majority of spouses are female, trailing male spouses face similar problems of adjustment.[25] These factors can contribute to a failure of the spouse

EXHIBIT 3–4   *Reasons for Expatriate Failure (in descending order of importance)[26]*

U.S. Firms	Japanese Firms
Inability of spouse to adjust	Inability to cope with larger international responsibility
Manager's inability to adjust	Difficulties with new environment
Other family reasons	Personal or emotional problems
Manager's personal or emotional maturity	Lack of technical competence
Inability to cope with larger international responsibility	Inability of spouse to adjust

to adjust, which may affect the performance of the expatriate manager. As Reynolds and Bennett explain:[27]

> The negative impact of the accompanying spouse's career continuity, self-esteem and identity can be personally and professionally devastating. Not only can the marriage partnership's balance and health be jeopardized by the psychological assault to the trailing spouse, but so can the performance level of the employee who has been transferred.

In fact, when one adds cultural adjustment problems to such a situation, it is perhaps not so surprising to find that some couples seek to return home prematurely.

Tung[28] notes that the relatively lower ranking of "inability of spouse to adjust" by Japanese respondents is not surprising, given the role and status to which Japanese society relegates the spouse. However, other social factors may contribute to this finding. Because of the competitive nature of the Japanese education system, the spouse commonly opts to remain in Japan with the children, particularly where male offspring are concerned. The Japanese word for these unaccompanied male expatriates is *tanshin funin*, or bachelors-in-exile.[29] Thus, in many cases, the spouse is not a factor in expatriate failure. However, one should not assume that adjustment is not a problem for the Japanese. A tragic case that received front-page news treatment in Melbourne, Australia, involved a Japanese spouse.[30] Police treated the incident as an apparent suicide—the unhappy, homesick woman drove her car, containing herself and her four-year-old son, off a pier into the water, drowning them both. An extreme, terrible event, it serves to remind us that the global movement of staff may produce severe adjustment problems for some families.

Other factors that appear to contribute or provoke "failure" include:

- *Length of assignment.* The average assignment for Japanese firms is four to five years, compared with two to three years for American firms. This longer assignment allows the expatriate more time to adjust to the foreign situation.[31] As well, Japanese firms do not expect the expatriate to perform up to full capacity until the third year; the first year of the foreign assignment is seen mainly as a period of adjustment to the foreign environment. Allen[32] examined the differences between Japanese postings to the United States and vice versa. He found that some Japanese firms post to the United States only those senior managers who have a significant history with the company and can make contact with top executives in Japan. He also found that Japanese firms sometimes send a younger potential successor with the senior manager, who acts as the junior manager's mentor while in the United States.

- *Willingness to move.* Respondents in Hamill's[33] study suggested that the reasons for the lower British expatriate failure rate were that British managers were more internationally mobile than U.S. managers, and that perhaps British companies had developed more effective expatriate policies (e.g., many international assignments were an integral part of individuals' career development). Welch[34] notes that the respondents in her study perceived an expatriate posting as a desirable appointment—an opportunity to travel and live abroad. This attitude is partly due to a feeling among Australians of being isolated from the rest of the world, and partly to a willingness to travel, similar to that reported by Hamill. This positive outlook on the foreign assignment may have assisted the Australians in the study to adjust to the demands of the foreign location.

  Willingness to relocate as a predictor of success should, however, include family members. From a survey of 405 U.S. managers and their spouse/partners, working in 20 Fortune 500 corporations, Brett and Stroh[35] found a significant causal relationship between the manager and the spouse's willingness to move. They conclude that managers who are most ready for international relocation are those whose spouses are also supportive of that move—a not surprising finding.

- *Work-environment related factors.* Gregersen and Black[36] studied 220 American expatriates in four Pacific Rim countries. They found a positive correlation between what they term "intent to stay in the international assignment" and the PCN's commitment to the local company, adjustment to interaction with HCNs, and adjustment to general living conditions. Adjustment to the work role itself, however, was negatively associated with "intent to stay."

Selection Criteria

Because of the high profile given to expatriate "failure," along with the multifaceted nature of expatriate assignments, predicting success factors and developing appropriate selection criteria for international operators has become a critical IHRM issue.

The challenge for those responsible for selecting staff for international assignments is to determine appropriate selection criteria, and the predictors of success have been reflected in the way firms approach this critical activity. It should be noted that selection is a two-way process between the individual and the organization. A prospective candidate may reject the expatriate assignment, either for individual reasons, such as family considerations, or for situational factors, such as the perceived toughness of a particular culture. Exhibit 3–5 illustrates the factors involved in expatriate selection, both in terms of the individual and the specifics of the situation concerned. We base the following discussion around this figure.

Technical Ability

essential/necessary but not sufficient

Naturally, the person's ability to perform the required tasks is an important consideration. Technical and managerial skills are therefore an essential criterion. Indeed, research findings consistently indicate that multinationals place heavy reliance on relevant technical skills during the expatriate selection process. For example, Hixon[37] found that selection was based on technical ability and willingness to reside abroad. Mendenhall, Dunbar, and Oddou[38] conclude that U.S.

EXHIBIT 3-5 *Factors in Expatriate Selection*

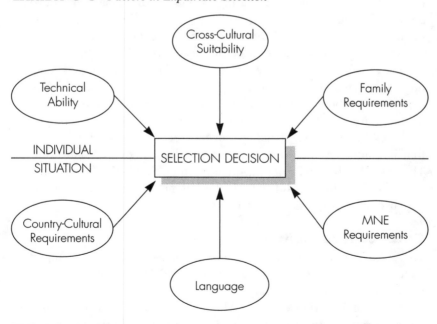

companies seem to focus their selection efforts on one single criterion—that of technical competence—despite the importance of all the other criteria correlated to international success. A survey of 40 Michigan firms by McEnery and DesHarnais[39] revealed that functional or technical skills were the most important selection criteria used. Björkman[40] and Gertsen report a comparable emphasis on technical skills in their survey of Scandinavian multinationals. More recently, a study of U.K. and German multinationals[41] found that the majority based their selection decision mainly on technical abilities. Similarly, the 1997–98 Price Waterhouse[42] survey of 184 European firms (nearly a quarter of which had their worldwide headquarters in the United States) reports that the most important selection criteria were job-related skills (99 percent) and leadership skills (76 percent).

Reinforcing the emphasis on technical skills is the relative ease with which the multinational may assess the potential candidate's potential, since technical and managerial competence can be determined on the basis of past performance. Since expatriates are usually internal recruits,[43] personnel evaluation records can be examined and checked with the candidate's past and present superiors. Of course, as can be demonstrated in the Vietnamese example in Exhibit 3–3, past performance may have little or no bearing on one's ability to achieve a task in a foreign cultural environment. In fact, *domestic does not equal international*—technical abilities that may make a person a good performer in the domestic environment may be liabilities abroad.

One should note here that while technical ability (or lack thereof) does not emerge as a critical precursor to "failure," job-related aspects may be a component in the expatriate's intention to stay in the foreign location, or with the firm upon return home after successful completion of the assignment. For instance, several recent U.S. studies[44] indicate that job autonomy is a powerful factor influencing expatriate turnover. The nature of the job itself (the situation in Exhibit 3–5) may counter the individual's technical ability to do the job, or interact with other factors to cause underperformance, even early recall.

Cross-Cultural Suitability

The cultural environment in which expatriates operate is an important factor in determining successful performance. According to the relevant literature, certain traits and characteristics have been identified as predictors of expatriate success. Although these traits may not guarantee an expatriate's success, without them the possibility of failure is enhanced. Apart from the obvious technical ability and managerial skills, expatriates require crosscultural abilities that enable the person to operate in a new environment. These include: cultural empathy, adaptability, diplomacy, language ability, positive attitude, emotional stability, and maturity.[45] Murray and Murray[46] advocate that, while managerial or technical competence is regarded as the primary competence for expatriate success, *effectiveness and coping skills* are also required. Effectiveness skills are defined as the ability to successfully translate the managerial or technical skills into the foreign environment, whereas coping skills enable the person to become reasonably comfortable, or at least survive, in a foreign environment. Reliance on technical skills as a predictor of success is, therefore, limiting—technical competence does not assist a person's ability to adapt to, and cope with, a new environment that involves dealing effectively with foreign coworkers.[47] Hence, the predictors of expatriate success have tended to stress the traits and characteristics of the candidate.

In practice, while inter-cultural competence is recognized as important, it is difficult to precisely define what this comprises, let alone assess a candidate's suitability in this regard. One has to take into consideration aspects such as the individual's personality, attitude to foreigners, ability to relate to people from another cultural group, and so on. As studies such as that by Tung[48] report, multinationals may indicate that, for example, relational abilities are an important expatriate selection criterion, but few will assess a candidate's relational ability through a formal procedure such as judgment by senior managers or psychological tests. As we will discuss shortly, testing procedures are not necessarily the answer.

Family Requirements

The contribution that the family, particularly the spouse, makes to the success of the international assignment is now well-documented, having been the subject of much research in the past decade or so. For example, Black and Stephens[49] examined the influence of the spouse on American expatriate adjustment. Surveying 220 U.S. expatriates and their spouses working in Japan, Taiwan, and Hong Kong, they found that a favorable opinion about the international assignment by the spouse is positively related to the spouse's adjustment. The adjustment of the spouse was found to be highly correlated to the adjustment of the expatriate manager. Despite this important link, however, Black and Stephens relate that only 30 percent of the firms in their study sought the spouse's opinion concerning the international assignment, and they conclude:

> Given (a) that spouse opinion about accepting the international assignment is related to spouse adjustment, (b) that spouse adjustment is positively related to expatriate adjustment and expatriate intentions to stay or leave and (c) that premature returns are quite costly, it seems that firms could benefit from more careful attention to the opinion of the spouse concerning the assignment before the expatriate is transferred overseas.

Likewise, Australian research into the psychological impact of relocation on the partners of 58 expatriate and repatriate managers[50] found that the amount of control the partner felt over the decision to relocate was significantly correlated to her satisfaction with life in the predeparture and early stages of expatriation. Another important finding was that the more comprehensive the company assistance, especially during the early stages of the expatriation process, the higher the level of psychological adjustment to relocation made by the expatriate partner. These results suggest the need for the inclusion of the family in the selection process. Yet, when one looks at more recent studies of the expatriation practices of various multinationals, the inclusion of the spouse and family in the selection process continues to be either overlooked or treated in a peripheral way. Brewster's[51] study of 25 European MNEs found that only 16 percent interviewed the spouse during the selection process. The 1997–98 Price Waterhouse[52] survey comments:

> Compared to our 1995 survey, the number of companies which routinely interview an employee's spouse or partner as part of the selection process has increased slightly, from 9% to 11%. However, overall, fewer companies involve the spouse or partner in the selection process under any circumstances, rising from half in 1995 to two-thirds currently. Of the companies which do interview the spouse or partner, 12% interview them on their own. Given that more than a third of the companies believe the assignments that either failed, or been ended prematurely, due to a spouse or partner's difficulties with adapting to life in the host location, it is perhaps a little surprising that companies are not attributing more importance to assessing their suitability.

We can speculate why companies appear to be reluctant to include families in the selection process, based on the separation between work and private life that occurs in most Western cultures. For example, Welch[53] found a reluctance on the part of Australian firms to include spouses in the formal selection process because it was considered to be outside their domain, and could evoke civil liberties concerns. What one finds in practice is that multinationals alert to the key role the family plays may resort to informal methods, such as taking the couple to dinner or putting the couple in contact with a repatriated couple who once lived in the location concerned. However, this understandable reluctance to become involved in an employee's private life constrains the multinational's ability to select the most appropriate couple.

Country/Cultural Requirements

The host country may be an important determinant. Some regions and countries are considered "hardship postings"—remote areas away from major cities or modern facilities, or war-torn regions with high physical risk. Accompanying family members may be an additional responsibility that the MNE does not want to bear. There may be a reluctance to select females for certain Middle East or South East Asian regions. Indeed some countries will not issue a work permit for a female. These aspects may result in the selection of HCNs rather than expatriates. Other country and cultural requirements, along with cultural adjustment issues, will be explored in Chapter 4.

MNE Requirements

As we examined in the previous chapter (Exhibit 2–11), situational factors have an influence on the selection decision. For instance, the multinational may consider the proportion of expatriates to local staff when making selection decisions, mainly as an outcome of its staffing philosophy. However, operations in particular countries may require the use of more PCNs and TCNs than would normally be the case, as multinationals operating in parts of Eastern Europe and China are discovering. This will affect the selection ratio—that is, PCN:TCN:HCN. Other situational factors include:

- *The mode of operation involved.* Selecting staff to work in an international joint venture may involve major input from the local partner, and be constrained by the negotiated agreement on selection processes.[54]
- *The duration of the assignment.*[55] Family members tend not to accompany an expatriate when the assignment is only for three to six

month's duration, so family requirements may not be a strong factor in
the selection decision.

- *The amount of knowledge transfer inherent in the expatriate's job in the foreign operation.* If the nature of the job is to train local staff, then the multinational may include training skills as a selection criterion.

Some support for including situation factors comes from the argument
proffered by Zeira and Banai.[56] They claim that a broadening of the
spectrum to include the host environment would make it possible for
multinationals to base the selection of their PCNs on the expectations of
the real environment in which expatriates work, and with which they
must cope. This, they argue, would allow better prediction of the extent
of the candidate's suitability for the host country.

Language

The ability to speak a second language is an aspect often linked with
crosscultural ability. We have chosen to stress language as situation-
determined in terms of its importance as a factor in the selection decision. Language skills may be regarded as of critical importance for some
expatriate positions, but lesser in others. In Tung's[57] initial study, U.S.
respondents listed "knowledge of the host-country's language" as important for functional head and operative jobs; whereas communication
skills, rather than specific language skills, was an important selection
criterion for the top subsidiary management position. Nevertheless,
some would argue that knowledge of the host-country's language is an
important aspect of expatriate performance, regardless of the level of
position. Differences in language are recognized as a major barrier to
effective crosscultural communication.[58] Yet, in terms of the other selection criteria we have examined above, from the multinational's perspective, language is placed lower down the list of desirable attributes.
For example, the 1997–98 Price Waterhouse survey ranks language
skills as the third most important selection criterion (behind job-related
and leadership skills). The U.K.-German study by Marx, referred to
above, ranks language skills as number five (behind social competence,
openness to other ways of thinking, cultural adaptation, and professional
excellence).

An explanation for this attitude may be drawn from a study of the foreign language needs of U.S. multinationals. Through her interviews with
people in nine companies of varying size and nature, Fixman[59] found

that foreign language skills were rarely considered an important part of international business success. She comments, "Language problems were largely viewed as mechanical and manageable problems that could be solved individually." From the perspective of some expatriates, though, language is a factor in cultural adjustment, as the Tung–Arthur Andersen survey indicates: Respondents (predominantly Americans) greatly valued the ability to speak the local language, regardless of how different the culture was from their home country.[60]

Another component to language as a situation factor in the selection decision is the role of the common corporate language. Most multinationals, at some point, whether consciously or not, adopt a common corporate language as a way of standardizing reporting systems and procedures. This is not, perhaps, an issue for PCN selection within multinationals from the United States, the United Kingdom, Canada, and Australia, where the chosen company language remains the same as that of the home country.[61] It becomes a PCN selection factor, though, for multinationals from non–English-speaking countries that adopt English as the corporate language, unless the posting is to a country with a shared language. For instance, a Spanish multinational, using Spanish as the corporate language, selecting a manager to head a new subsidiary in Mexico, does not face the same language issue as a Spanish multinational, with English as its corporate language, selecting a manager to its U.S. facility. For the latter, fluency in English is important.

Inter-Relatedness of Criteria

As we will explore further in the next chapter, the above individual and situational factors involved in expatriate selection interact with each other in terms of performance. For example, in their discussion of the significance of the work role and intent to stay, Gregersen and Black[62] link challenges at work with cultural adjustment. They argue that once the expatriate has mastered, or nearly completed, the assigned work, other factors may surface and assume relative importance. For instance, if the work becomes less demanding and no longer so time-consuming, the expatriate may have time to pay more attention to negative crosscultural experiences that the family is encountering. These negative experiences can become distorted when combined with lack of challenge at work and thus sow seeds for early recall, or underperformance. This adds to the dilemma of designing and using appropriate selection criteria that will predict performance in the foreign location.

The Use of Selection Tests

Although there is a consensus among scholars and practitioners that personal characteristics (or traits) are important, there is considerable debate about how such personal characteristics can be reliably and accurately measured. Personality and psychological tests have been used in the selection process, but the effectiveness of such tests as predictors of cultural adjustment is questioned. For example, Torbiörn[63] comments that though desirable personality traits are specified and recommended, the tests or criteria to assess these traits are seldom convincingly validated. Likewise, Willis[64] states that if tests are used they should be selected with care and regard for reliability and validity because, while some tests may be useful in suggesting potential problems, there appears to be little correlation between test scores and performance. He further adds that most of the relevant tests have been devised in the United States and, therefore, may be culture-bound. Use of such tests without careful modification on non–American nationals adds another question mark to their reliability and validity as predictors of expatriate success.

Another constraint is that in some countries (the United Kingdom and Australia, for instance) there is controversy about the use of psychological tests.[65] There is also a different pattern of usage across countries—the use of such tests is very low in Germany.[66] The 1997–98 Price Waterhouse survey reports only 12 percent used formal assessment centers, and some companies "indicated through their comments that they also use psychometric tests." A clear majority of respondents (85 percent) mainly assessed expatriate suitability through the traditional interview process.

The difficulty of predicting success, then, seems to be related to the lack of valid and reliable screening devices to identify, with certainty, managers who will succeed in a foreign assignment. The crucial variables affecting the adjustment of the individual and family are not only difficult to identify or measure, but the complex relationship between personality factors and ability to adjust to another culture is not well understood.[67] Discussing this problem, Gertsen[68] points out that the use of personality traits to predict intercultural competence is further complicated by the fact that personality traits are not defined and evaluated in the same way in different cultures. She states, "The most serious problem, however, is that attitudes do not always result in the implicitly expected behavior. If a person has very positive attitudes towards a culture but is unable to express this in his behavior, it has no effect." She concludes that attitudes are relevant only to the extent that they determine a person's actual communicative behavior in another culture and that other personality traits are relevant in the same way. Another drawback of expatriate selection based on traits or characteristics is the subjective nature of the scoring of abilities, especially those classified as personal and environmental characteristics.

Nevertheless, models derived from this approach have value in that they provide some guidelines that can be applied during the selection process, rather than mere reliance on the potential manager's domestic record as a predictor.[69] One such model is offered by Mendenhall and Oddou.[70] They propose a four-dimensional approach that attempts to link specific behavioral tendencies to probable international performance:

- *The self-oriented dimension* reflects the degree to which the expatriate expresses an adaptive concern for self-preservation, self-enjoyment, and mental hygiene. These could be measured through certain psychometric tests (such as stress tolerance and Type A behavior).
- *The perceptual dimension* reflects the expertise the expatriate possesses in accurately understanding why host nationals behave the way they do. Psychological tests with established validity could assess the flexibility of an individual's perceptual and evaluative tendencies. They could be used in conjunction with in-depth evaluations from other sources such as a consultant psychologist and the applicant's superiors. Use of testing may also encourage self-reflection regarding motivation for the assignment.
- *The others-oriented dimension* reflects the degree to which the expatriate is concerned about host-national coworkers and desires to affiliate with them. This could be evaluated through similar techniques for the perceptual dimension.
- *The cultural-toughness dimension* reflects a mediating variable that recognizes that acculturation is affected by the degree to which the culture of the host country is incongruent with that of the home country. This could be assessed by comparing the host-country's political, legal, socioeconomic, and business systems to those in the parent country. If there is considerable disparity (i.e., if the host country is "culturally tough"), only applicants with high scores on a battery of the various evaluation devices available should be considered for the assignment. For assignments to countries similar to the parent country (e.g., an assignment to Australia from the United

States), applicants with more marginal evaluation scores may be considered.[71]

The evaluation of the candidate's strengths and weaknesses on these four dimensions, Mendenhall and Oddou suggest, will focus appropriate attention on crosscultural ability and behavior, thus complementing technical ability assessment.

Other Factors in Expatriate Selection

Our examination so far has revealed that establishing criteria for expatriate selection remains problematic. Predictors of success have been identified, but it remains unclear as to how these should be measured. Part of the problem is the design of appropriate tests, but other factors are involved. One is *time*—expatriates are often selected quickly to staff unexpected international vacancies, precluding a lengthy screening process. Torbiörn[72] has noted the impact of lack of planning in this area: "The mass of possible selection criteria proposed in the literature is rarely likely to be matched by a wide range of available candidates and the man [sic] chosen is often simply the man who happens to be there."

Another is that of *availability*. After going through the selection process, the multinational may find that the preferred candidate rejects the offered assignment. The main reasons for refusal, or nonavailability, include dual-career couples and family considerations.

Dual-Career Couples

Accepting the international assignment will impact upon the career of the potential candidate's spouse or partner. The increase in the number of dual-career couples is a worldwide trend, one that is posing a dilemma for both companies and employees alike. In the past, working spouses were less common, spouses were generally female, and they were prepared to follow their partner's work transfers, both domestic and international. This past situation is reflected in the use of terms such as "the trailing spouse" to refer to the housebound female who accompanied her husband. But this situation has changed. Fewer families in Western countries could be classified as "traditional." As Reynolds and Bennett[73] point out, fewer U.S. employees are willing to relocate, either domestically or internationally, without the support of their spouses, to the extent that the career-couple challenge is now an issue that multinational employers cannot ignore. A U.K.-based study[74] supports this contention: 67 percent of respondents listed "spouse/partner reluctant to give up own career" as a major constraint to international staff transfers. A 1993 study, conducted by Royal Dutch Shell into its own expatriate management practices, revealed that more than half of all spouses were in employment prior to the assignment, yet fewer than 10 percent were able to work in the foreign location.[75]

Similar results were found in the 1997–98 Price Waterhouse survey mentioned previously, where the majority of companies (86 percent) admitted they had assignment offers turned down. The main reasons for refusals were domestic/family concerns (77 percent) and dual-career issues (58 percent). The increasing number of refusals indicates that:

- More people are immobile, and are prepared to state the grounds as family concerns. That this is acceptable as a reason reflects a significant shift in thinking about the role of non-work aspects impinging on work-related matters.
- Multinationals are being forced to select from a diminishing pool of candidates who may be less qualified. This has strategic implications for staffing policies. Harzing found that companies in her survey who experienced problems with dual-career couples sent out less PCNs and employed more HCNs and TCNs. Such findings confirm the inclusion of staff availability as a barrier to developing a geocentric staffing policy, as illustrated in Exhibit 3–1.

Reflecting this global trend, the impact of the accompanying spouse's or partner's career orientation upon the international assignment is an emerging area of research. It seems that career orientation not only affects the couple's willingness to move, but may also negatively affect performance and retention in the foreign location. For example, a study of the impact of a spouse's career orientation on managers during transfers from the United States to Japan[76] found that, although most spouses who worked before the international assignment did not find employment, a significantly higher proportion of career-oriented spouses did. In their discussion of this finding, Stephens and Black suggest that career-oriented spouses may have had a higher employment rate in the foreign country because:

- They were more qualified;
- They had more to lose and therefore tried harder to find employment; or, perhaps,

- Their spouses' companies provided job-finding and work visa assistance.

They caution that this finding should not necessarily lead companies to believe that job-finding assistance for spouses is not important. They conclude, "If organizations wish to take advantage of the career development aspects of international transfers and the benefits to the firm inherent in effective relocation programmes, they must consider the impact of international transfers on both partners in dual-career couples."

In late 1994, Harvey[77] surveyed 325 members of the Institute for International HRM of the U.S. Society for Human Resource Management to examine the international relocation issues associated with dual-career families. Harvey's key findings, from a 36 percent response rate to a self-administered questionnaire, were:

- Confirmation of the shift to a more prevalent co-provider role for the "trailing spouse." Dual-career couples are two income families. His finding reminds us that monetary factors (i.e., the potential loss of the second income) combine with fears about the spouse's career progression in a couple's refusal to move.
- Refusal to relocate or related issues with dual-career couples is forcing U.S. companies to select from "secondary" candidates. This is similar to the conclusions we drew from the 1997–98 Price Waterhouse data (the European subsidiaries of U.S. multinationals were included in this survey). Harvey found that, for executive positions, HRM managers looked from within the PCN pool first, shifting the search to TCNs when refusal rates from PCNs were above 10 percent. For lower level managers, they continue to select second choice candidates from the PCN pool, before moving to look at possible HCN candidates.
- Related issues emerged as important in dual-career relocation, such as the level of position concerned (e.g., managerial versus supervisory), the career attractiveness of the position, country of destination, stage in career life cycle, and significant increase in real income.
- Corporate assistance, such as training programs and education support, differed according to the category of the potential candidate. Spouses of supervisory personnel received less support than did those of middle and executive management level.

- Personnel managers surveyed indicated that the complications associated with dual-career couples would increase as more female managers were selected for international assignments.

Some multinationals are endeavoring to come up with solutions to the dual-career challenge. According to Reynolds and Bennett:[78]

> Most companies still use informal or *ad hoc* approaches to addressing the problems of their expatriate career couples. In isolation or with industry colleagues, companies are beginning to generate innovative programs and interventions to assist this special breed of couples.

Strategies multinationals have experimented with include:

- *Intercompany networking.* Here the multinational attempts to place the accompanying spouse or partner in a suitable job with another multinational—sometimes in a reciprocal arrangement. To illustrate, a U.S. multinational may enter into an agreement with a German multinational also operating in, say, China, that they find a position within their respective Chinese facilities for each other's accompanying partner (i.e., "you find my expatriate's spouse a job and work visa, and I will do likewise for you"). Alternatively, a local supplier, distributor, or joint venture partner may agree to employ the accompanying spouse/partner.
- *Job-hunting assistance.* Here the multinational provides spouse or partner assistance with the employment search in the host country. This may be through employment agency fees, career counseling, or simply work permit assistance. The 1997–98 Price Waterhouse survey found that 25.5 percent of the firms surveyed provided job-finding assistance. Some may provide a fact-finding trip to the host location before the actual assignment.
- *Intracompany employment.* This is perhaps a logical but often a somewhat difficult solution. It means sending the couple to the same foreign facility, perhaps the same department. Not all multinationals are comfortable with the idea of having a husband and wife team in the same work location, nor do all couples wish it either. A large Australian multinational sent a couple into its Vietnamese operation, knowing that this would create a delicate situation—the wife reported directly to her husband. The selection decision was not undertaken

lightly. HRM staff provided counseling before the assignment, and the situation was monitored carefully by headquarters.

- *Support for "commuter marriages."* The spouse/partner may decide to remain in the home country, and the couple works out ways to maintain the relationship with the help of the firm. In a case known to the authors, when a major U.S. multinational assigned a female expatriate to its Australian subsidiary for 18 months, her husband remained in Chicago. The multinational supported this arrangement through subsidized telephone bills and three return airline tickets. Alternatively, couples may move to jobs in adjoining countries, or within the same geographical region. For instance, one may work in Hong Kong (the original posting), the other in Bangkok. This makes commuting (relationship maintenance) easier than from the United States.[79] Multinationals adjust the compensation benefits to fit with the agreed arrangements.

- *On-assignment career support.* Motorola[80] is an example of how a multinational may assist spouses to maintain and even improve career skills through what Motorola calls its Dual-Career Policy. This consists of a lump-sum payment for education expenses, professional association fees, seminar attendance, language training to upgrade work-related skills, and employment agency fees. There are conditions attached, such as the spouse must have been employed before the assignment. Thus, if the spouse is unable to find suitable employment, the time can be spent on career development activities.

These attempts demonstrate that creative thinking can assist multinationals overcome this potential barrier. However, it is worthy of note that 64.6 percent of the firms in the 1997–98 Price Waterhouse survey did not have a dual-career policy, and only 15.8 percent indicated they had a formal, written policy on this issue. Reynolds and Bennett found the attitude that "this is a problem the couples responsible should resolve" still prevails in many U.S. firms. Such an attitude contributes to the problem of staff immobility rather than solving it. Where assistance is lacking from multinationals, dual-career couples often obtain help from voluntary agencies such as the Federation of American Women's Clubs Overseas (FAWCO) in the host location.

Female International Managers

The selection of females for international postings is a related issue. It would appear that, in the past, relatively few women were sent on expatriate assignments. For example, in 1984, Adler[81] reported a survey of international HR practices in over 600 U.S. and Canadian companies that found only 3 percent (402) of the 13,338 expatriates identified were female. She found that female expatriates tended to be employed by companies with over 1,000 employees in the banking, electronics, petroleum, and publishing industries. There are various explanations for her findings:

- The data simply reflect the preferences of males and females, and the majority of females do not wish to be sent on an expatriate assignment. Such an explanation assumes that both males and females are offered the opportunity of expatriate assignments, which Adler reports is not the case.
- The data reflect the limited number of females with sufficient experience to be sent abroad.
- Many multinationals are concerned with the various social norms with regard to women that prevail in many countries. For example, some Middle Eastern countries would not issue a work visa to a female expatriate even if the multinational selected her. Adler argues that such examples are the exception rather than the rule, and that, in many countries, social norms regarding the role of women do not apply to female expatriates because locals regard them as foreigners. This did appear to be the situation for female members of the U.S. armed forces stationed in Saudi Arabia during the Gulf War. However, there may be some gender-related constraints. For example, some of the traditional methods of entertainment in Asian business culture involve the sexual exploitation of women and clearly exclude female colleagues.[82]

We could add another attitudinal explanation: a somewhat externalized belief that men in some cultures, such as certain Asian countries, do not like reporting to female managers, particularly foreign women, and therefore women should not be posted abroad. Such beliefs help create what has been termed *the glass border that supports the glass ceiling*. There is a paucity of empirical studies surrounding this issue, and what exists presents somewhat inconclusive data. For example, a recent study[83] of 70 U.S. women expatriates, working in 31 countries (mostly in Europe and Far East Asia), reports that 52.9 percent acknowledged the existence of discrimination in the local company, but 47.1 percent said that they did not encounter local discrimination because they were women.

There is a suggestion in some of the literature that, as the proportion of women in the domestic workforce continues to increase, and as international experience becomes an essential criterion for career progression within multinationals, we will see more international managers who are female. However, the 1997–98 Price Waterhouse survey found that only 6 percent of expatriates were female.

Family Considerations

Apart from the accompanying partner's career, there are family considerations that can cause a potential expatriate to decline the international assignment. Disruption to children's education is an important consideration, and the selected candidate may reject the offered assignment on the grounds that a move at this particular stage in his or her child's life is inappropriate. The care of aging or invalid parents is another consideration (see Case 2: Exhibit 3–3). While these two reasons have been noted in various studies, what has been somewhat overlooked is the issue of single parents. Given the increasing divorce rates, this may become a critical factor in assignment selection and acceptance where the custody of children is involved. This is not necessarily an additional barrier for prospective female international managers only. An increasing number of males in the United States are being granted custody of the children of the marriage.[84] The associated legal constraints, such as obtaining the consent of the other parent to take the child (or children) out of the home country, and visiting/access rights, may prove to be a major barrier to the international mobility of both single mothers and single fathers.

Work Permit Refused

As discussed in Chapter 1, international firms are usually required to demonstrate that a HCN is not available before the host government will issue the necessary work permit and entry visa for the desired PCN or TCN. In some cases, the multinational may wish to use an expatriate and has selected a candidate for the international assignment, only to find the transfer blocked by the host government. Some countries, such as the United States, are changing their legislation to facilitate employment-related immigration,[85] which will make international transfers somewhat easier. As we will see in Chapter 8, the Social Charter allows for free movement of citizens of member countries within the European Union. It is therefore important that HR staff keep up-to-date with changing legislation in the countries in which the multinational is involved. Exhibit 3–6 shows how one U.S. multinational's careful planning allowed it to obtain the required number of PCN visas.

An important, related point is that generally a work permit is granted to the expatriate only. The accompanying spouse or partner may not be permitted to work in the host country. Increasingly, multinationals are finding that the inability of the spouse to work in the host country may cause the selected candidate to reject the offer of an international assignment. If the international assignment is accepted, the lack of a work permit for the accompanying spouse or partner may cause difficulties in adjustment and even contribute to failure. For these reasons, as reported above, some multinationals provide assistance in this regard.

Selecting Third-Country Nationals

Surprisingly, there is little in the literature regarding the selection process for this group of international employees. Apart from discussions surrounding the motives for the use of TCNs, and the advantages and disadvantages involved (see Exhibit 3–2), there is a paucity of information regarding specific TCN selection issues and policies.[87] It is safe to

EXHIBIT 3–6 *Citibank Plans for Changing Staffing Needs*[86]

Banks, along with oil and construction companies, remain heavy users of PCN employees, because these industries require very specific (sometimes firm-specific) skills frequently not found in foreign locations. In the mid-1980s Australia offered a once-only opportunity for foreign banks to enter the local market. Citibank already held a limited banking license that allowed it to operate in Australia as a merchant banking operation and finance company. A year before the licenses were to be awarded, Citibank sent one of its senior HR managers on a year-long assignment to Sydney to assess the staffing implications of an application to the Australian government for a banking license. First, an assessment was made as to how many PCN visas would be required. Then, a detailed summary was prepared for the Australian immigration department that demonstrated the history of Citibank's investment in training Australian nationals, with career examples of HCNs who were now employed by Citibank in Australia, in other foreign locations, and in the United States. This proved to be a successful strategy: Citibank received one of the sixteen licenses on offer and all of the PCN work permits it requested.

assume, however, that much of what we have covered in our treatment of expatriate selection issues applies to both PCNs and TCNs. Thus, when selecting TCNs from within its own operations, the individual factors identified in Exhibit 3–5—technical ability, crosscultural adaptability, and family requirements—would apply equally to PCNs and TCNs.

Situational factors may dominate the selection decision—such as lack of suitably qualified or available PCNs. However, the issue of work permits may be a crucial determinant in the ability to use TCNs, as governments would prefer to see their own nationals employed. It may be harder to justify the use of TCNs than PCNs. For companies developing a geocentric staffing policy, transferring subsidiary staff to other subsidiaries, as well as to headquarters, is an important part of creating an international team (or cadre). High profile transfers can provide a powerful signal. Creating the means for such transfers is not easy. As Percy Barnevik, Chairman and former CEO of the Swedish–Swiss conglomerate Asea Brown Boveri (ABB)[88] commented recently:

> The difficulty is that bosses tend to attract clusters of people from their own nationality around them. They do this not because they are racists, but because they feel comfortable with people they know best. You get a German cluster or a Swedish cluster. So you must make sure that when a boss selects managers, he considers people from other countries. And you must make sure good people from other countries are available to him. Managers have to be asked to supply lists of potential candidates for work outside their countries. Then if a German manager selects four Germans for a task, you will be in a position to suggest an Italian or an American and ask him to think again. There's a disadvantage in doing this because you lose a little since maybe they will all have to speak in bad English instead of in German or whatever. But the advantage is that you get the best people in place. And you build a global company.

Language ability as a selection criterion may be more critical because the TCN would need to be fluent in at least the common corporate language ("bad English" in the ABB case).

When recruiting and selecting external candidates for TCN positions, there may be a danger that the multinational will place more emphasis on the potential candidate's ability to fit into the multinational's corporate culture rather than on crosscultural ability. Whether selection is from an international or external pool, it would be important for HRM staff in all locations to be aware of the debate surrounding the use of selection tests, particularly the culture-bound nature of psychometric tests designed for PCNs.

Techniques for recruiting TCNs vary. Some U.S. multinationals recruit potential TCNs from among the foreign student body at various U.S. business schools. In Europe, for example, in October 1997, Nokia, the Finnish telecommunications multinational ran advertisements in local newspapers in Denmark and The Netherlands for young graduates to take positions in its growing Asian operations. Stress was placed on technical skills and fluency in English (the company language). For internal recruiting for TCN positions, companies such as IBM use their internal communication media, such as electronic bulletin boards, in-house journals, and so on, to advertise vacancies.

An emerging trend is the use of *foreign-born* nationals, recruiting from ethnic groups living abroad. For example, a U.K. multinational may select a Canadian-born Chinese to head up its Chinese facility. It was estimated that, in 1996, the majority of expatriate managers working in China were overseas Chinese from Malaysia, Singapore, Hong Kong, and Taiwan.[89] The underlying assumption appears to be that such appointments will reduce crosscultural difficulties. It is also a partial solution to the dearth of qualified local managers. Eastman-Kodak is one company using people from surrounding regions—though Kodak's HR director of the Greater China region regards this as a Band-Aid measure: "We could take everybody from our organizations in Hong Kong and Taiwan and put them in China and we still wouldn't come close to getting the number of managers we need." The company estimates that it will take at least 10 years to fully localize its Chinese management.[90]

Selecting Host-Country Nationals

When it comes to HCNs, we should distinguish between the selection of staff for positions in the local facility and the selection of staff for transfer into the parent's facilities in the home country.

Staffing the Local Subsidiary

We will begin with the issues surrounding recruiting and selecting HCNs for subsidiary operations. It is obvious that the multinational must observe the host-country's legal requirements and social customs for hiring staff. In some countries, questions regarding a person's family, hobbies, parents, or religious convictions are unacceptable, since these are considered private areas. In the absence of local hiring experience, the multinational may localize the HR function, or employ a local recruiting source. Appointing a HCN as the HR manager is attractive when the strategy is to appear as localized as possible (part of a polycentric staffing policy, for example). It is sometimes seen as a way of ensuring that the local operation conforms to local standards, thus avoiding the "bad press" that can result from nonadherence. The sexual harassment allegations at Mitsubishi Motor Manufacturing of America (MMMA), and at Astra USA, a Swedish subsidiary, in 1996 are cases in point.[91]

There is a paucity of empirical studies on how the multinational approaches the recruitment and selection of local staff, though we can make some inferences from recent research that examines the standardization versus localization of HR practices. One such study, by Rosenzweig and Nohria, examined HRM practices in U.S. affiliates of foreign multinationals. The authors found a high level of localization of HR practices (i.e., adoption of U.S. work-related practices), though the precise degree depended on various factors such as founding, nationality of parent company, presence of expatriates, and extent of communication of the parent.[92] Unfortunately, recruitment and selection activities were not specifically included in this study, nor was the nationality mix within the HR department revealed. Another study by Lu and Björkman[93] examined the HRM localization issue in 65 Sino-Western international joint ventures (IJVs). They report a variety of approaches, depending on mode of establishment, ownership, and the contribution of critical resources to the venture. The type of HR activity involved was also important. Recruitment and training were the two activities that were most likely to be localized: HR managers commented during follow-up interviews that recruitment in IJVs closely resembled the practices utilized by local firms. Both used job advertisements, job fairs, and job exchange centers. Criteria for selection also were similar, with an emphasis on education background, skills, and work experience.

Mode of entry, then, is an important consideration. If the multinational establishes its own facility (i.e., builds its own plant—what is termed a "greenfield site"), it may have more discretion in its hiring practices. Entry through acquisition generally means a ready-made workforce initially. South Korean multinationals have tended to follow a "growth-through-acquisition" strategy, and have generally encountered more staffing and labor problems than have Japanese multinationals that preferred a "greenfield sites" strategy.[94] An international joint venture can be even more difficult, as the host-country partner will have specific goals regarding hiring. This is further complicated when the local joint venture partner is the host government. Some Western firms entering into China have found staffing to be somewhat problematical, as state-owned partners often insist that all, or almost all, existing employees are utilized by the joint venture.

Monks[95] took a slightly different approach in her study of Irish subsidiaries of foreign multinationals. While she too was interested in the standardization–localization issue, Monks confined her sample to the HR department. In all of the nine companies, the HR managers were Irish, though other top subsidiary management positions were not necessarily localized. The Irish HR managers interviewed considered their control over local staffing issues as almost total. The exception was the Japanese firm in the sample—a finding which Monks considered consistent with Japanese subsidiary practices in other countries. Overall, Monks found that HCN selection remained in the domain of the Irish HR managers, but there was minimal input into HR decisions and strategies at the corporate level. None of the HR managers attended meetings at headquarters; controls, where they existed, were through the monitoring of financial implications of staffing decisions.

Selecting HCNs for Transfers to Headquarters

The second issue is the selection of HCNs for international transfer into the parent-company's domestic operations. Motives for utilizing HCNs in this way tend to be for training and development purposes, which we will discuss in Chapter 5. Among the reasons for HCN transfers is that so-called "inpatriates" can assist in breaking down the uniculture of the U.S. multinational. Related to this point, in a somewhat controversial article published in 1988, Kobrin[96] argued that many U.S. firms have overdone the replacement of U.S. expatriates with HCNs, in response to the difficulties that Americans have had in adjusting to other cultural environments, rather than for reasons of effectiveness and efficiency. In doing so, Kobrin warned that U.S. multinationals could become composed primarily of employees who identify with the local subsidiary rather than the worldwide organization. An influx of "inpatriates" is one way of preventing or overcoming such a problem. In their article, Harvey and Buckley[97] advocate careful selection and management of "inpatriates" to ensure that the advantages of such transfers are obtained. They highlight similar factors to those we include in Exhibit 3–5 for the selection of expatriates.

Other types of HCN transfers into parent operations can be to facilitate subsidiary learning and integration. As you will recall from the case of General Electric (Exhibit 2–1) the transfer of HCN staff into the United States was an important part of its attempts to integrate the Hungarian facilities into the GE family. HCNs may be transferred for technical and operative skills training, as well as to acquire a sense of belonging—part of building a global corporate culture. Of course, these transfers may be of a shorter duration than a general expatriate posting, and the reason for the transfer will affect selection. Some South Korean *chaebols* have encountered problems finding and keeping local management,[98] particularly in the United States. As a counter to this, HCN managers were transferred into South Korean facilities in an attempt to expose foreigners to the Korean way of doing business. Transfers of HCNs to the foreign partner's headquarters are playing an important training role in developing Chinese staff.[99] As we will demonstrate in the following chapters, language becomes more important as a selection criterion for HCN transfers. Ability to communicate in the common corporate language, and the language of the parent company (where these are different), may determine a potential candidate's suitability.[100]

Equal Employment Opportunity Issues

In the recruitment and selection process, multinationals must address the issue of equal employment opportunity (EEO) for employees in all employment locations. The legal definition and coverage of relevant laws are immediate problems since the multinational must take into consideration the increasingly conflicting national laws on employment. For example, mandatory retirement and hiring ages are illegal in the United States and some other countries but remain a legal requirement in other countries.

As we mention in Chapter 8, determining which law applies where, and which has precedence, is a problem without a specific solution. The United States has a comprehensive statute (Title VII of the Civil Rights Act of 1964) to cover many EEO situations. However, it should be noted here that the U.S. Supreme Court[101] has held that this act does not apply outside the territorial borders of the United States. The case involved an American citizen who claimed that he had been illegally discriminated against while working abroad for a U.S. corporation. A naturalized citizen born in Lebanon, the plaintiff began working for Aramco Corporation in Texas in 1979 and was transferred by the company to work in Saudi

Arabia in 1980, where he worked until 1984, when he was discharged. The Court rejected the person's claim that he had been harassed and ultimately discharged by Aramco Corporation on account of his race, religion, and national origin. The decision has important implications for the status and protection of Americans working abroad for U.S. firms.

Equal employment opportunity laws are expressions of social values with regard to employment and reflect the values of a society or country. In parts of the Middle East, Africa, Asia, and Latin America, women have tended to have a lower social status and are not universally employed. On the other hand, with the increasing rate of female entry into the workforce, many Western countries have introduced legislation to cover sex discrimination. Multinationals must be aware of legislation and ensure subsidiary compliance where appropriate. The selection procedures must be defended against illegality. Exhibit 3–7 demonstrates this point through the experience of an international hotel chain.

SUMMARY

This chapter identified a number of issues and trends in the area of international staffing. The interaction with the multinational's staffing approach and the pool of nationalities from which it selects key managers were reviewed. We also discussed the debate surrounding the definition and degree of expatriate failure before looking at the factors involved in

EXHIBIT 3-7 *Obeying Local EEO Laws*

In 1993, one of the Hyatt hotels in Australia had to explain to the Equal Employment Opportunity Commissioner on national TV as to why it was circulating an internal memo that violated Australian Equal Employment (EE) legislation.[102] The internal memo concerned was from a Japanese Hyatt hotel that had vacancies for two young single males. Under Australian EE law, these constitute age, marital status, and sex discrimination, respectively, so the memo violated Australian law on three counts. The hotel's defense that such circulation of internal job vacancies was normal company practice was not acceptable. The EE Commissioner did recognize that special circumstances may have been behind the internal memo—that the positions were traineeships and that the persons would share accommodation in a male-only dormitory.

expatriate selection. An evaluation of the common criteria used revealed the difficulty of selecting the right candidate for an international assignment and the importance of including family considerations in the selection process. Societal trends such as dual-career families will continue to constrain the firm's ability to attract the best candidate for the international assignment. Ensuring that high-potential employees are available is a major challenge for multinationals.

It is also clear that, while our appreciation of the issues surrounding expatriate recruitment and selection has deepened in the past decade, much remains to be explored. One such area is how firms approach the TCN and HCN management selection process. Are we right in assuming that the same criteria are used for PCNs and TCNs? Another area is the continuing low level of female international managers. Despite the suggestion that more female managers will be used in the future, it may be that the dual-career issue, coupled with single-parent families, will prove to be major constraints to their mobility.

It is apparent, though, that staff selection remains critical. Finding the right people to fill positions, particularly key managers—whether PCN, TCN, or HCN—can determine international expansion. As the American in charge of McDonald's Russian operations commented in a 1997 CNN interview,[103] staff availability remained a major constraint to further expansion in the region. However, effective recruitment and selection is only the first step. As we will explore in the next chapter, maintaining and retaining productive staff is equally important.

QUESTIONS

1. Outline the main characteristics of the ethnocentric, polycentric, regiocentric, and geocentric approaches to international staffing.
2. Try to estimate the total cost to the respective companies for each case of "failure" detailed in Exhibit 3–3—both direct and indirect. Could these instances have been prevented?
3. What are the most important criteria multinationals should use when selecting expatriates? What factors may influence these criteria?
4. There are widely held beliefs regarding the use of foreign females in international management positions, particularly in Asian countries, yet the South Korean manager in Exhibit 3–3 was female. Discuss this case and consider this question: Female international managers

are desirable, but is the risk of posting them to some countries too great?

5. What strategies can companies develop to overcome the potential barrier that dual-career couples may become in terms of staff availability for international assignments?

FURTHER READING

1. Birdseye, M., and J. Hill, 1995. Individual, organizational/work and environmental influences on expatriate turnover tendencies: An empirical study, *Journal of International Business Studies*, vol. 26, no. 4, pp. 787–813.

2. Black, J.S., and G.K. Stephens, 1989. The influence of the spouse on American expatriate adjustment and intent to stay in Pacific Rim overseas assignments, *Journal of Management*, vol. 15, no. 4, p. 541.

3. De Cieri, H., P.J. Dowling, and K.F. Taylor, 1991. The psychological impact of expatriate relocation on partners, *The International Journal of Human Resource Management*, vol. 2, no. 3, pp. 377–414.

4. Harvey, M.G., 1995. The impact of dual-career families on international relocations, *Human Resource Management Review*, vol. 5, no. 3, pp. 223–244.

5. Harzing, A-W.K., 1995. The persistent myth of high expatriate failure rates, *International Journal of Human Resource Management*, vol. 6, no. 2, p. 458.

6. Monks, K., 1996. Global or local? HRM in the multinational company: The Irish experience, *International Journal of Human Resource Management*, vol. 7, no. 3, pp. 721–735.

7. Rosenzweig, P., and N. Nohria, 1994. Influences on human resource management practices in multinational corporations, *Journal of International Business Studies*, vol. 25, no. 2, pp. 229–251.

8. Selmar, J., ed., 1995. *Expatriate Management: New Ideas for International Business*, Westport, CT: Quorum Books.

ENDNOTES

1. R.S. Schuler, and V.L. Huber, 1993. *Personnel and Human Resource Management*, 5th ed. St. Paul, MN: West Publishing Co.

2. Y. Zeira, 1976. Management development in ethnocentric multinational corporations, *California Management Review*, vol. 18, no. 4, pp. 34–42.

3. The Conference Board, 1997. *Managing Expatriates Return*, Report No. 1148-96RR.

4. A.V. Phatak, 1995. *International Dimensions of Management*, 4th ed. Cincinnati, OH: South-Western, p. 205. See also, M. Borg, 1987. *International Transfers of Managers in Multinational Corporations*, Sweden: University of Uppsala.

5. D. Welch, 1994. HRM implications of globalization, *Journal of General Management*, vol. 19, no. 4, pp. 52–68.

6. D.A. Heenan, and H.V. Perlmutter, 1979. *Multinational Organization Development*, Reading, MA: Addison-Wesley.

7. A.J. Morrison, D.A. Ricks, and K. Roth, 1991. Globalization versus regionalization: Which way for the multinational?, *Organizational Dynamics*, Winter, pp. 17–29.

8. R.D. Robinson, 1978. *International Business Management: A Guide to Decision Making*, 2d ed. Hinsdale, IL: Dryden.

9. A-W.K. Harzing, 1995. The persistent myth of high expatriate failure rates, *International Journal of Human Resource Management*, vol. 6, no. 2, p. 458.

10. R.L. Tung, 1981. Selection and training of personnel for overseas assignments, *Columbia Journal of World Business*, vol. 16, no. 1, pp. 68–78. See also, R.L. Tung, 1982. Selection and training procedures of U.S., European and Japanese multinationals, *California Management Review*, vol. 25, no. 1, pp. 57–71; and R.L. Tung, 1984. Human resource planning in Japanese multinationals: A model for U.S. firms?, *Journal of International Business Studies*, Fall, pp. 139–149.

11. C. Brewster, 1988. *The Management of Expatriates*, Human Resource Research Centre Monograph Series, No. 2, Cranfield School of Management, Bedford, U.K. In a pilot study, Hamill investigated the IHRM practices and policies of seven British multinationals. He found that the failure rate among British expatriates was significantly lower (less than 5 percent) than that reported for U.S. multinationals (J. Hamill, 1989. Expatriate policies in British multinationals, *Journal of General Management*, vol. 14, no. 4, pp. 19–33).

12. N. Forster, 1997. The persistent myth of high expatriate failure rates, *International Journal of Human Resource Management*, vol. 8, no. 4, p. 430.

13. E. Marx, 1996. *International Human Resource Practices in Britain and Germany*, London: Anglo-German Foundation.

14. Price Waterhouse, 1997. *International Assignments: European Policy and Practice 1997/1998*, Europe.

15. I. Björkman, and M. Gertsen, 1990. Corporate expatriation: An empirical study of Scandinavian firms, in *Proceedings of the Third Symposium on Cross-Cultural Consumer and Business Studies*, Honolulu, December. Danish firms did not respond to Tung's survey, but the Swedish and Norwegian firms did.

16. P.J. Dowling, and D. Welch, 1988. International human resource management: An Australian perspective, *Asia-Pacific Journal of Management*, vol. 6, no. 1, pp. 39–65. A further study by Welch of three Australian multinationals and one U.S. subsidiary found that, although precise records were not kept, the four companies estimated failure rates of less than 5 percent (D. Welch, 1994. Determinants of international human resource management approaches and activities: A suggested framework, *Journal of Management Studies*, vol. 31, no. 2, pp. 139–164).

17. For example, Enderwick and Hodgson explain that the absence of "expatriate failure" in their study of New Zealand firms may be due to their early stages in internationalization. See P. Enderwick, and D. Hodgson, 1993. Expatriate management practices of New Zealand business, *International Journal of Human Resource Management*, vol. 4, no. 2, pp. 407–423.

18. E. Mendenhall, and G. Oddou, 1988. The overseas assignment: A practical look, *Business Horizons*, September–October, pp. 78–84.

19. Y. Zeira, and M. Banai, 1984. Present and desired methods of selecting expatriate managers for international assignments, *Personnel Review*, vol. 13, no. 3, pp. 29–35.

20. M. Mendenhall, and G. Oddou, 1985. The dimensions of expatriate acculturation: A review, *Academy of Management Review*, vol. 10, pp. 39–47. See also, R.L. Desatnick, and M.L. Bennett, 1978. *Human Resource Management in the Multinational Company*, New York: Nichols.

21. A. Schwartz, 1995. Love thy neighbour?, *Far Eastern Economic Review*, August 10, p. 63.

22. This case is one encountered in 1989 by the second author of this text during research on expatriate management practices in Australian companies. Names and places have been changed to respect anonymity.

23. P. Guptara, 1986. Searching the organization for the cross-cultural operators, *International Management*, August, p. 40.

24. Tung, Selection and training procedures.

25. M. Harvey, 1985. The executive family: An overlooked variable in international assignments, *Columbia Journal of World Business*, Spring, pp. 84–93. See also, A. Thompson, 1986. Australian expatriate wives and business success in South East Asia, *Euro-Asian Business Review*, vol. 5, no. 2, pp. 14–18; and J.E. Harris, 1989. Moving managers internationally: The care and feeding of expatriates, *Human Resource Planning*, vol. 12, no. 1, pp. 49–53.

26. Tung, Selection and training procedures.

27. C. Reynolds, and R. Bennett, 1991. The career couple challenge, *Personnel Journal*, March, p. 48.

28. Tung, Selection and training procedures.

29. Focus Japan, 1990. Tanshin funin: Bachelors in exile, December, p. 4.

30. 1992. The lonely mother who chose death before disgrace, *The Age*, October 25, p. 4.

31. Tung, Selection and training procedures.

32. L.A. Allen, 1988. Working better with Japanese managers, *Management Review*, vol. 77, no. 11, pp. 55–56.

33. Hamill, Expatriate policies in British multinationals.

34. Welch, Determinants of international human resource management approaches. One U.S. personnel director who was interviewed by Dowling and Welch pointed out that attributing expatriate recall to "failure of spouse to adjust" was at times a simplistic explanation. He postulated that, apart from the probability of the expatriate blaming his wife (all the expatriates in this study were male) for his own failure to adjust, some astute spouses may see the expatriate's poor performance and trigger the early recall to limit damage to the expatriate's career. See Dowling and Welch, International human resource management: An Australian perspective.

35. J.M. Brett, and L.K. Stroh, 1995. Willingness to relocate internationally, *Human Resource Management*, vol. 34, no. 3, pp. 405–424.

36. H.B. Gregersen, and J.S. Black, 1990. A multifaceted approach to expatriate retention in international assignments, *Group & Organization Studies*, vol. 15, no. 4, pp. 461–485.

37. A.L. Hixon, 1986. Why corporations make haphazard overseas staffing decisions, *Personnel Administrator*, vol. 31, no. 3, pp. 91–94.

38. M.E. Mendenhall, E. Dunbar, and G. Oddou, 1987. Expatriate selection, training and career-pathing: A review and a critique, *Human Resource Planning*, vol. 26, no. 3, pp. 331–345.

39. J. McEnery, and G. DesHarnais, 1990. Culture shock, *Training and Development Journal*, vol. 44, no. 4, pp. 43–47.

40. I. Björkman, and M. Gertsen, 1993. Selecting and training Scandinavian expatriates: Determinants of corporate practice, *Scandinavian Journal of Management*, vol. 9, no. 2, pp. 145–164.

41. Marx, *International Human Resource Practices in Britain and Germany*.

42. Price Waterhouse, *International Assignments: European Policy and Practice*.

43. For example, according to the *Price Waterhouse Cranfield Project on International Human Resource Management 1991 Report*, most organizations surveyed filled management vacancies predominantly from among current employees.

44. See, for example, M. Birdseye, and J. Hill, 1995. Individual, organizational/work and environmental influences on expatriate turnover tendencies: An empirical study, *Journal of International Business Studies*, vol. 26, no. 4, pp. 787–813; and E. Naumann, 1993. Organizational predictors of expatriate job satisfaction, *Journal of International Business Studies*, vol. 24, no. 1, pp. 61–79.

45. Harvey, The executive family: An overlooked variable; Phatak, *International Dimensions of Management*.

46. F.T. Murray, and A.H. Murray, 1986. Global managers for global businesses, *Sloan Management Review*, vol. 27, no. 2, pp. 75–80.

47. Mendenhall, and Oddou, The overseas assignment.

48. Tung, Selection and training procedures.

49. J.S. Black, and G.K. Stephens, 1989. The influence of the spouse on American expatriate adjustment and intent to stay in Pacific Rim overseas assignments, *Journal of Management*, vol. 15, no. 4, p. 541.

50. H. De Cieri, P.J. Dowling, and K.F. Taylor, 1991. The psychological impact of expatriate relocation on partners, *The International Journal of Human Resource Management*, vol. 2, no. 3, pp. 377–414.

51. Brewster, *The Management of Expatriates*.
52. Price Waterhouse, *International Assignments: European Policy and Practice*.
53. Welch, Determinants of international human resource management approaches.
54. S.N. As-Saber, P.J. Dowling, and P.W. Liesch, 1998 (forthcoming). The role of human resource management in international joint ventures: A study of Australian-Indian joint ventures, *International Journal of Human Resource Management*.
55. D. Welch, and L. Welch, 1994. Linking operation mode diversity and IHRM, *International Journal of Human Resource Management*, vol. 5, no. 4, pp. 911–926.
56. Y. Zeira, and M. Banai, 1985. Selection of expatriate managers in MNCs: The host-environment point of view, *International Studies of Management and Organization*, vol. 15, no. 1, pp. 36–37.
57. Tung, Selection and training procedures.
58. D. Victor, 1992. *International Business Communication*, New York: HarperCollins.
59. C. Fixman, 1990. The foreign language needs of U.S.-based corporations, *ANNALS, AAPSS*, vol. 511, September, p. 25.
60. R.L. Tung, and Arthur Andersen, 1997. *Exploring International Assignees' Viewpoints: A Study of the Expatriation/Repatriation Process*, Arthur Andersen.
61. R. Marschan, D. Welch, and L. Welch, 1997. Language: The forgotten factor in multinational management, *European Management Journal*, vol. 15, no. 5, pp. 591–598.
62. Gregersen, and Black, A multifaceted approach to expatriate retention.
63. I. Torbiörn, 1982. *Living Abroad: Personal Adjustment and Personnel Policy in the Overseas Setting*, New York: John Wiley.
64. H.L. Willis, 1984. Selection for employment in developing countries, *Personnel Administrator*, vol. 29, no. 7, p. 55.
65. See, for example, P. Sparrow, and J-M. Hiltrop, 1994. *European Human Resource Management in Transition*, Hemel Hempstead, Herts, Prentice Hall; P.J. Dowling, 1988. Psychological testing in Australia: An overview and an assessment, in *Australian Personnel Management: A Reader*, G. Palmer, ed. Sydney: Macmillan.
66. Marx found that only 4.4 percent of the Germany companies in her survey used such tests, compared with 15.2 percent in the U.K.

firms. See Marx, *International Human Resource Practices in Britain and Germany*.

67. Hixon, Why corporations make haphazard overseas staffing decisions.

68. M. Gertsen, 1989. Expatriate selection and training, in *Proceedings of the Fifteen Annual Conference of the European International Business Association*, R. Luostarinen, ed. Helsinki, December, p. 1257.

69. G.M. Baliga, and J.C. Baker, 1985. Multinational corporate policies for expatriate managers: Selection, training, evaluation, *Advanced Management Journal*, vol. 50, no. 4, pp. 31–38. See also J.S. Black, 1990. The relationship of personal characteristics with the adjustment of Japanese expatriate managers, *Management International Review*, vol. 30, no. 2, pp. 119–134, for a review and discussion of crosscultural adjustment.

70. Mendenhall, and Oddou, The dimensions of expatriate acculturation. For a review of the Type A literature, see V.A. Price, *Type A Behavior Pattern: A Model for Research and Practice*, New York: Academic Press.

71. This point is very similar to the notion of similarity/dissimilarity between cultures as a selection factor proposed by Tung in her selection model. See Tung, Selection and training procedures.

72. Torbiörn, *Living Abroad*, p. 51. See also, Welch, Determinants of international human resource management approaches.

73. Reynolds, and Bennett, The career couple challenge.

74. K. Barham, and M. Devine, 1990. *The Quest for the International Manager: A Survey of Global Human Resource Strategies*, Ashridge Management Resource Group/The Economist Intelligence Unit, Special Report No. 2098.

75. S. Murray, 1998. Overseas stints can exact toll on all parties, *The Wall Street Journal Europe*, March 26, p. 4. One should note that Shell posts staff into somewhat remote areas—Oman, Brunei, Nigeria, Syria, Gabon, for example—as well as the United Kingdom, The Netherlands, and the United States, which may affect work possibilities for spouses.

76. G.K. Stephens, and S. Black, 1991. The impact of spouse's career-orientation on managers during international transfers, *Journal of Management Studies*, vol. 28, no. 4, p. 425.

77. M.G. Harvey, 1995. The impact of dual-career families on international relocations, *Human Resource Management Review*, vol. 5, no. 3, pp. 223–244.
78. Reynolds, and Bennett, The career couple challenge, p. 48.
79. Ibid.
80. The Conference Board, 1996. *Managing Expatriates' Return*, Report Number 1148-98-RR, New York.
81. N.J. Adler, 1984. Women in international management: Where are they?, *California Management Review*, vol. 26, no. 4, pp. 78–89.
82. Similar results were found by R. Stone 1989. Expatriate selection and failure, *Proceedings of the Second International Conference on Personnel and Human Resource Management*, Hong Kong, December, in his study of Australian and Asian managers' attitudes toward female expatriate managers working in Asia.
83. O. Culpan, and G. Wright, 1997. An examination of human resource policies of MNCs and job satisfaction of expatriate women managers, Paper presented at the 12th Workshop on Strategic Human Resource Management, Turku, Finland, March. More than half the women surveyed (68 percent) considered their present positions as a promotion. Discrimination may also come from the home organization: While 80 percent of the women believed that their selection for the foreign assignment was made on the basis of gender equality, 50 percent agreed that they were paid less than their male colleagues.
84. R. Johnson, 1998. Daddy dearest, *The Guardian*, March 2, pp. G2:2.
85. C. Shusterman, 1991. A welcome change to immigration law, *Personnel Journal*, September, pp. 44–48.
86. This case was prepared by Peter Dowling.
87. A recent article focuses on the TCN manager but does not include selection issues. See W.F. Chadwick, 1995. TCN expatriate manager policies, in *Expatriate Management: New Ideas for International Business*, J. Selmar, ed. Westport, CT: Quorum Books.
88. P. Barnevik, 1997. A multinational cadre of managers is the key, *Financial Times*, October 8, p. 12.
89. 1996. China Survey, *Financial Times*, June 27, p. VI.
90. 1997. Cover Story: Managing, barely, *Far Eastern Economic Review*, August 28, p. 56.

91. M. Nakamoto, 1996. Mitsubishi sued in US over sex harassment allegations, *Financial Times*, April 11, pp. 1, 10; M. Maremont, 1996. Abuse of power, *Business Week*, May 13, pp. 36–41.

92. P. Rosenzweig, and N. Nohria, 1994. Influences on human resource management practices in multinational corporations, *Journal of International Business Studies*, vol. 25, no. 2, pp. 229–251.

93. Y. Lu, and I. Björkman, 1997. HRM practices in China-Western joint ventures: MNC standardization versus localization, *International Journal of Human Resource Management*, vol. 8, no. 5, pp. 614–628.

94. 1996. *The Economist*, September 14, p. 70.

95. K. Monks, 1996. Global or local? HRM in the multinational company: The Irish experience, *International Journal of Human Resource Management*, vol. 7, no. 3, pp. 721–735.

96. S.J. Kobrin, 1988. Expatriate reduction and strategic control in American multinational corporations, *Human Resource Management*, vol. 27, no. 1, pp. 63–75.

97. M.Harvey, and M.R. Buckley, 1997. Managing inpatriates: Building a global core competency, *Journal of World Business*, vol. 32, no. 1, pp. 35–52.

98. 1996. *The Economist*, September 14, pp. 69–70.

99. R. Verburg, 1996. Developing HRM in foreign-Chinese joint ventures, *European Management Journal*, vol. 14, no. 5, pp. 518–525.

100. Marschan, Welch, and Welch, Language: The forgotten factor in multinational management.

101. E.E.O.C. vs. Arabian American Oil Co., 111 S. Ct. 1227 (1991). For an excellent commentary on this case, see G.L. Clark, 1992. The geography of civil rights, *Environment and Planning D: Society and Space*, no. 10, pp. 119–121.

102. Interview with Sydney Hyatt Hotel representative and the EE Commissioner for New South Wales on the "7.30 Report" current affairs program, Australian Broadcasting Corporation TV, October 10, 1993.

103. *Cable Network News (CNN)*, Business Report segment, May 26, 1997. The number of McDonald's outlets in Russia has grown to 15, and the number of expatriates reduced from 80 to 10

Performance Management

O ne of the most challenging aspects for a firm operating internationally is managing the performance of its various international facilities. As we discussed in Chapter 2, control matters increase in complexity as the geographical spread, product, and operation mode become more diversified. Staffing decisions are only part of the picture; the multinational requires an effective system for managing the performance of its global operations that assists strategic cohesion and competitiveness but, at the same time, does not impose burdensome reporting procedures that impinge on local responsiveness. Monitoring performance and ensuring conformance to agreed standards are important elements.

The aim of this chapter is to draw together the relevant literature on performance management as it relates to IHRM. Through such a review, we can identify similarities to performance management in the domestic context, yet highlight those aspects that require a substantial modification of the traditional performance management (especially appraisal criteria) imposed by international operations.

Exhibit 4–1 illustrates the basic components of international performance management. It provides a convenient starting point for our exploration of the link between the multinational's internationalization strategies, its goals for individual international operations in terms of contribution to global profitability, and individual performance management, whether PCN, TCN, or HCN. This link is important since an individual's performance is evaluated according to expectations of appropriate outcomes and behavior that contribute to organizational goal attainment.

EXHIBIT 4-1   *Basic Components of Performance Management*

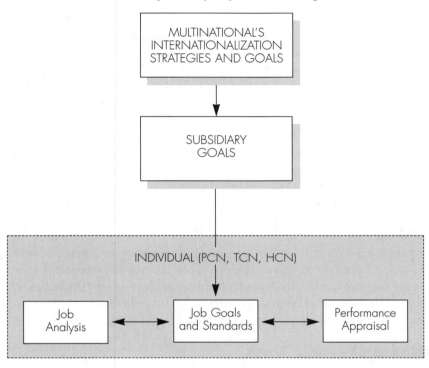

Source: Adapted from M. Tahvanainen, and D. Welch, 1995. Expatriate job performance management: A review and a critique, in *New Challenges for European and International Business*, R. Schiattarella, ed. Proceedings of the 21st Annual Meeting of the European International Business Academy, Urbino, Italy, December.

MULTINATIONAL PERFORMANCE MANAGEMENT

While its general strategic position may be international, multinational, global, or transnational[1] (depending on its size, industry, geographic dispersal, etc.), a multinational makes strategic choices based on economic and political imperatives. Within this context, as indicated in Exhibit 4–1, the multinational has specific expectations for each of its foreign affiliates in terms of market performance and contribution to total profits and competitiveness. When evaluating subsidiary performance against these expectations, however, it is important to recognize various constraints that may affect goal attainment. We identify five major constraints.

Whole versus Part

By its very nature, a multinational is a single entity that faces an international environment, which means that it simultaneously confronts differing national environments. Integration and control imperatives often place the multinational in the position where it decides that the good of the whole is more important than one subsidiary's short-term profitability. In an example provided by Pucik,[2] a multinational establishes an operation in a particular market where its main global competitor has a dominant position. The objective of entering the market is to challenge the competitor's cash flow with aggressive pricing policies. Pucik explains that "The balance sheet of this particular subsidiary might be continually in the red, but this strategy, by tying up the competitor's resources, may allow substantially higher returns in another market. The difficulties in quantifying such a global strategy in terms of the usual return-on-investment objectives are obvious." In another situation the multinational establishes a joint venture in a particular market in order to have a presence there, even though it has low expectations in the short term, and may provide minimum resources to the venture. Undoubtedly, the consequences of such global decisions for subsidiary management must be taken into consideration for performance evaluation.

Noncomparable Data

Frequently, the data obtained from subsidiaries may be neither interpretable nor reliable. As Garland et. al. illustrate:[3]

- Sales in Brazil may be skyrocketing, but there are reports that the Brazilian government may impose tough new exchange controls within a year, thus making it impossible for the multinational to repatriate profits. Does this mean that the MNE is performing effectively? Is the subsidiary performing effectively?
- Sales in Peru may be booming, but headquarters management was unaware that under Peruvian accounting rules, sales on consignment are counted as firm sales. How should the headquarters accounting system handle these sales relative to sales from other subsidiaries that do not consider sales on consignment as firm sales?

Garland et. al. further explain that physical measures of performance may be easier to interpret than in the above examples, but difficulties may still arise. For instance, notions of what constitutes adequate quality control checks can vary widely from one country to another, import tariffs can distort pricing schedules, a dock strike in one country can unexpectedly delay supply of necessary components to a manufacturing plant in another country, and local labor laws may require full employment at plants that are producing at below capacity. These factors can make an objective appraisal of subsidiary performance problematic, and may complicate the evaluation of individual subsidiary managers.

Volatility of the International Environment

The turbulence of the international environment requires that long-term goals be flexible in order to respond to potential market contingencies. According to Pucik,[4] an inflexible approach may mean that subsidiaries could be pursuing strategies that no longer fit the new environment. Consider, for example, the impact on international business of major events in the last decade such as the collapse of communist rule beginning in 1989 throughout Eastern Europe and the former Soviet Union, the Persian Gulf War in 1991, the formation of the Single European Market in 1992, recent market reforms in China, the handover in 1997 of the British colony of Hong Kong to the control of the People's Republic of China (PRC), and the current economic downturn in the so-called "tiger" economies of South-East Asia. Each of these events has had profound implications for the global and local strategies of multinationals operating in these countries. Because subsidiaries operate under such volatility and fluctuation, they must tailor long-term goals to the specific situation in a given market. Problems arise when subsidiary managers perceive goals and deadlines set by a distant headquarters strategy team as unrealistic and inflexible—failing to take into account local conditions that change as a result of a volatile environment. Obviously, involving regional and subsidiary managers in strategic planning assists in overcoming this perception.

Separation by Time and Distance

Judgments concerning the congruence between the multinational and local subsidiary activities are further complicated by the physical distances involved, time-zone differences, the infrequency of contact between the corporate head-office staff and subsidiary management, and the cost of the reporting system.[5] Developments in sophisticated worldwide communications systems, such as fax machines, video telephone conferences, and e-mail, do not fully substitute for "face-to-face" contacts between subsidiary managers and corporate staff. In some areas, the telecommunications system may be so overloaded, or underdeveloped, that reliable telephone, fax services, and Internet connections cannot be assumed. Meeting personally is often necessary to fully understand each person's situation. For this reason many multinational corporate managers spend a considerable amount of time traveling in order to meet expatriate and local managers in foreign locations. It is then possible for HR corporate staff, when designing performance management systems, to take account of country-specific factors.

Variable Levels of Maturity

According to Pucik,[6] without the supporting infrastructure of the parent, market development in foreign subsidiaries is generally slower and more difficult to achieve than at home where established brands can support new products, and new business areas can be crosssubsidized by other divisions. More time may be needed to achieve results than is customary in a domestic market, and this fact ought to be considered in the performance management process. Further, variations in customs and work practices between the parent-country and the foreign subsidiary need to be recognized. For example,

> one does not fire a Mexican manager because worker productivity is half the American average. In Mexico, that would mean that this manager is working at a level three or four times as high as the average Mexican industrial plant. Here we need relevant comparative data, not absolute numbers; our harassed Mexican manager has to live with Mexican constraints, not European or American ones, and these can be very different. The way we measure worker productivity is exactly the same, but the numbers come out differently because of that environmental difference.[7]

In summary, there are a number of significant constraints that must be considered when evaluating the performance of a foreign subsidiary. Because this evaluation is primarily based on strategic factors, it most directly affects the evaluation and success of the subsidiary chief executive.

FACTORS ASSOCIATED WITH INDIVIDUAL PERFORMANCE AND APPRAISAL

The remainder of this section deals with the key factors surrounding individual performance management that pertain to three categories of employees—PCNs, TCNs, and HCNs—at various management and operative levels. As you can see from Exhibit 4–1, we differentiate between "performance management" and "performance appraisal." Performance management is a process that enables the multinational to evaluate and continuously improve individual, subsidiary unit, and corporate performance, against clearly defined, pre-set goals and targets. As Tahvanianen[8] points out, strong goal setting and appraisal are key elements of a performance management system that also may include training and development and performance-related pay. In a sense, by adopting a performance management approach, multinationals are building on the goal-setting strengths of management-by-objectives and more traditional methods of performance appraisal. Its proponents argue, somewhat convincingly, that effective performance management is beneficial to both the individual and the firm.

Expatriate Performance Management

Performance can be viewed as a combination of several variables, such as motivation, ability, working conditions, and expectations. When attempting to determine expatriate performance, it is important to consider the impact of the following variables and their interrelationship since the assessment of expatriate performance is enhanced by a consideration of the variables that influence success or failure in a foreign assignment.[9]

- The compensation package;
- The task (assignment task variables and role of the expatriate);
- Headquarters' support;
- The environment in which performance occurs (subsidiary or foreign facility); and
- Cultural adjustment of the individual and the accompanying family members.

Exhibit 4–2 depicts these variables and forms the basis on which we will explore both the nature of the expatriate assignment, how performance is managed, the criteria for assessment, and the other elements that comprise an effective performance management system. Generally, we will use the term *expatriate* to cover both PCNs and TCNs, since much of the following is applicable to both.

EXHIBIT 4-2   *Variables Affecting Expatriate Performance*

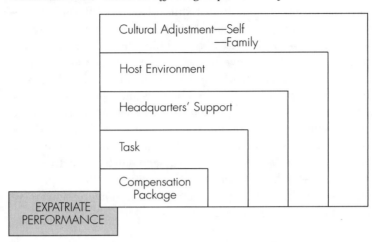

Compensation Package

We will examine in greater detail the issues surrounding compensation in Chapter 6; however, it is essential that we first recognize the importance of remuneration and reward in the performance equation. Perceived financial benefits, along with the career progression potential associated with an international assignment, are often important motives for accepting the posting. If these expectations are not realized during the assignment, the level of motivation and commitment is likely to decrease, thus affecting performance.

Task

As you will have begun to appreciate, expatriates are assigned to foreign operations to fulfill specific tasks. Hays[10] identifies four expatriate task roles:

1. The *chief executive officer*, or subsidiary manager, oversees and directs the entire foreign operation.
2. The *structure reproducer* carries the assignment of building or reproducing in a foreign subsidiary a structure similar to that which he or she knows from another part of the company. He or she could be building a marketing framework, implementing an accounting and

financial reporting system, or establishing a production plant, for example.
3. The *troubleshooter* is the individual sent to a foreign subsidiary to analyze and solve a particular operational problem.
4. The *operative* performs functional job tasks in an existing operational structure, in generally lower-level, supervisory positions.

In her study of expatriate performance management in the Finnish multinational, Nokia Telecommunications, Tahvanainen[11] identifies five categories of personnel: top managers, middle managers, business establishers, project employees, and research and development (R&D) project personnel. There are clear differences in the way performance management is approached within these groups. For example, middle managers play a moderate role in establishing performance goals, whereas business establishers play a strong role in establishing their performance goals and job descriptions.

Task variables are generally considered to be more under a multinational's control than are environmental factors. Because of this relative control, task variables can be better assessed and more easily changed, depending, of course, on the level of position and the nature of the task assignment. Along with the specifics of the task, the multinational, like any other organization, determines the role that accompanies each task position. A role is the organized set of behaviors that are assigned to a particular position. Although an individual may affect how a role is interpreted and performed, the role itself is predetermined.[12] For the expatriate (role recipient), the parent company (role sender) predetermines his or her role in the foreign assignment, and role expectations may be clearly communicated to the expatriate before departure. Black and Porter[13] found that American expatriates working in Hong Kong exhibited similar managerial behavior to those employees remaining in the United States. In their discussion of this finding, these authors suggest that the U.S. multinationals involved communicated role expectations by omitting to provide crosscultural training before departure. In the absence of incentives to modify their role behavior when abroad, it is not surprising that the expatriates concerned performed as they did. This study reminds us that the transmission of expatriate role conception is culturally bound. As Torbiörn[14] explains:

> The content of the managerial role, as perceived by both the individual manager and the parent company, is affected by organizational norms, in terms of

parent-company expectations of the manager, and by the set of cultural norms that the manager holds in relation to other cultural and organizational norms that may be represented by other role senders. Organizational and cultural norms thus interactively determine the role content of the manager.

The difficulty this presents for the expatriate manager is that the role is defined in one country but performed in another; that is, the cultural norms regarding the set of behaviors that define a manager in the United States may not be the same as those considered appropriate for a manager's role in Indonesia.

Communication of role conception from the multinational to the expatriate is indicated by the straight arrows in Exhibits 4–3 and 4–4. Role conception is also communicated to the role recipient by host-country stakeholders (e.g., subsidiary employees, host government officials, customers, suppliers, etc.) as shown by the dashed arrows. This, however, crosses a cultural boundary. Role behavior provides the feedback loop, again at two levels: the parent- and host-country stakeholders. Trying to perform to differing expectations may cause role conflict. If the PCN manager adapts his role behavior according to the role conception communicated in the host environment, it may conflict with that predetermined at headquarters. Janssens'[15] study of expatriate performance indicated that role conflict is likely to result in situations where the international manager has an understanding of the host-country culture

EXHIBIT 4-3 *PCN Role Conception*

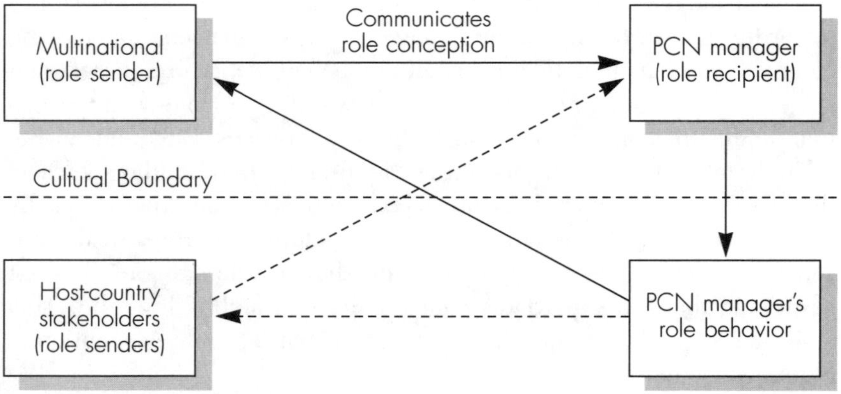

Source: Adapted from I. Torbiörn, 1985. The structure of managerial roles in cross-cultural settings, *International Studies of Management & Organization*, vol. 15, no. 1, p. 60.

EXHIBIT 4-4 *TCN Role Conception*

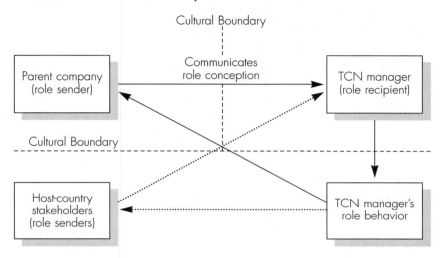

Cultural Boundary

Parent company
(role sender)

Communicates
role conception

TCN manager
(role recipient)

Cultural Boundary

Host-country
stakeholders
(role senders)

TCN manager's
role behavior

Source: Adapted from I. Torbiörn, 1985. The structure of managerial roles in cross-cultural settings, *International Studies of Management & Organization*, vol. 15, no. 1, p. 60.

and realizes that the use of headquarters' procedures or actions may lead to ineffective management. She postulates that the higher the degree of intercultural interaction, the more problems the expatriate has with role conflict.

From the perspective of headquarters, commitment to the parent is perceived as important, given the part that the PCN plays in transferring know-how and "the company way of doing things" into the subsidiary. This helps to explain the preference for using headquarters' standards in expatriate performance evaluation as a control mechanism.[16] If the PCN is perceived to identify too closely with host subsidiary concerns, he or she may be recalled (the term *going native* is often used to describe this perception). Some multinationals will restrict the length of stay to no more than three years to contain the possibility of PCN identification with local concerns. Because of the importance given to the parent as role sender in performance evaluation, a PCN may elect to ignore role communication sent from the host-country stakeholders if she or he considers that performance evaluation is determined by how role behavior conforms to headquarters' expectation. After all, the expatriate's career is with the parent, not the host subsidiary. Some empirical support for this comes from work by Gregersen and Black[17] in their study of U.S. expatriate retention and dual commitments (to the parent and the local organizations). They found that, at the correlational level commitment to the parent and to the local operation were both positively related to intent to stay. However, "regression analysis indicated that when controlling for certain demographic and attitudinal variables, commitment to the parent company appears to be slightly more relevant to expatriates' intention to stay." Role conflict was found to affect commitment to the parent company, but was unrelated to commitment to the host company.

Another intervening variable may be that of role autonomy. For instance, job discretion emerged as an important aspect in a recent survey by Birdseye and Hill[18] of 115 U.S. expatriates working in various countries. They found that "Foreign work methods may be more structured than their American counterparts (perhaps more procedures and protocols) and that individuals have less discretion in how they approach tasks and problems." These authors conclude that individuals are likely to blame this lack of discretion on the organization, the job, and the location—in that order. A similar finding emerged from a study of U.S. domestic and international relocation by Feldman and Tompson.[19] The degree of change in job duties was positively related to adjustment, while the degree of change in the organization was negatively related to adjustment. Thus, role conflict and role autonomy appear to be important elements in job satisfaction and task performance.

Role expectations are likely to be more complex for the TCN than the PCN, because the role is defined by and performed in two countries other than the TCN's own; that is, role conception crosses two cultural boundaries, as shown in Exhibit 4–4. Parent- and host-country role senders may have differing expectations of role behavior that, in turn, are different to the accepted managerial behavior defined by the prevailing norms in the TCN's own country. For example, a U.S. manager working for a Dutch multinational posted as a TCN in Indonesia may face added difficulties. The American's role behavior may be deemed inappropriate by both the parent (Dutch multinational) and the host nationals (Indonesians). As Torbiörn points out:

> The task of the PCN manager could be described as one of realizing the expectations of a psychologically close, but physically distant stakeholder [parent] in an environment containing other role senders [host country

stakeholders] who are psychologically distant, but physically close ... The TCN manager must try to meet the expectations of role senders who are all psychologically distant in a context that is also psychologically distant.

However, as you will recall from our discussion of the rationale for using TCNs, often the country of assignment is perceived by headquarters as culturally close (i.e., a German multinational decides to transfer a Canadian into the United States rather than a German). Whether cultural closeness lessens the potential for TCN role-conflict situations has yet to be empirically investigated.[20]

Since there are very few studies that specifically examine TCN performance management issues,[21] we can only assume that many of the aspects relating to PCNs discussed above will apply to the TCN situation. An American manager working in Indonesia, for instance, whether as a PCN or TCN, may encounter lack of job discretion—with perhaps the same effect in terms of performance—depending on the strength of other intervening variables. For example, differing role senders may exacerbate the situation through conflicting role expectations.

The preceding discussion demonstrates the importance of considering the role that accompanies each task position. Given that task performance is a core component of expatriate evaluation, it is also necessary to recognize that it does not occur in isolation. Many individuals and firms rank job ability as the primary ingredient relating to their expected probability of success in the international assignment (the "domestic equals international performance equation" mentioned in Chapter 3). Certain types of tasks, however, require significantly more interaction with host-country stakeholders. Thus the task variables should not be evaluated in isolation from the subsidiary environment context.

Another factor relating to task variables that warrants consideration is the similarity of the job the individual is assigned abroad to the job he or she held domestically. Some types of tasks require an individual to operate within a given structure, while other tasks demand the creation of the structure. Individuals vary greatly in their ability to conceive and implement a system and their tolerance for lack of structure and ambiguity. Some multinationals have experienced failure abroad because they assumed that an individual could be effective in setting up a structure, such as a marketing system, based on evidence of good performance within the existing marketing structure in the domestic corporation.[22]

Headquarters' Support

The expatriate assignment differs from a domestic relocation because it involves the transfer of the individual and accompanying family members into a foreign environment, which is outside their normal, cultural comfort zones. The individual's primary motivation for accepting the assignment may be career or financially orientated, but this is often mixed with a genuine feeling of loyalty and commitment to the sending organization. As we will explore later in this section, the process of adjustment to the foreign location typically produces, to varying degrees, a range of emotional and psychological reactions to unfamiliar situations encountered over the period of the stay in the host country. The level of headquarters' support provided to the individual and the family is an important performance variable that involves more than the tangible, monetary support contained in the compensation package. To appreciate this interaction, we need to consider the elements that comprise the employment contract and its relationship to organizational commitment and performance.

As depicted in Exhibit 4–5, the employment contract comprises two components—the transactional and the relational—contained within a broader social contract. The latter represents an implicit contract to execute the employment exchange according to a set of values, beliefs, and norms.[23] The transactional contract comprises the specific, short-term, monetizable obligations; the relational contract is characterized by broad, open-ended, long-term obligations based on both exchanges around monetizable elements (e.g., pay for service) and socioemotional elements (e.g., loyalty and support). For expatriates, the transactional contract is the terms and conditions of the assignment itself. It is the relational contract, combined with the social contract in which it is embedded, that underlies expatriate expectations regarding organizational support while in the foreign location.

The relational element of the employment contract is connected to the concept of the *psychological contract*: The "beliefs that individuals hold regarding promises made, accepted, and relied upon between themselves and another."[24] It is based on perceived reciprocal obligations pertaining to both formal contracts and implicit agreements and is, by nature, very subjective and specific to the individual. Violation of the psychological contract occurs when an individual feels that the organization has not fulfilled its obligations in return for the efforts and contributions made by the individual; perceived violation has a negative effect on commitment and loyalty to the organization.

EXHIBIT 4–5 *The Employment Contract*

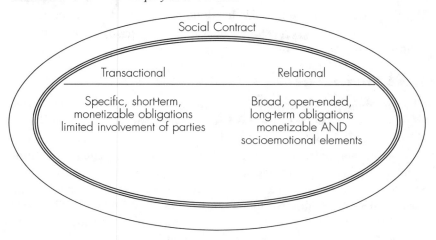

Social Contract

Transactional

Specific, short-term,
monetizable obligations
limited involvement of parties

Relational

Broad, open-ended,
long-term obligations
monetizable AND
socioemotional elements

Source: D. Welch, 1998. The psychological contract and expatriation: A disturbing issue for
IHRM?, Paper presented at the 6th Conference on International HRM, June, Paderborn, Germany.

In one of the few studies that examines the effect of the psychological
contract on expatriate behavior, Guzzo, Noonan, and Elron[25] found that
retention in the foreign location was influenced by expatriates' subjective evaluations of employer practices. More importantly, there was no
significant correlation between how much multinationals provided in
terms of benefits and services, and expatriate retention. Rather, it is the
perception of insufficient support provided in the host location that is the
critical factor, especially that provided to the family, such as job-search
assistance for the partner, adequate access to schooling for the children,
and so on. Thus, if the expatriate perceives that the multinational has not
provided the promised level of support, violation of the psychological
contract may affect performance and organizational loyalty, and trigger
an early recall. A perception of lack of adequate support for the family
may decrease commitment to the point that the expatriate resigns from
the organization.

Other studies also indicate the importance of headquarters' support.
For example, Harvey[26] reports that support during foreign assignments
is a critical aspect for dual-career couples. Likewise, De Cieri, Dowling,
and Taylor[27] found that company assistance to be one of the most consistent and strong predictors of psychological adjustment of expatriate
partners to relocation. The way in which the expatriate and family are

received and supported by subsidiary staff is also important.[28] We may, therefore, conclude that perhaps headquarters' support in the foreign location is a more powerful explanatory variable in expatriate performance than is generally recognized.

Host Environment

The environment has an impact on any job, but it becomes of primary importance with regard to expatriate management. According to Gregersen et. al.,[29] the international context—with its differing societal, legal, economic, technical, and physical demands—can be a major determinant of expatriate performance. Consequently, expatriate performance should be placed within its international as well as its organizational context. Therefore, the five major constraints identified earlier in terms of multinational strategy and goal setting for the subsidiary are important considerations for expatriate performance management.

The type of operation to which the expatriate is assigned is important. For instance, in China it may be relatively easier to perform in a wholly owned subsidiary than in a joint venture with a state-owned enterprise. Conflicting goals between the parent companies are a common problem within international joint ventures and can make the expatriate's job more difficult. An expatriate IJV manager may have difficulty trying to serve two masters and experience a high level of uncertainty regarding the effect of differing goal expectations for the IJV upon her or his performance evaluation. Similarly, the stage of the international business will influence the success of the expatriate. An expatriate overseeing the establishment of a new facility in a foreign country, especially in a developing or emerging market, will face different challenges and constraints than one who is posted in a mature operation.

Cultural Adjustment

The process of cultural adjustment may be a critical determinant of expatriate job performance, as we discussed in the context of "expatriate failure" in Chapter 3. Indeed, much of the literature reviewed in our discussion of the cause of expatriate "failure" covers the process of adjustment. It is likely that expatriates and their families will have some difficulty adjusting to a new environment, and this will impact on the manager's work performance. The dilemma is that adjustment to a foreign culture is multifaceted, and individuals vary in terms of their reaction and coping behaviors. Determining the relevance of adjustment to the new environment when assessing expatriate work performance may be problematical.

The concept of an adjustment cycle, or curve, depicted in Exhibit 4–6, is helpful in demonstrating the typical phases that may be encountered during cultural adjustment. The curve (sometimes referred to as the U-Curve) is based on psychological reactions to the assignment and comprises certain phases.[30]

Phase 1 begins with reactions prior to the assignment—the expatriate may experience a range of positive and negative emotions such as excitement, anxiety, fear of the unknown, sense of adventure, and so on. There can be an upswing of mood upon arrival in the assignment country that produces what has been referred to as the "honeymoon" or "tourist" phase. Then, as the novelty wears off, realities of everyday life in the foreign location begin to intrude, homesickness sets in, and a downswing may commence—a feeling that "the party is over"[31]—which can create negative appraisals of the situation and the location leading to a period of crisis (Phase 2). This can be a critical time, and how the individual copes with the psychological adjustment at this phase has an important outcome in terms of success or failure. There is a suggestion that "failure as an early recall" may be triggered at this point (indicated by the dotted line in Exhibit 4–6). Once past this crisis point, as the expatriate comes to terms with the demands of the new environment,

EXHIBIT 4–6 *The Phases of Cultural Adjustment*

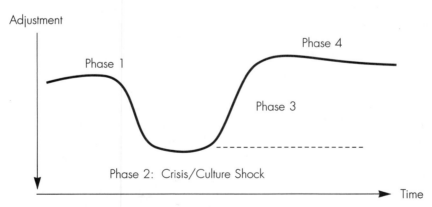

Source: Adapted from H. De Cieri, P.J. Dowling, and K.F. Taylor, 1991. The psychological impact of expatriate relocation on partners, *International Journal of Human Resource Management*, vol. 2, no. 3, p. 380.

there is a pulling up (Phase 3) as the person begins to adjust to the new environment. This levels off over time to what has been described as healthy recovery (Phase 4).

One should remember, though, the following points:

- The U-Curve is **not** normative. Some people do not experience this U-Curve. Individuals will differ in their reactions to the foreign location.
- The time period involved varies, and there is no conclusive statistical support for the various phases. Black and Mendenhall[32] point out that the U-Curve describes these phases but does not explain how and why people move through the various phases.
- There may be other critical points during the assignment—beyond Phase 4—that may produce downturns, negative reactions, and upswings (i.e., a cyclical wave rather than a U-Curve).
- As we will discuss in Chapter 7, the return home after completion of the assignment may require some psychological adjustment.

Despite these limitations, however, expatriates often relate experiencing these phases, and awareness of the psychological adjustment process can assist the expatriate adopt positive coping behaviors. We should also note that family members will experience the phases differently, and not necessarily move through the various phases at the same time as each other. How accompanying family members handle cultural adjustment is important, since there can be a spill-over effect—an unhappy spouse may affect the expatriate's ability to adjust, and thus impact on performance. For example, in their study of American managers in Japan, Korea, Taiwan, and Hong Kong, Black and Stephens[33] found a high correlation between spouse and expatriate adjustment. Firms can assist in the cultural adjustment of the expatriate and family members. Recognizing that cultural adjustment is a major problem when bringing HCNs (including Americans) into its home operations, the Norwegian multinational, Norsk Hydro, has developed a family mentoring program. Supervised by Corporate Expatriate Services staff, Norsk Hydro employees volunteer to "adopt" a visiting family. The volunteers are generally employees who have worked abroad as expatriates and thus have an understanding of what it is like to move a family unit into another country.

Personality factors appear to play a role in explaining an international manager's ability to adapt to a foreign environment and, therefore, increase the probability of successful performance. Much of the expatriate effectiveness literature is concerned with assessing personality variables, particularly in the context of staff selection and performance. For example, an individual's position along the dogmatism/authoritarianism scale, which can be determined with some accuracy, has a significant influence on his or her performance as an international manager. Dogmatism is a relatively closed conception of beliefs and disbeliefs about reality; authoritarianism is a preoccupation with power and status considerations and a general hostility toward out-groups. Authoritarian personality traits and dogmatism tend to represent one end of the scale; the other end is represented by the corresponding opposites of openness, social sensitivity, and empathy[34]. These variables are relevant to the performance of international managers because open-minded individuals seem to adapt more easily to new environments. Those who score high on authoritarianism/dogmatism often have difficulty accepting and adjusting to a new culture and, therefore, may be somewhat less effective in accomplishing tasks within the local cultural setting.[35]

The five variables—compensation package, task, headquarters' support, host environment and cultural adjustment—reviewed above and shown in Exhibit 4–2 are not mutually exclusive; they interact in a way that has significant implications for the evaluation of international employees' performance. Designers and users of performance management systems need to be conscious of, and responsive to, the impact of these variables.

CRITERIA USED FOR PERFORMANCE APPRAISAL OF INTERNATIONAL EMPLOYEES

Now that we have an understanding of the variables likely to influence expatriate performance, we can discuss the criteria by which performance is to be evaluated, or appraised (the terms are used interchangeably in the relevant literature). As you will recall from Exhibit 4–1, individual performance management involves job analysis, job goals and standards, and performance appraisal. Traditionally, it comprises a formal process of goal setting, performance appraisal, and feedback. Data from this process is often used to determine pay and promotion, and training and development requirements. Company goals, against which job goals and standards are established and measured, influence the individual's job analysis and job description. There are differences in the way this process is handed within companies. For example, in Germany

and Sweden it is common for employees to have input into job goal setting, whereas in other countries such as the United States, job goals tend
to be assigned.[36]

Performance Criteria

Goals tend to be translated into performance appraisal criteria so specificity and measurability issues are important aspects, and we need to
recognize that hard, soft, and contextual goals are often used as the basis
for performance criteria. **Hard goals** are objective, quantifiable, and can
be directly measured such as return-on-investment (ROI), market share,
and so on. **Soft goals** tend to be relationship- or trait-based, such as leadership style or interpersonal skills. **Contextual goals** attempt to take into
consideration factors that result from the situation in which performance
occurs. For example, multinationals commonly use arbitrary transfer
pricing and other financial tools for transactions between subsidiaries in
order to minimize foreign-exchange risk exposure and tax expenditures.
Another consideration is that all financial figures are generally subject
to the problem of currency conversion, including sales and cash positions. Further complications arise because host governments can place
restrictions on repatriation of profits and currency conversion. The nature of the international monetary system and local accounting differences may preclude an accurate measurement of results. This poses a
dilemma. The use of transfer pricing and other financial tools is necessary because of the complexity of the international environment. Multinationals cannot allow subsidiaries to become autonomous in financial
management terms, and place controls on subsidiary managers. Thus,
the financial results recorded for any particular subsidiary do not always
reflect accurately its contribution to the achievements of the corporation
as a whole. For this reason such results should not be used as a primary
input in performance appraisal.[37] A performance management approach,
rather than a traditional performance appraisal, is now advocated since
it allows clarification of goals and expectations of performance against
those goals.

Janssens[38] suggests that performance evaluation of subsidiary managers against hard criteria is often supplemented by frequent visits
by headquarter staff and meetings with executives from the parent
company. Soft criteria can be used to complement hard goals, and take
into account areas that are difficult to quantify, such as leadership skills,
but their appraisal is somewhat subjective and, in the expatriate context,

more complicated due to cultural exchanges and clashes. However, relying on hard criteria such as financial data to evaluate how well an expatriate manager operates a foreign subsidiary does not consider the way results are obtained and the behaviors used to obtain these results.[39] Concern with questionable ethical practices led to the enactment of the U.S. Foreign Corrupt Practices Act (FCPA), which may prompt an increased use of behavioral as well as results data to appraise the performance of expatriate managers in foreign subsidiaries.[40] However, an appraisal system that uses hard, soft, and contextual criteria builds on the strengths of each while minimizing their disadvantages;[41] using multiple criteria wherever possible is recommended in the relevant literature.

Who Conducts the Performance Appraisal?

Another issue concerns who conducts the performance appraisal. Typically, employees are appraised by their immediate superiors, and this can pose problems for subsidiary managers. They work in countries geographically distant, yet are evaluated by superiors back at headquarters who are not in the position to see on a day-to-day basis how the expatriate performs in a particular situation. Consequently, subsidiary managers tend to be assessed according to subsidiary performance, with a reliance on hard criteria similar to that applied to heads of domestic units or divisions. Of course, there is a danger that a PCN or TCN subsidiary manager will make decisions and implement local strategies that favor short-term performance to the detriment of longer-term organizational goals—her or his subsidiary performance will not be affected if the expatriate assignment has been completed before the consequences of those decisions and strategies begin to take effect.

Appraisal of other expatriate employees is likely to be conducted by the subsidiary's chief executive officer, the immediate host-country supervisor, or the individual's home-country manager, depending on the nature and level of the position concerned.[42] Host-country managers may have a clearer picture of expatriate performance and can take into consideration contextual criteria, but they may have culturally bound biases (e.g., about role behavior) and lack an appreciation of the impact of the expatriate's performance in the broader organizational context.

Some expatriates may prefer to have parent-company evaluators given that their future career progression may depend on how the evaluation data is utilized back at headquarters; this may be especially so in cases where foreign operations are relatively less important than domestic U.S. operations.[43] Others may prefer host-country evaluation if they perceive it as a more accurate reflection of their performance.

Multiple raters are sometimes used in the domestic context—such as the technique referred to as "360-degree feedback."[44] It has been argued that, given the crosscultural complexity of the foreign assignment, a team of evaluators should be used for expatriate performance evaluation. Gregersen et. al.[45] found that most firms (81 percent) in their survey of HR directors in 58 U.S. multinationals used more than one rater when assessing expatriate performance. The immediate superior (in either the home- or host-country), the expatriate as self-rater, and the HR manager (either home or host country-based) were commonly used as multiple evaluators of U.S. expatriate performance. Likewise, a survey of 99 Finnish internationally operating companies reports that 79 percent of respondents indicated that expatriate performance evaluation was conducted by the superior located in Finland.[46] Often though, this was simply because there was no suitable person in the host country to conduct such evaluations. The availability of knowledgeable, trained raters may constrain the approach taken in the international context.

Standardized or Customized Performance Appraisal Form

Domestic companies commonly design performance appraisal forms for each job category, particularly those using a traditional performance appraisal approach rather than performance management. Such standardization assists in the collection of accurate performance data on which personnel decisions can be made and allows for cross-employee comparisons. The question often posed is, Should these standardized forms be adapted when used for evaluating international managers? As Gregersen et. al.[47] argue:

> In principle, performance appraisal systems are designed carefully and often presumed to be static. Valid reasons exist for maintaining standard, traditionally used appraisals (e.g., when the system has been tested, has identified baselines, and reduces future development costs). These reasons are valid as long as the context of the performance does not change. In the expatriate setting, however, the performance context does change, and sometimes it changes dramatically. Given a global context, previous testing and established baselines grounded in domestic situations can become meaningless.

Despite this, they found in their sample of U.S. firms that 76 percent, in fact, used the same standardized appraisal forms for expatriate evaluation.[48]

Frequency of Evaluation

In practice, evaluation is commonly performed on a yearly basis, and this appears to extend to international performance systems, even though the domestic-oriented literature on this topic recommends more frequent performance evaluation and feedback. For example, the majority of U.S. firms in the Gregersen et. al. study referred to earlier reported annual appraisal practices. It is interesting to note that the U.S. firms using annual appraisal systems were more likely to use standard appraisal forms and hard criteria. In their discussion of this finding, Gregersen et. al. commented that replicating domestic practices requires less effort in collecting and interpreting the data, and that the preference for following the domestic system might reflect lack of international experience within the firms in the sample. Since only 28 percent of the HR respondents in their study reported having been on international assignments themselves, they might not be aware of the need to take contextual criteria into consideration, or see a need for the customization of their expatriate appraisal systems.

Performance Feedback

An important aspect of an effective performance management system is the provision of timely feedback of the evaluation process. One of the problems with annual appraisal is that employees do not receive the consistent frequent feedback considered critical in order to maintain or improve their performance. It is also suggested in the performance literature that regular feedback is an important aspect in terms of meeting targets and revising goals, as well as assisting in motivation of work effort. The difficulty for the expatriate who is being evaluated by a geographically distant manager is that timely, appropriate feedback is only viable against hard criteria.

A Contextual Model of Expatriate Performance Management

One of the few studies that examines expatriate performance management, as opposed to those that focus solely on appraisal, is that conducted by Tahvanainen. Taking a grounded theory approach and using qualitative case methodology, Tahvanainen explored the international, domestic, and organizational context in which expatriate performance evaluation occurred within the Finnish multinational, Nokia Telecommunications. From this study, Tahvanainen[49] developed a comprehensive model that illustrates the interrelationships between the various elements discussed so far in this chapter. The model (see Exhibit 4–7) illustrates how performance evaluation is both an outcome of the company's strategies and goals (through goal setting), and an important source of information on which other personnel-related activities, such as training and development and performance-related pay, are based.

As you can see from Exhibit 4–7, the organizational context is comprised of the nature of the job, the organizational structure, a standard performance management system, top-management support, size of the receiving unit (subsidiary), and the style and skills of the manager and subsidiary employees. The mediating effect of any of these elements varies according to the strength of its interaction with other elements. In Nokia, for example, the organizational structure emerged as important. Like some of its Nordic counterparts, Nokia has adopted a global matrix form that prevails at the top-management level of the multinational as an overarching structure. However, in some divisions, and particularly at lower organizational levels, a traditional line-management organization remains. The multinational also uses project teams. Tahvanainen found that employees within these different organizational configurations were managed differently. For example, expatriates in line positions were evaluated by their host-country managers, whereas product managers, who reported through the matrix structure, were evaluated by host- and home-country superiors. As Tahvanainen points out, the matrix structure can, in fact, resolve inherent conflict between differing expectations, as the two superiors evaluating an expatriate's performance are, in the normal course of their work, required to recognize commonality of global and area goals in other areas besides employee performance.

Another aspect of the model shown in Exhibit 4–7, is that clarification of performance expectations is an important element linking company strategies and goals with performance evaluation. Individual goal setting does not always occur within all job categories, but performance expectations may be conveyed in informal ways. Likewise, a concept—daily management—is added as a critical component of the organizational context. For example, expatriates working in customer project operations tended to rely more on guidance, performance review, feedback, and coaching on an ongoing, informal basis rather than

EXHIBIT 4-7   *Contextual Model of Expatriate Performance Management*

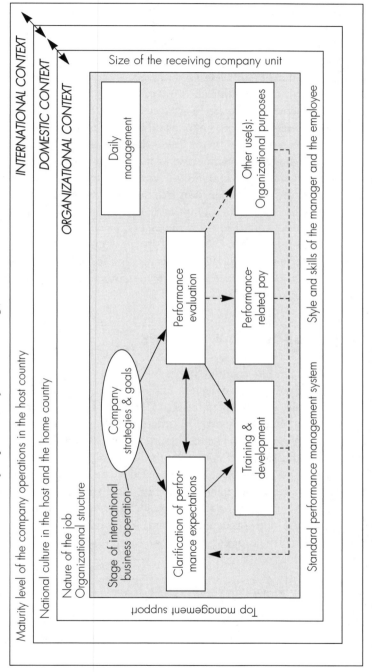

Source: M. Tahvanainen, 1998. *Expatriate Performance Management: The Case of Nokia Telecommunications*, Helsinki: Helsinki School of Economics. Reproduced with permission of the author.

Nokia's standardized performance management system. The model also indicates, through the use of dotted lines and arrows connecting the various elements, that performance management varies across job categories and expatriate situations, and the extent to which data collected through the performance management system is utilized.

A somewhat surprising finding of the Nokia study is the seemingly irrelevance of national culture as a contingency variable. While the Finnish culture indirectly affected expatriate performance management, it was not evident as a powerful factor that influenced general expatriate performance management. Tahvanainen explains that this finding may reflect the implementation of a standard, global performance management system within Nokia, rather than extending an existing domestic system to expatriates. Another explanation is that, in general, Nokia expatriates either did not report to HCN managers, or only to PCN managers, so their performance was evaluated in the Finnish context. For these reasons, and in recognition that the framework is limited by its empirical grounding in a single case study, Tahvanainen includes national context in her contextual model.

APPRAISAL OF HCN EMPLOYEES

The discussion so far has omitted the issue of appraising the performance of HCN employees. To a certain extent, this reflects the limited research on the topic in the context of IHRM, though there is a growing body of literature on comparative HRM practices (we will cover some of this in Chapter 9). What is important to mention here is that the practice of performance appraisal itself confronts the issue of cultural applicability.[50] Performance appraisal in different nations can be interpreted as a signal of distrust or even an insult. In Japan, for instance, it is important to avoid direct confrontation to "save face," and this custom affects the way in which the performance appraisal is conducted. A Japanese manager cannot directly point out a work-related problem or error committed by a subordinate.

> Instead, he is likely to start discussing with the subordinate about the strong points of that person's work, continuing with a discussion about the work on a relatively general level. Then he might continue to explain the consequences of the type of mistake committed by the subordinate, still without directly pointing out the actual mistake or the individual employee. From all

this, the subordinate is supposed to understand his mistake and propose how to improve his work.[51]

One way to overcome the dilemma of cultural adaptation is to use host-country nationals to assist in devising a suitable system for appraising the local staff in the subsidiary and to advise on the conduct of the appraisal. The need for local responsiveness may affect the multinational's ability to effectively implement a standardized approach to performance management at all levels within the global operation.

As we discussed in relation to PCNs and TCNs, the level of position involved is an important consideration. Should a multinational appoint a HCN as its subsidiary manager, then much of what we covered in terms of goals (particularly hard goals) and performance measures could be expected to apply to the HCN. In terms of task performance and potential role conflict, as seen in Exhibit 4–8, Torbiörn[52] recognizes that HCN managers face particular role concerns that are different from those of the PCN and TCN managers. The HCN manager is expected to perform a role that is conceptualized by a psychologically and physically distant parent company, but enacted in an environment with other role senders who are both psychologically and physically close.

Parent-company role conception is communicated to the HCN, but it crosses the cultural boundary, as does feedback expressed as the HCN's role behavior (the straight arrows in Exhibit 4–8). Input from host-country role senders, though, does not cross a cultural boundary. The HCN receives role expectations and enacts role behaviors in his or her own cultural environment (as depicted by the shaded area in Exhibit 4–8). For subsidiary staff below the top-management level, one would expect that the performance management system is localized to take into consideration local behavioral norms of work behavior. Torbiörn's model depicts only HCN managerial role conception and communication.

Conflict may arise in cases where HCNs report to a PCN expatriate manager who also conducts their performance evaluation. In a way, this is the reverse of the discussion surrounding local managers evaluating the performance of expatriates in terms of cultural bias. The difference, of course, is the impact that parent-company standards have on the performance management system and the degree to which localization is permitted in a standardized approach. It may not be culturally sensitive to use evaluation techniques such as 360-Degree Feedback, for instance. In practice, U.S. multinationals have often used the same

EXHIBIT 4-8   *HCN Role Conception*

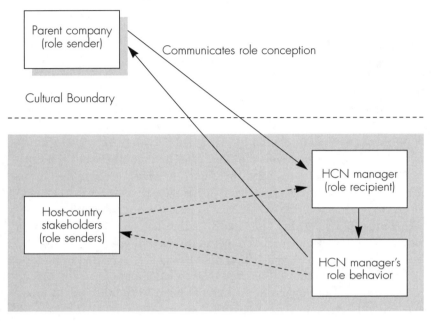

Source: Adapted from I. Torbiörn, 1985. The structure of managerial roles in cross-cultural settings, *International Studies of Management & Organization*, vol. 15, no. 1, p. 61.

appraisal form for HCNs as for their domestic employees. Sometimes the forms are translated from English; sometimes they are not. Both approaches have drawbacks. While some companies are developing information systems to assist in performance appraisal, the widespread use of computer-generated data is hampered by the legal constraints imposed by some host governments or by concerns about personal privacy. This is, however, a dynamic issue. Despite these problems, it is possible to devise a standardized appraisal system that caters for local concerns, as you will see from the approach taken by Pepsi-Cola International detailed in Exhibit 4–9.

An aspect often overlooked in the limited literature is the potential for role conflict for those HCNs transferred into the parent-company's operations.[54] For that period, the HCN may be evaluated according to role behavior expectations communicated by role senders that are physically close but psychologically distant, in an environment that is also psychologically distant. The HCN is then transferred, usually back into

EXHIBIT 4-9 *Performance Appraisal at Pepsi-Cola International*[53]

good

Pepsi-Cola International (PCI), with operations in over 150 countries, has devised a common performance appraisal system that focuses on motivating managers to achieve and maintain high standards of performance. Administrative consistency is achieved through the use of a performance appraisal system of five feedback mechanisms—Instant Feedback, coaching, accountability based performance appraisals, development feedback, and a human resource plan.

The common system provides guidelines for performance appraisal yet allows for modification to suit cultural differences. For example, the first step—Instant Feedback—is based on the principle that any idea about any aspect of the business or about an individual's performance is raised appropriately and discussed in a sensitive manner. The Instant Feedback message can be delivered in any culture; the important thing is not *how* it is done but *that* it is done.

In practice at PCI, the successful delivery of Instant Feedback requires some adjustment to local cultures. Americans use it because it fits the fast-paced way of doing business. In most Asian cultures, feedback may be tough and direct but is never given in public; nor, in some Asian cultures, does head-nodding during Instant Feedback signify agreement, only that the message has been heard. Some Latins will argue very strongly if they do not agree with the feedback, and some employees, Indian nationals, for example, will insist on a great deal of specificity. The purpose of Instant Feedback is always to improve business performance, not to criticize cultural styles. Using this system, PCI tries to balance the cultural and administrative imperatives of successfully managing the performance of a diverse workforce.

her or his home country, and may experience difficulties in readjusting role behavior (as we will examine in Chapter 7).

SUMMARY

As we discussed in Chapter 3, HR management needs to recognize that technical competence is a necessary but not sufficient condition for successful performance in international management positions. Crosscultural interpersonal skills, sensitivity to foreign norms and values, and ease of adaptation to unfamiliar environments are just a few of the managerial characteristics most multinational firms seek when selecting international managers. The added challenge is the effective evaluation of performance across all of the multinational's operations, through a system that is conscious of, and responds to, the organizational, national, and international elements we have explored in this chapter.

The focus of this chapter—mainly as a reflection of its dominance in the relevant literature—has been on performance management issues relating to international managers. An effective performance management system also has to deal with the challenges of comparing subsidiary managers in different countries. For example, it is difficult to compare the performance of a French subsidiary manager with that of a Singapore subsidiary manager because each manager works under quite different environmental conditions. It is equally as challenging to evaluate the performance of the various subsidiary employees (the majority of whom are HCNs). However, performance management, with its emphasis on goal setting and agreement of performance goals between managers and employees, may assist in overcoming some of these difficulties.

An aspect of performance management not addressed in the current IHRM literature is the effect that constant international travel has on those employees who are not expatriates, yet whose job involves frequent journeys abroad. For example, heads of international divisions typically spend a large proportion of time travelling to various countries in order to oversee international projects, evaluate subsidiary performance, coordinate activities, and advise on strategic issues. Export managers may also travel to control and coordinate foreign agent activities. The performance effects of factors associated with constant air travel on the person's health, and the stress of long absences from family and home, have been the subject of little investigation in HR or IHRM performance management literature.[55] A survey by the World Bank on the effect of frequent travel on its staff revealed an increase in psychological disorders, such as depression, nervous anxiety, and sleep disturbance. "We first attributed these symptoms to jet lag, but we realised that other significant factors were involved. The three main influences are separation from home and family, workload and lack of back-up abroad."[56] Among 500 frequent fliers surveyed by Hyatt Hotel, 18 percent said that their absences had a negative impact on their marriages.[57]

Related to this, the 1997–1998 Price Waterhouse survey identifies a trend to what is being called "virtual assignments" to overcome staff immobility. Instead of moving into the host environment, the person manages the international position from the home country using a combination of regular communication link-ups and frequent trips to the foreign location. Forty three percent of the companies in the Price

Waterhouse survey[58] have agreed to such assignments instead of the traditional expatriate posting. Half of the companies report that their use of virtual assignments has increased over the last two years, and 53 percent anticipate the trend to increase over the next five years. These emerging trends serve to remind us that there are many dimensions to international business operations—all of which have performance management implications.

QUESTIONS

1. Discuss the major factors associated with appraisal of expatriate managerial performance.
2. One of the dangers of performance appraisal is that, because the focus is so much on a particular individual, the teamwork aspect gets lost. In an international location, it is perhaps desirable to focus more on how the PCN has settled in and is operating as part of a team rather than as an individual at the possible detriment of the team. Do you agree or disagree with this statement? Explain.
3. Why is it important to include hard, soft, and contextual goals when assessing expatriate managerial performance?
4. In what ways would the role of a manager working in a less-developed country (LDC) differ from that of a manager in a developed Western economy?
5. It is often claimed that U.S. managers are less skilled in crosscultural interaction than are their European counterparts. In your view, is this a fair comment? Explain.

FURTHER READING

1. Adsit, D.J., M. London, S. Crom, and D. Jones, 1997. Cross-cultural differences in upward ratings in a multinational company, *International Journal of Human Resource Management*, vol. 8, no. 4, pp. 384–401.
2. Arthur, W., and W. Bennett, 1995. The international assignee: The relative importance of factors perceived to contribute to success, *Personnel Psychology*, vol. 48, no. 1, pp. 99–114.
3. Black, J.S., and M. Mendenhall, 1991. The U-Curve adjustment hypothesis revisited: A review and theoretical framework, *Journal of International Business Studies*, vol. 22, no. 2, pp. 225–247.

4. Harvey, M., 1997. Focusing the international personnel performance appraisal process, *Human Resource Development Quarterly*, vol. 8, no. 1, pp. 41–62.

5. Jackson, E., ed., 1992. *Human Resource Management Approaches for Effectively Managing Diversity*, New York: Guilford Publications.

6. Janssens, M., 1994. Evaluating international managers' performance: Parent company standards as control mechanism, *International Journal of Human Resource Management*, vol. 5, no. 4, pp. 853–873.

7. Kamoche, K., 1992. Human resource management: An assessment of the Kenyan case, *International Journal of Human Resource Management*, vol. 3, no. 3, pp. 497–520.

8. Rao, A., and K. Hashimoto, 1996. Intercultural influence: A study of Japanese expatriate managers in Canada, *Journal of International Business Studies*, vol. 27, no. 3, pp. 443–466.

ENDNOTES

1. C.A. Bartlett, and S. Ghoshal, 1987. Managing across borders: New strategic requirements, *Sloan Management Review*, Summer, pp. 7–17.

2. V. Pucik, 1985. Strategic human resource management in a multinational firm, in *Strategic Management of Multinational Corporations: The Essentials*, H.V. Wortzel, and L.H. Wortzel, eds. New York: John Wiley, pp. 429, 430.

3. J. Garland, R.N. Farmer, and M. Taylor, 1990. *International Dimensions of Business Policy and Strategy*, 2d ed. Boston: PWS-KENT.

4. Pucik, Strategic human resource management in a multinational firm, p. 430.

5. Ibid.

6. Ibid.

7. Garland, Farmer, and Taylor, p. 193.

8. M. Tahvanainen, 1998. *Expatriate Performance Management*. Helsinki: Helsinki School of Economics Press.

9. S.F. Slater, and N.K. Napier, 1989. Human resource competence as a source of competitive advantage in multinational companies: Issues affecting the transfer of distinctive competence, Working paper, Boise State University.

10. Richard Hays, 1974. Expatriate selection: Insuring success and avoiding failure, *Journal of International Business Studies*, vol. 5, no. 1, pp. 25–37. Tung appears to have based her initial studies on these categories (see R. Tung, 1991. Selection and training of personnel for overseas assignments, *Columbia Journal of World Business*, vol. 16, no. 1, pp. 68–78).

11. Tahvanainen, *Expatriate Performance Management*.

12. H. Mintzberg, 1973. *The Nature of Managerial Work*, Englewood Cliffs, N.J.: Prentice Hall.

13. J.S. Black, and L.W. Porter, 1991. Managerial behaviors and job performance: A successful manager in Los Angeles may not succeed in Hong Kong, *Journal of International Business Studies*, vol. 22, no. 1, pp. 99–113.

14. I. Torbiörn, 1985. The structure of managerial roles in cross-cultural settings, *International Studies of Management & Organization*, vol. 15, no. 1, pp. 52–74.

15. M. Janssens, 1994. Evaluating international managers' performance: Parent company standards as control mechanism, *International Journal of Human Resource Management*, vol. 5, no. 4, pp. 853–873.

16. Ibid.

17. H.B. Gregersen, and J.S. Black, 1990. A multifaceted approach to expatriate retention in international assignments, *Group & Organization Studies*, vol. 15, no. 4, p. 478.

18. M.G. Birdseye, and J.S. Hill, 1995. Individual, organization/work and environmental influences on expatriate turnover tendencies: An empirical study, *Journal of International Business Studies*, vol. 26, no. 4, p. 800.

19. D.C. Feldman, and H.B. Tompson, 1993. Expatriation, repatriation, and domestic geographical relocation: An empirical investigation of adjustment to new job assignments, *Journal of International Business Studies*, vol. 24, no. 3, pp. 507–529.

20. A study of Finnish expatriates working in European contexts reveals interesting examples of culturally close postings and role behavior. One Finnish expatriate posted to nearby Sweden found it difficult to adjust because Swedes were used to more subordinate participation in decision making than is common practice in Finnish companies. One can assume that Finns posted to Sweden as TCNs would relate similar reactions. See V. Suutari and C.

Brewster, 1997. The adaptation of expatriates in Europe: Evidence from Finnish companies, Paper presented at the 12th Workshop of Strategic Human Resource Management, March, Turku, Finland.

21. For example, in one of the few articles on this topic, Chadwick looks at the TCN assignment in general, and does not specifically address performance. Rather, the focus is on fair treatment and equity regarding compensation (W.F. Chadwick, 1995. TCN expatriate manager policies, in *Expatriate Management: New Ideas for International Business*, Jan Selmer, ed. Westport, CT: Quorum Books.

22. M. Conway, 1984. Reducing expatriate failure rates, *Personnel Administrator*, July, pp. 31–37.

23. D.M. Rousseau, and K.A. Wade-Benzoni, 1994. Linking strategy and human resource practices: How employee and customer contracts are created, *Human Resource Management*, vol. 33, no. 3, pp. 463–489.

24. Ibid., p. 466.

25. R.A. Guzzo, K.A. Noonan, and E. Elron, 1994. Expatriate managers and the psychological contract, *Journal of Applied Psychology*, vol. 79, no. 4, pp. 617–685.

26. M. Harvey, 1997. Dual-career expatriates: Expectations, adjustment and satisfaction with international relocation, *Journal of International Business Studies*, vol. 28, no. 3, pp. 627–658.

27. H. De Cieri, P.J. Dowling, and K.F. Taylor, 1991. The psychological impact of expatriate relocation on partners, *International Journal of Human Resource Management*, vol. 2, no. 3, pp. 377–414.

28. M. Kauppinen, 1994. *Antecedents of Expatriate Adjustment: A Study of Finnish Managers in the United States*, Helsinki: Helsinki School of Economics Press.

29. H.B. Gregersen, J.M. Hite, and J.S. Black, 1996. Expatriate performance appraisal in U.S. multinational firms, *Journal of International Business Studies*, vol. 27, no. 4, pp. 711–738.

30. For a review and assessment of the U-Curve, see J.S. Black, and M. Mendenhall, 1991. The U-Curve adjustment hypothesis revisited: A review and theoretical framework, *Journal of International Business Studies*, vol. 22, no. 2, pp. 225–247.

31. H. De Cieri, P.J. Dowling, and K.F. Taylor, The psychological impact of expatriate relocation on partners.

32. Black, and Mendenhall, The U-Curve adjustment hypothesis revisited.

33. J.S. Black, and G.K. Stephens, 1989. The influence of the spouse on American expatriate adjustment and intent to stay in Pacific Rim overseas assignments, *Journal of Management*, vol. 15, no. 4, pp. 529–544. See also, M. Kauppinen, *Antecedents of Expatriate Adjustment*, for support of this finding.

34. See E. Dapsin, 1985. Managing expatriate employees, *Management Review*, July, pp. 47–49; W. Davidson, 1984. Administrative orientation and international performance, *Journal of International Business Studies*, Fall, pp. 11–23; and M. Mendenhall, and G. Oddou, 1988. The overseas assignment: A practical look, *Business Horizons*, September–October, pp. 78–84.

35. See M. Harvey, 1985. The executive family: An overlooked variable in international assignments, *Columbia Journal of World Business*, Spring, pp. 84–92; M. Harvey, 1982. The other side of foreign assignments: Dealing with the repatriation dilemma, *Columbia Journal of World Business*, vol. 17, no. 1, pp. 53–59; and Hays, Expatriate selection.

36. Tahvanainen, *Expatriate Performance Management*.

37. Pucik, Strategic human resource management.

38. Janssens, Evaluating international managers' performance.

39. R.W. Beatty, 1989. Competitive human resource advantages through the strategic management of performance, *Human Resource Planning*, vol. 12, no. 3, pp. 179–194.

40. K.F. Brickley, 1992. *Corporate Criminal Liability: A Treatise on the Criminal Liability of Corporations, Their Officers and Agents*, Cumulative supplement, Deerfield, IL: Clark Boardman Callaghan. Enacted in 1977, the FCPA addresses the problem of questionable foreign payments by U.S. multinationals and their managers. The act was amended by Congress in 1988 to include substantial increases in the authorized criminal fines for organizations and new civil sanctions for individuals violating the FCPA. This issue is discussed further in Chapter 9.

41. Tahvanainen, *Expatriate Performance Management*; and Gregersen, Hite, and Black, Expatriate performance appraisal in U.S. multinational firms.

42. Tahvanainen, *Expatriate Performance Management*.

43. E. Naumann, 1993. Organizational predictors of expatriate job satisfaction, *Journal of International Business Studies*, vol. 24, no. 1, pp. 61–80.

44. For further details about this technique, see the Special Issue on 360-Feedback, *Human Resource Management*, vol. 32, nos. 2, 3 (191993).

45. Gregersen, Hite, and Black, Expatriate performance appraisal in U.S. multinational firms.

46. Tahvanainen, *Expatriate Performance Management*.

47. Gregersen, Hite, and Black, Expatriate performance appraisal in U.S. multinational firms, p. 716.

48. It should be remembered that these authors take a traditional performance appraisal approach, rather than utilize the newer performance management literature that we discuss in this chapter. It may be that the goal setting stressed in the performance management literature will assist standardization.

49. Tahvanainen, *Expatriate Performance Management*, p. 226.

50. See, for example, N.J. Adler, 1997. *International Dimensions of Organizational Behavior*, 3rd ed. Cincinnati, OH: South Western. S. Schneider, 1988. National vs. corporate culture: Implications for human resource management, *Human Resource Management*, vol. 27, pp. 231–246; and G.P. Latham, and N.K. Napier, 1989. Chinese human resource management practices in Hong Kong and Singapore: An exploratory study, in *Research in Personnel and Human Resource Management*, G. Ferris, K. Rowland, and A. Nedd, eds. vol. 6, Greenwich, CT: JAI.

51. J.V. Koivisto, 1992. Duality and Japanese management: A cosmological view of Japanese business management, Paper presented at the European Institute of Advanced Studies in Management Workshop, *Managing in Different Cultures*, Cergy, Group Essec, France, November 23–24.

52. Torbiörn, The structure of managerial roles in cross-cultural settings.

53. For a complete description of PCI's system, see R.S. Schuler, J.R. Fulkerson, and P.J. Dowling, 1991. Strategic performance measurement and management in multinational corporations, *Human Resource Management*, vol. 30, no. 3, pp. 365–392.

54. The performance appraisal of "inpatriates" is briefly covered in M.G. Harvey, and M.R. Buckley, 1997. Managing inpatriates: Building a global core competency, *Journal of World Business*, vol. 32, no. 1, pp. 35–52.

55. D. Welch, and L. Welch, 1994. Linking operation mode diversity and IHRM, *International Journal of Human Resource Management*, vol. 5, no. 4, pp. 911–926.
56. F. Kahn, 1997. Living in fear of frequent flying, *Financial Times*, November 3, p. 14.
57. Ibid. The term *Intermittent Spouse Syndrome (ISS)* has been coined to explain the effect that the rapid and unrelenting cycle of partings and reunions can have on family members.
58. Price Waterhouse, 1997–98. *International Assignments: European Policy and Practice*, Europe.

C H A P T E R 5
Training and Development

I n order to compete successfully in a global market, more firms are focusing on the role of human resources as a critical part of their core competence and a source of competitive advantage. As Kamoche[1] reminds us: "the human resource refers to the accumulated stock of knowledge, skills, and abilities that the individuals possess, which the firm has built up over time into an identifiable expertise." The question for the multinational firm is how to maintain and leverage its human resources so that suitably trained, internationally oriented personnel are available to support its strategic responses and contribute to its core competencies. An indication of the importance of training and developing staff is the increasing number of multinationals that establish their own "universities," or "schools." Motorola, McDonald's Hamburger, and Disney universities are good examples of these in-house training centers; several European, Japanese, and Korean firms have similar arrangements.

Exhibit 5–1 is a schematic representation of the structure of this chapter. It shows the link between international recruitment and selection (Chapter 3) and training and development activities. As we discussed in Chapter 4, training and development programs are an integral part of an effective performance management system. However, new employees generally undergo some form of training upon selection; for example, you may recall from the account of McDonald's entry into Russia in Chapter 2 that crew members were each given 60 hours of training prior to the opening of the Moscow outlet. In this chapter, we distinguish

154

EXHIBIT 5-1   *International Training and Development*

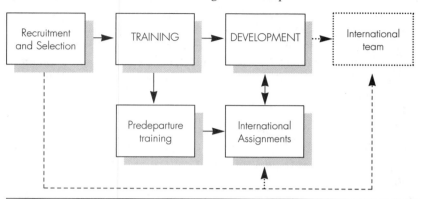

between the terms *training* and *development*. Training aims to improve current work skills and behavior, whereas development aims to increase abilities in relation to some future position or job—usually managerial. We will begin by examining the training approaches and issues for each of the three categories of staff—PCNs, TCNs, and HCNs. Development aspects, especially the impact of international assignments upon career paths within a multinational, will then be addressed.

EXPATRIATE TRAINING

Most expatriates, whether PCNs or TCNs, are selected from within the multinational's existing operations, though, as indicated by the dotted arrow in Exhibit 5–1, some expatriates may be hired externally. Given that the primary selection criterion is technical ability, it is not surprising to find that most of the literature is devoted to expatriate predeparture training activities that are mainly concerned with developing cultural awareness. Once an employee has been selected for an expatriate position, predeparture training is considered to be the next critical step in attempting to ensure the expatriate's effectiveness and success abroad, particularly where the assignment country is considered culturally tough. Some form of cultural preparation is indicated because, as you may recall from our discussion of expatriate failure in Chapter 3, functional ability alone does not determine success. Effective cultural training also enables individuals to adjust more rapidly to the new culture. As Earley[2] points out, "A major objective of intercultural training is to help people cope with unexpected events in a new culture." For these performance-related reasons, investing resources in training for international assignments can be justified easily.[3]

The limited, predominately U.S.-based, research into this area reveals that a large number of U.S. multinationals have been reluctant to provide even a basic level of predeparture training. Tung[4] asked respondents to indicate the frequency of use of training programs. The results showed that the U.S. multinationals tended to use training programs for expatriates less frequently than the European and Japanese firms (32 percent compared with 69 percent and 57 percent, respectively). According to Ronen[5] this finding was consistent with earlier research.

Our review of extant literature shows that the rate of predeparture training provision has been slow to increase in the intervening years since Tung's 1982 study. A 1984 study of 1,000 U.S. multinationals found that only 25 percent offered extensive predeparture training programs.[6] Another study, conducted in 1989, surveyed U.S. firms regarding relocation programs and found that only 13 percent of respondents indicated that they would offer expatriates a predeparture program.[7] In their 1990 review of U.S. practices, McEnery and DesHarnais[8] estimated that between 50 and 60 percent of U.S. companies operating abroad at that time did not provide any predeparture preparation. The various authors report that, among the various reasons cited by firms for the low use of crosscultural training, top management does not believe predeparture training is necessary or effective.[9] So, while the potential benefits of cultural awareness training are widely acknowledged, such training is not offered by a large number of U.S. multinationals.[10] The emphasis placed by European (including Scandinavian) multinationals on predeparture training, particularly language training, has been found to be stronger than that of U.S. multinationals.[11]

More recently, the 1997–98 Price Waterhouse[12] survey of European firms (including subsidiaries of non–European multinationals) revealed that cultural awareness training remains the most common form of predeparture training, and that it is still offered on a voluntary basis rather than as a mandatory requirement. Only 13 percent of the firms surveyed always provided their expatriates with access to cultural awareness courses, though a further 47 percent now provided briefings for culturally "challenging" postings (compared with 21 percent in their 1995 survey). In the past, regardless of country of origin,[13] firms placed less priority on providing predeparture training for the spouse and family. However, perhaps due to increasing recognition of the interaction between expatriate performance and family adjustment, more multi-nationals are now extending their predeparture training programs to include the spouse or partner and children.

Components of Effective Predeparture Training Programs

Studies indicate that the essential components of predeparture training programs that contribute to a smooth transition to a foreign post include cultural awareness training, preliminary visits, language instruction, and assistance with practical, day-to-day matters.[14] We will look at each of these in turn.

Cultural Awareness Programs

It is generally accepted that to be effective the expatriate employee must adapt to and not feel isolated from the host country. A well-designed cultural awareness training program can be extremely beneficial, as it seeks to foster an appreciation of the host-country's culture so that expatriates can behave accordingly, or at least develop appropriate coping patterns. Sieveking, Anchor, and Marston[15] cite the culture of the Middle East to emphasize this point. In that region, emphasis is placed on personal relationships, trust, and respect in business dealings; coupled with this is an overriding emphasis on religion that permeates almost every aspect of life. As discussed in Chapters 3 and 4, without an understanding (or at least an acceptance) of the host-country culture in such a situation, the expatriate is likely to face some difficulties during the international assignment.

The components of cultural awareness programs vary according to country of assignment, duration, purpose of the transfer, and the provider of such programs.[16] As part of her study of expatriate management, Tung[17] identified five categories of predeparture training, based on different learning processes, type of job, country of assignment, and the time available:

- Area studies programs that include environmental briefing and cultural orientation;
- Culture assimilators;
- Language training;
- Sensitivity training; and
- Field experiences.

To understand possible variations in expatriate training, Tung[18] proposed a contingency framework for deciding the nature and level of rigor of training. Two determining factors were the degree of interaction required in the host culture and the similarity between the individual's native culture and the new culture. The related training elements in her framework involved the content of the training and the rigor of the training. Essentially, Tung argued that:

- If the expected interaction between the individual and members of the host culture was low, and the degree of dissimilarity between the individual's native culture and the host culture was low, then training should focus on task- and job-related issues rather than culture-related issues. The level of rigor necessary for effective training should be relatively low.
- If there was a high level of expected interaction with host nationals and a large dissimilarity between the cultures, then training should focus on crosscultural skill development as well as on the new task. The level of rigor for such training should be moderate to high.

Tung's model specifies criteria for making training method decisions—such as degree of expected interaction and cultural similarity. One limitation though is that it does not assist the user to determine which specific training methods to use or what might constitute more or less rigorous training.

Mendenhall and Oddou proposed a model that builds upon Tung's. It was refined subsequently by Mendenhall, Dunbar, and Oddou.[19] They propose three dimensions—training methods, low, medium, and high levels of training rigor, and duration of the training relative to degree of interaction and culture novelty—as useful guidelines for determining an appropriate program. For example, if the expected level of interaction is low and the degree of similarity between the individual's native culture and the host culture is high, the length of the training should probably be less than a week. Methods such as area or cultural briefings via lectures, movies, or books would provide the appropriate level of training rigor.[20] On the other hand, if the individual is going overseas for a period of two to twelve months and is expected to have some interaction with members of the host culture, the level of training rigor should be higher and its length longer (one to four weeks). In addition to the information-giving approaches, training methods such as culture assimilators and roleplays may be appropriate.[21] If the individual is going to a fairly novel and different host culture and the expected degree of inter-action is high, the level of crosscultural training rigor should be high and training should last as long as two months. In addition to the less rigor-ous methods already discussed, sensitivity training, field experiences, and inter-cultural experiential workshops may be appropriate training methods in this situation.

In their literature review, Black and Mendenhall[22] concluded that the Mendenhall, Dunbar, and Oddou model, like that of Tung, is primarily "cultural" in nature, with little integration of the individual's new tasks and the new host culture. Black and Mendenhall proposed what they described as an extensive theoretically based model using Bandura's so-cial learning theory and prior cultural awareness training models. They take three aspects of social learning theory—attention, retention, and reproduction—and show how these are influenced by individual differ-ences in expectations and motivation, and the incentives to apply learned behaviors in the foreign location. This approach recognizes that effective training is only the first step and that the expatriate's willing-ness and ability to act on that training in the new environment is crucial to effective performance. However, their theoretical model and related propositions have yet to be rigorously tested.

An obvious practical limitation of Black and Mendenhall's model is that insufficient time is often given as a reason why multinationals do not provide predeparture training; it would be difficult to develop appropri-ate predeparture training programs in such cases. Other contextual and situational factors—such as cultural toughness, length of assignment, and the nature/type of the job—may have a bearing on the content, method, and processes involved in the cultural awareness training pro-gram. More importantly, monitoring and feedback should be recognized as important components of individual skill development, particularly as adjustment and performance are the desired outcomes of cultural aware-ness training.

Exhibit 5–2 draws together the components of the three models re-viewed above. It stresses the importance of attention paid by the poten-tial expatriate to the behaviors and probable outcomes of a cultural awareness training program, the individual's ability and willingness to retain learned behaviors, and their reproduction as appropriate in the host location. Based on our review of performance management in Chap-ter 4, it seems important that adjustment and performance be linked to the multinational's performance management system. For instance, one could expect that poor performance could be addressed by clarifying

EXHIBIT 5-2 *Cultural Awareness Training and Assignment Performance*

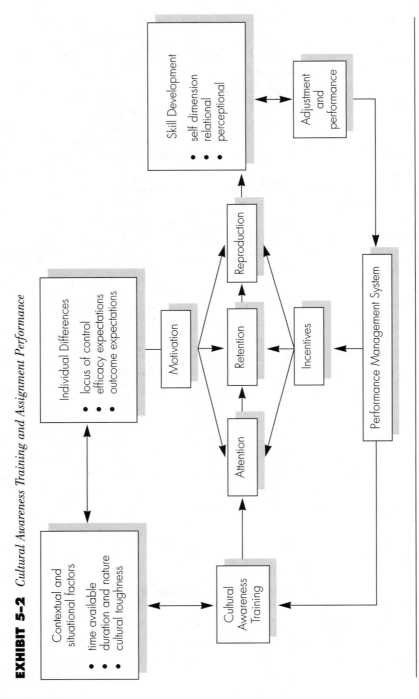

Source: Adapted from Tung (1981), Mendenhall, Dunbar, and Oddou (1987), and Black and Mendenhall (1989, 1990, 1991).

incentives for more effective reproduction of the required level of behavior, or by providing additional cultural awareness training. We combine adjustment and performance and link it to the performance management system; Black and Mendenhall have adjustment and performance as separate outcomes, with adjustment leading to performance. We would argue that performance may affect adjustment in some instances.

Preliminary Visits

One useful technique in orienting international employees is to send them on a preliminary trip to the host country. A well-planned overseas trip for the candidate and spouse provides a preview that allows them to assess their suitability for and interest in the assignment. Such a trip also serves to introduce expatriate candidates to the business context in the host location and helps encourage more informed predeparture preparation. When used as part of a predeparture training program, visits to the host location can assist in the initial adjustment process. The 1997–98 Price Waterhouse survey mentioned earlier reports that 53 percent of firms always provided preliminary visits and a further 38 percent indicated such use in certain circumstances. The average length of visit was about a week. The country of assignment was a determining factor; visits were not provided if the country concerned was already known to the expatriate (perhaps from a previous visit either on firm-related business or as a tourist), or was perceived as culturally close (e.g., Zurich to Frankfurt, or New York to Toronto).

Obviously, the couple may reject the assignment on the basis of the preliminary visit. As one firm in the 1997–98 Price Waterhouse survey admits: "We do not provide pre-assignment visits where conditions are so poor that nobody would want to go." Most firms that utilize preliminary visits, though, weigh their cost against premature recall and underperformance risks. A potential problem exists in that the aim of the preliminary visit is often twofold—part selection decision and part predeparture training. The multinational could send mixed signals if it offers the preliminary visit as part of the selection process but the couple find upon arrival in the proposed country of assignment that they are expected to make decisions regarding suitable housing and schools. The couple may interpret such treatment as "accepting the preliminary visit equals accepting the assignment," thus negating its role in the decision-making process. When multinationals use the preliminary visit to allow the couple to make a more informed decision about accepting the overseas assignment, it should be used solely for that purpose. From the couple's perspective, they often find it difficult to reject the assignment in spite of negative impressions gained during the visit when they have been flown to the prospective location at the multinational's expense.

Combined with cultural awareness training, the preliminary visit is a useful component of a predeparture program. Exposure to the expatriate community, if one exists in the proposed host location, can also be a positive outcome of the preliminary visit. Brewster and Pickard[23] found that an expatriate community has an influence on expatriate adjustment. Perhaps the welcome received from, and interaction with, current expatriates may assist in developing a positive attitude to the assignment, confirm acceptance of the assignment, and even provide motivation to reproduce appropriate behaviors retained from cultural awareness training.

Language Training

Language training is a seemingly obvious, desirable component of a predeparture program. However, there are three interrelated aspects related to language ability that need to be recognized.

1. The Role of English as the Language of World Business. It is generally accepted that English is the language of world business, though the form of English is more "international English" than that spoken by native speakers of English.[24] Multinationals from English-speaking countries such as the United States, the United Kingdom, and Australia often use this fact as a reason for not considering language ability in the selection process, and for not stressing language training as part of predeparture programs. Such an attitude may lead to the downplaying of the importance of foreign language skills. For example, in a 1989 survey by Columbia University[25] of 1,500 senior executives in twenty countries, participants were asked to rate the importance of a number of attributes "for the CEO of tomorrow." For the attribute "trained in a foreign language" 19 percent of the U.S. respondents gave a rating of very important compared to 64 percent of non-U.S. respondents. Fixman's[26] study of U.S. multinationals' foreign language needs, conducted the same year, found that foreign language skills were seldom included as part of cross-cultural understanding, and that language problems were largely viewed as mechanical and manageable problems that could easily be solved.

However, as Pucik[27] comments, an exclusive reliance on English diminishes the multinational's linguistic capacity. The resultant lack of language competence has strategic and operational implications as it limits the multinational's ability to monitor competitors and process important information. For example, translation services, particularly those external to the firm, cannot make strategic inferences and firm-specific interpretations of language specific data. Fixman[28] raises the question of protecting important technology in international joint venture activities: "It would seem that the less one understands of a partner's language, the less likely one is to detect theft of technology." Perhaps more importantly, as Wright and Wright[29] in their study of British firms point out, to accept English as the *de facto* language of international business gives the advantage to the other person:

> The other speaker controls what is communicated and what is understood. The monolingual English speaker has less room to manoeuvre, no possibility of finding out more that he [or she] is given. His position forces him to be reactive rather than proactive in the relationship. What he says and understands is filtered through the other speaker's competence, over which he has no control.

Disregarding the importance of foreign language skills may reflect a degree of ethnocentrism. A study by Hall and Gudykunst has shown that the lower the level of perceived ethnocentrism in an MNE, the more training it provides in cultural awareness and language training.[30]

Firms are including language training as evidenced by recent surveys, such as the 1997–98 Price Waterhouse survey referred to above. Firms in that survey reported that language training was not only provided where necessary to the expatriate but generally extended to the spouse or partner (81 percent) and children (42 percent). Perhaps as a result of the increased global competitive pressures, and growing awareness of its strategic and operational importance, more U.S. multinationals are requesting that U.S. business schools include foreign languages in their curricula and are giving hiring preference to graduates with foreign language skills. A similar trend is evident in the United Kingdom and in Australia.

2. Host-Country Language Skills and Adjustment. Clearly, the ability to speak a foreign language can improve the expatriate's effectiveness and negotiating ability. As Baliga and Baker[31] point out, it can improve managers' access to information regarding the host-country's economy, government, and market. Of course, the degree of fluency required may depend on the level and nature of the position that the expatriate holds in the foreign operation, the amount of interaction with external stake-holders such as government officials, clients, trade officials, as well as with host-country nationals.

The importance of language skills was identified as a critical component in assignment performance in a recent survey of over 400 expatriates conducted by Tung–Arthur Andersen.[32] Respondents indicated that the ability to speak the local language, regardless of how different the culture was to their home country, was as important as cultural awareness in their ability to adapt and perform on assignment. Knowledge of the host-country language can assist expatriates and family members gain access to new social support structures outside of work and the expatriate community.

Language skills, therefore, are important in terms of task performance and cultural adjustment. Its continued omission from predeparture training can be partly explained by the length of time it takes to acquire even a rudimentary level of language competence. Hiring language competent staff to enlarge the "language pool" from which potential expatriates may be drawn is one answer, but its success depends on up-to-date information being kept on all employees, and frequent language auditing to see whether language skills are maintained.[33]

3. Knowledge of the Corporate Language. In the literature reviewed, where language skills and fluency are considered, it tends to be in the context of crosscultural communication. Recent work by Marschan, Welch, and Welch[34] highlights what appears to be a somewhat neglected issue—the impact that the adoption of a common corporate language has upon HRM activities within the multinational. As you recall from our discussion on the path to multinational status in Chapter 2, at a certain stage in its internationalization process, multinationals confront control and coordination concerns that force changes upon processes and procedures. Marschan et. al. argue that, for multinationals from non–English-speaking countries, the standardization of information and reporting systems tends to be handled in the language of the parent's country of origin until geographical dispersal makes that problematical. The multinational then adopts (either deliberately or by default) a common company language to facilitate reporting standardization and other control mechanisms, particularly normative control.

As we mention above, English has become the language of international business, and quite often, English becomes the common language within these multinationals. Marschan et. al.[35] suggest that the question of a common corporate language does not consciously arise to the same extent within multinationals from English-speaking countries such as the United States—English is automatically the chosen corporate language. Regardless, the authors argue that language skills become an important aspect. PCNs can find themselves performing as communication conduits between subsidiary and headquarters, due to their ability to speak the corporate language. It also can give added power to their position in the subsidiary as PCNs often have access to information that those not fluent in the corporate language are denied. Marschan et. al. also point out that a PCN fluent in the parent-company language and the language of the host subsidiary can perform a gatekeeping role, whatever the formal position the expatriate may hold. What this line of research suggests is that for multinationals that have adopted a corporate language, predeparture training programs may need to include both language of the host country and the corporate language.

Practical Assistance

Another component of a predeparture training program is that of providing information that assists in relocation. Practical assistance makes an important contribution toward the adaptation of the expatriate and his or her family to their new environment. Being left to fend for themselves may result in a negative response toward the host-country's culture, and/or contribute to a perceived violation of the psychological contract. Many multinationals now take advantage of relocation specialists to provide this practical assistance. Further language training for the expatriate and family could be provided, particularly if such training was not possible before departure. While local orientation and language programs are normally organized by the personnel staff in the host country, it is important that corporate HRM staff liaize with the sending line manager as well as the HR department in the foreign location to ensure that practical assistance is provided.

Job-Related Factors

Although the literature reviewed has concentrated almost exclusively on the cultural awareness and adjustment components of predeparture training, it is important that we note that there may be some job-related aspects that need to be addressed in an effective predeparture training program. As we discussed earlier in Chapter 3, expatriates are often used because of a lack of suitably trained staff in the host location. Consequently, expatriates often find themselves training HCNs as their replacements. The obvious question is How are expatriates prepared for this training role? Our review of extant literature indicates that this aspect has yet to be specifically addressed. We do know from the cross-cultural management literature that there are differences in the way people approach tasks and problems, and that this can have an impact on the learning process.[36] The ability to transfer knowledge and skills in a culturally-sensitive manner perhaps should be an integral part of predeparture training programs. A related issue is that an international assignment can be a promotion to a managerial role for which the preparation is effectively the international assignment. We will take up this in our section on career development.

The bulk of this chapter has so far focused on the expatriate, and we have not distinguished between PCNs and TCNs. In theory, all staff should be provided with the necessary level of predeparture training given the demands of the international assignment. Anecdotal evidence does suggest, however, that in some firms predeparture training may not be provided to TCNs—at least to the extent of that available to PCNs. This omission could create perceptions of inequitable treatment in situations where PCNs and TCNs work in the same foreign location. As an Australian working in the Japanese subsidiary of a U.S. multinational remarked, "We were third-class nationals in Japan. The Americans received cultural training about Japan before they left the United States. We were just given our plane tickets."[37]

HCN Training

There are many issues related to HCN training. Consider the following case. A multinational, as part of its cost leadership strategy, decides to build a production facility in Country X where labor costs are low. It then finds it needs to invest heavily in training local employees, thereby automatically increasing the cost of that labor (the paradox referred to as "the expense of cheap labor"). Not only does the unit cost of labor rise over time, but trained employees may well become attractive to its foreign and local competitors, who simply offer higher wages to lure them away. If this "poaching" of HCNs is successful, the multinational discovers that its competitors reap the training benefits while it receives little return for its investment in human capital. Thus, the level of HCN competence has important training and cost consequences although these may not be initially recognized during country selection.

Mode of operation is another issue related to HCN training. For instance, entering into a joint venture arrangement can lead to unexpected training costs if the local partner regards the joint venture operation as a convenient way of re-deploying surplus employees who may not have the skills required. The multinational has to invest heavily in the training of the joint venture HCNs in order to achieve its strategic objectives for the foreign market, leading to costs perhaps not "factored in" the original market-entry decision. These costs may, however, be offset by intangible factors. For example, in some Chinese joint ventures, training programs are regarded by HCNs as incentives to work for foreigners.[38] Thus the provision of HCN training can help in retaining qualified HCN employees, thereby assisting the multinational to recoup its training costs.

When it comes to HCN training programs, given our understanding of cultural differences, it could be assumed that this is an area that the multinational would automatically delegate to the local operation. To a certain extent, training programs are localized, but there are many cases where multinationals have successfully replicated work practices in their foreign subsidiaries through intensive training programs designed and implemented by headquarters. This is particularly true regarding technical training for operating employees in areas where certain skills and work practices are regarded as strategically essential. Japanese multinationals such as Nissan and Honda have been able to train substantial numbers of HCNs in their U.S., U.K., and European subsidiaries with reasonable success.[39] To save on costs, some multinationals are now using satellite technology to deliver custom-designed training courses from home-country locations.[40]

International Training of HCNs

HCNs can be transferred into the parent country, into either its headquarters or home-subsidiary operations. There are various motives for HCN staff transfers:

- It facilitates specific firm-based training. You may recall from the GE case presented in Chapter 2, that Tungsram staff were transferred to GE plants in the United States for technical and operative training.

Likewise, the Pepsi-Cola International Management Institute is an umbrella system for the delivery of training programs such as sales force management or production techniques for the manufacturing of Pepsi brands. Part of this approach is the "Designate Program," which brings HCNs to the United States for a minimum of eighteen months of training in the domestic U.S. Pepsi system. Fiat, the Italian automobile manufacturer, uses staff transfers as part of its training program, with HCN recruits spending time at corporate headquarters.

- While technical and managerial training may be the primary goal, there is often a secondary, yet equally important, objective of building a sense of corporate identity. The Swedish telecommunications company, L.M. Ericsson,[41] has two levels of formal management programs. One caters to the top 300 managers in the group, the other to the 1,500 middle managers. While the focus of course content differs for these two programs, there is a common aim to develop informal networks among Ericsson managers throughout the entire global company. As part of its approach, the company established the Ericsson Management Institute. These types of corporate training centers serve as a useful venue for HCNs from various countries to meet and develop personal networks that facilitate informal communication and control (see Exhibit 2–10).

- Particular skills may be required in the subsidiary and the most cost-effective way is to bring certain HCN staff into the parent operations. For example, in the late 1980s when Ford Australia began manufacturing the Capri model—a sports car aimed at the U.S. market—Australian production and engineering employees spent time in Ford's U.S. factories to quickly gain the necessary knowledge required to meet U.S. safety regulations.

- As discussed in Chapter 3, the presence of HCNs may assist in broadening the outlook of parent-company employees. Also, it may be that HCNs have particular knowledge and skills that can be transferred into parent operations. The "importing" by Matsushita of 100 overseas managers a year to work alongside their Japanese counterparts is perhaps an extreme strategy.[42] In Matsushita's case, the necessity of having to use English with the "imported foreigners" improved the parent-company's language base.

In a recent article, Harvey[43] advocates that "inpatriates" (HCNs) need the same predeparture training programs as those designed for expatriate assignments. This is perhaps an obvious point. After all, cultural adjustment is inherent in international staff transfers, regardless of the direction of the transfer—that is, whether it is the PCN moving to a subsidiary, a HCN coming into parent operations, or transferring to another subsidiary. Harvey's suggested model for "inpatriate" predeparture training appears to mirror those proposed for U.S. expatriate cultural-awareness training. In order to design and implement HCN predeparture training, local management, particularly those in the HR department, need to be conscious of the demands of an international assignment—just as we have discussed in terms of corporate/headquarters HR staff. There perhaps also needs to be recognition and encouragement of this from headquarters, and monitoring to ensure that sufficient subsidiary resources are allocated for such training.

A related aspect is that HCNs require adequate language skills in order to gain the maximum benefit from parent-based training. Lack of language competence may be a major barrier in terms of access to corporate training programs since these are conducted in the parent/corporate language. As a study[44] of a Finnish multinational—Kone Elevators—found, subsidiary staff who would have benefited from attendance at the corporate training center in Finland were often excluded on the ground of lack of competence in English, the corporate language. Provision of corporate language training may be an important component of HCN training.

DEVELOPING INTERNATIONAL STAFF AND MULTINATIONAL TEAMS

Foreign assignments have long been recognized as an important mechanism for developing international expertise—for both management and organizational development.[45] As we discussed in Chapter 2, establishing truly global operations means having a team of international managers (PCNs, HCNs, and TCNs) who are available to go anywhere in the world. To develop such teams, many multinationals are conscious that they need to provide international experience to many levels of managers (regardless of nationality) and not just to a small cadre of PCNs. One technique used to develop larger pools of employees with international experience is through short-term development assignments ranging from a few months to several years. However, some very successful multinationals, such as the Swedish-Swiss conglomerate ABB, have carried on the practice of developing a small cadre of international employees rather than internationalizing everyone.

International job rotation, therefore, is one well-established technique for developing multinational teams and international operators. It may be supported by PCN, TCN, and HCN attendance at common training and development programs held either in the parent country, or regional centers, or both. The Global Leadership Program at the University of Michigan is an example of externally provided training programs. For a period of five weeks, teams of American, Japanese, and European executives learn global business skills through action learning. To build crosscultural teams, the program utilizes seminars and lectures, adventure-based exercises, and field trips to investigate business opportunities in countries such as Brazil, China, and India. The overall objective of the Global Leadership Program is to produce individuals with a global perspective.[46] The success of such programs depends on participants being able to apply these skills in their home location and assist in the development of multinational, crossborder, crossfunctional teams.

International meetings in various locations have also become important forums for fostering interaction and personal networks that also may be used later to build global teams.[47] In line with a general trend towards an emphasis on work teams,[48] there is a suggestion in the literature that multinationals would benefit from building on their inherent diversity to foster innovation, organizational learning, and the transfer of knowledge. Fostering a sense of corporate identity and teamwork seems an important aspect of leverage resources and ideas from all parts of the multinational. The following remark from Jack Welch, CEO of GE, reflects this line of thinking:[49]

> The aim in a global business is to get the best ideas from everywhere. Each team puts up its best ideas and processes—constantly. That raises the bar. Our culture is designed around making a hero out of those who translate ideas from one place to another, who help somebody else. They get an award, they get praised and promoted.

Individual Career Development[50]

The above discussion has been from the multinational's perspective. We now briefly look at the impact that an international assignment has on an individual's career. There is an implicit assumption that an international assignment has *per se* management development potential; perceived career advancement is often a primary motive for accepting such postings. However, there is a paucity of research that demonstrates the link between an international assignment and career advancement. Two exceptions are studies by Feldman and Thomas, and Naumann;[51] while these studies confirm career expectations as motives, the expatriates involved were taken from those currently on assignment. There is a need for research that examines career paths as a direct consequence of international assignments.

It is possible to trace the typical assignment and identify critical decision points that may have career-related outcomes for a particular individual. Exhibit 5–3 attempts to illustrate a sequence that may be common to all expatriates—PCNs as well as HCNs who accept assignments to either the parent operations, or to other subsidiaries (thus becoming TCNs). For ease of discussion, though, we will simply use the term *expatriate* and refer to the sending unit or subsidiary as *parent*.

Exhibit 5–3 follows the stages of expatriation from recruitment and selection to completion of the particular assignment. The numerals are

EXHIBIT 5-3 *Expatriate Career Decision Points*

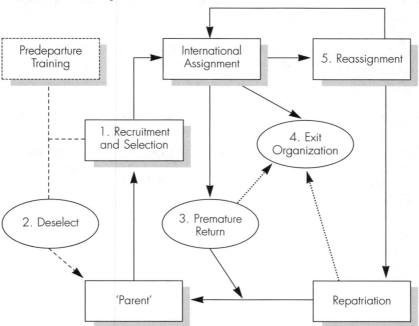

Source: D. Welch, 1997. Expatriation and career development in the changing global workscape, Paper presented at the 23rd Annual EIBA Conference, Stuttgart, December 14–16.

positioned at what have been identified as critical decision points. For example, Decision Point 1 occurs during recruitment and selection for a specific assignment, where the expatriate either applies, or is informally selected, for an international assignment. Further information about the host location during the recruitment and selection process (including predeparture training if that is available), or family considerations, may prompt the potential candidate to withdraw at this point. Hence Decision Point 2 is "deselect." There may be some career considerations as to whether a voluntary withdrawal at the point would have a negative consequence upon the person's future. Such a perception may influence the individual's decision to accept rather than reject the assignment.

As we discussed earlier in terms of adjustment and performance overseas, the expatriate may decide to leave the international assignment (as indicated in Decision Point 3—Premature Return). The individual then is assigned a position back in the "parent" operation. The premature return may or may not have career advancement consequences. Alternatively, as indicated by Decision Point 4, the expatriate may decide to exit the organization—prompted by a perceived violation of the psychological contract, or perhaps as a result of another job offer that is perceived to be better in terms of the person's career. This may be with a domestic firm back in the home country or with another foreign multinational.

Decision Point 5, Reassignment, can be either back into the "parent" organization or the person may accept another overseas assignment. Those who elect to take a consecutive international assignment may, upon subsequent reassignment return to the "parent" operation, or become part of what is often referred to as the international "cadre," or team. As we will discuss in Chapter 7, reassignment (or repatriation) back into the "parent" operation is a common ending to an international assignment and may or may not be to a position that leads to career advancement. There is a suggestion that turnover among repatriates may be as a consequence of a perceived lack of career advancement on the basis of the international experience. Decision Point 4 can be relevant at this stage, as indicated by the dotted arrow connecting "repatriation" with "exit organization."

These decision points are based on the issues we have discussed in the preceding chapters, as well as on the suggestions in the literature regarding the management development potential of international assignments. How individuals react at each point may vary according to the perceived value of the assignment; that is, whether the perceived benefits outweigh the costs in terms of family disruption (including a spouse or partner's career) and the factors that we have identified as important to performance while on an international assignment. Of course, the actual benefits will also depend on the multinational's willingness and ability to utilize the experiences the expatriate has gained during the international assignment. We will return to some of these aspects in Chapter 7.

SUMMARY

This chapter has concentrated on the issues relating to training and developing PCN, TCN, and HCN staff. We have placed emphasis on expatriate predeparture training mainly because of its emphasis in the relevant literature. Cultural-awareness training does appear to assist in adjustment and performance and should be made available to all categories of staff selected for overseas postings, regardless of duration and location. Predeparture training can also prevent costly mistakes such as that of the highly paid expatriate who brought two miniature bottles of brandy with him into Qatar (a Muslim country in the Middle East). The brandy was discovered by customs, and the expatriate was promptly deported, causing his firm to be "disinvited" and ordered never to return. It is worth noting here that despite the widely recognized value of predeparture training, in the 1997–98 Price Waterhouse survey previously mentioned, only one in ten of the firms measured the success of their programs.

The international assignment emerges as an important way of training international operators, developing the international team, or "cadre," as well as helping to build personal networks to support soft-control mechanisms. In this sense, an international assignment is both training (gaining international experience and competence) and managerial and organizational development. Thus, multinationals must address the growing need for international training and development and deal with controversial questions concerning which employees to train and the overall purpose of the training.

We also have mentioned briefly that mode of operation has an impact on training needs in relation to international joint ventures, and this will be further explored in our final chapter. There has, however, been little reference in the international HRM literature on issues connected with other forms of operation such as exporting, management contracts, and project operations. Again, as mentioned in Chapter 2, this omission is consistent with the preoccupation to date with subsidiary operations. However, analysis of broader training and development issues would provide parameters for corporate HR staff, enabling them to plan training and developmental activities that are congruent with the multinational's often diverse forms of international business operations.

QUESTIONS

1. What are some of the challenges faced in training expatriate managers?
2. Identify the key aspects of a successful expatriate predeparture training program.
3. What steps can be taken to ensure that trained, skilled HCNs are not lured away by foreign or local competitors?
4. What are the issues and challenges facing multinationals in developing a cadre of global managers?
5. List the key reasons for bringing HCNs into the parent operations for training.
6. Why do some multinationals appear reluctant to provide basic predeparture training?

FURTHER READING

1. Cyr, D.J., and S. Schneider, 1996. Implications for learning: Human resource management in East-West joint ventures, *Organization Studies*, vol. 17, no. 2, pp. 207–226.
2. Harris, P.R., and R.T. Moran, 1996. *Managing Cultural Differences: Leadership Strategies for a New World Business*, 4th ed. Houston: Gulf.
3. Harvey, M., 1996. Developing leaders rather than managers for the global marketplace, *Human Resource Management Review*, vol. 6, no. 4, pp. 279–304.
4. Kamoche, K., 1997. Knowledge creation and learning in international HRM, *International Journal of Human Resource Management*, vol. 8, no. 2, pp. 213–225.
5. Naumann, E., 1993. Organizational predictors of expatriate job satisfaction, *Journal of International Business Studies*, vol. 24, no. 1, pp. 61–80.

6. Snow, C.C., S.A. Snell, and S.C. Davison, 1996. Use transnational teams to globalize your company, *Organizational Dynamics*, Spring, pp. 50–67.
7. Vance, C., and Y. Paik, 1995. Host-country workforce training in support of the expatriate management assignment, in *Expatriate Management: New Ideas for International Business*, J. Selmer, ed. Westport, CO: Quorum Books.
8. Weiss, J.W., and S. Bloom, 1990. Managing in China: Expatriate experiences and training recommendations, *Business Horizons*, May-June, pp. 23–29.

ENDNOTES

1. K. Kamoche, 1996. Strategic human resource management with a resource-capability view of the firm, *Journal of Management Studies*, vol. 33, no. 2, p. 216.
2. P.C. Earley, 1987. Intercultural training for managers: A comparison, *Academy of Management Journal*, vol. 30, no. 4, p. 686.
3. S.H. Robock, and K. Simmons, 1989. *International Business and Multinational Enterprises*, 4th ed. Homewood, IL: Richard D. Irwin; Copeland, 1984. Making costs count in international travel, *Personnel Administrator*, vol. 29, no. 7, p. 47.
4. R. Tung, 1982. Selection and training procedures of United States, European, and Japanese multinationals, *California Management Review*, vol. 25, no. 1, pp. 57–71. Tung also asked those respondents who reported no formal training programs to give reasons for omitting these programs. Again, differences were found between the three regions. The U.S. companies cited a trend toward employment of local nationals (45%), the temporary nature of such assignments (28%), the doubtful effectiveness of such training programs (20%), and lack of time (4%). The reasons given by European multinationals were the temporary nature of such assignments (30%), lack of time (30%), a trend toward employment of local nationals (20%), and the doubtful effectiveness of such programs. Responses from the Japanese companies were lack of time (63%) and doubtful effectiveness of such programs (37%).
5. S. Ronen, 1986. *Comparative and Multinational Management*, New York: John Wiley.

6. J.C. Baker, 1984. Foreign language and departure training in U.S. multinational firms, *Personnel Administrator*, July, pp. 68–70.

7. D. Feldman, 1989. Relocation practices, *Personnel*, vol. 66, no. 11, pp. 22–25.

8. J. McEnery, and G. DesHarnais, 1990. Culture shock, *Training and Development Journal*, April, pp. 43–47. Of those multinationals that did provide only brief environmental summaries and some cultural and language preparation, only around half of these programs lasted longer than a week.

9. M. Mendenhall, and G. Oddou, 1985. The dimensions of expatriate acculturation, *Academy of Management Review*, vol. 10, pp. 39–47; H. Schwind, 1985. The state of the art in cross-cultural management training, in *International Human Resource Management Annual*, vol. 1, Robert Doktor, ed. Alexandria, VA: ASTD; and Y. Zeira, 1975. Overlooked personnel problems in multinational corporations, *Columbia Journal of World Business*, vol. 10, no. 2, pp. 96–103.

10. J.S. Black, and M. Mendenhall, 1990. Cross-cultural training effectiveness: A review and a theoretical framework for future research, *Academy of Management Review*, vol. 15, no. 1, pp. 113–136.

11. C. Brewster, 1988. *The Management of Expatriates*, Human Resource Research Centre Monograph Series, no. 2, Bedford, United Kingdom: Cranfield School of Management.

12. Price Waterhouse, 1997–98. *International Assignments: European Policy and Practice*, Price Waterhouse Europe.

13. K. Barham, and M. Devine, 1990. *The Quest for the International Manager: A Survey of Global Human Resource Strategies*, Ashridge Management Research Group, Special Report No. 2098, London; The Economist Intelligence Unit. See also, D. Welch, 1994. Determinants of international human resource management approaches and activities: A suggested framework, *Journal of Management Studies*, vol. 31, no. 2, pp. 139–164; I. Björkman, 1990. Expatriation and repatriation in Finnish companies: A comparison with Swedish and Norwegian practice, Working Paper No. 211, Helsinki: Swedish School of Economics and Business Administration.

14. See, for example, M. Mendenhall, and G. Oddou, 1986. Acculturation profiles of expatriate managers: Implications for cross-cultural training programs, *Columbia Journal of World Business*, Winter, pp. 73–79; R.W. Brislin, *Cross Cultural Encounters*; and D. Landis and R.W. Brislin, *Handbook on Intercultural Training*.

15. N. Sieveking, B. Anchor, and R. Marston, 1981. Selecting and preparing expatriate employees, *Personnel Journal*, March, pp. 197–202. See also N. Sievoking, and R. Marston, 1978. Critical selection and orientation of expatriates, *Personnel Administrator*, April, pp. 20–23.

16. A growing number of websites dealing with these topics appear on the Internet. See, for example: http://www.hbsp.harvard.edu, for a CD-ROM interactive program on managing across different cultures.

17. R. Tung, 1981. Selecting and training of personnel for overseas assignments, *Columbia Journal of World Business*, vol. 16, pp. 68–78.

18. Ibid.

19. Mendenhall, and Oddou, Acculturation profiles of expatriate managers; M. Mendenhall, E. Dunbar, and G. Oddou, 1987. Expatriate selection, training and career-pathing: A review and critique, *Human Resource Management*, vol. 26, pp. 331–345.

20. Earley advocates the use of both documentary and interpersonal methods to prepare managers for intercultural assignments. See P. Earley, 1987. International training for managers: A comparison of documentary and interpersonal methods, *Academy of Management Journal*, vol. 30, pp. 685–698. Baliga and Baker suggest that the expatriate receives training that concentrates on the assigned region's culture, history, politics, economy, religion, and social and business practices. They argue that only with precise knowledge of the varied components of their host culture can the expatriate and family grasp how and why people behave and react as they do (see G. Baliga, and J.C. Baker, 1985. Multinational corporate policies for expatriate managers: Selection, training, and evaluation, *Advanced Management Journal*, Autumn, pp. 31–38).

21. For further information on the use of cultural assimilators, see R.W. Brislin, 1986. A culture general assimilator: Preparation for various types of sojourns, *International Journal of Intercultural Relations*, vol. 10, pp. 215–234; and K. Cushner, 1989. Assessing the impact of a culture general assimilator, *International Journal of Intercultural Relations*, vol. 13, pp. 125–146.

22. J.S. Black, and M. Mendenhall, 1989. A practical but theory-based framework for selecting cross-cultural training methods, *Human Resource Management*, vol. 28, no. 4, pp. 511–539.

23. C. Brewster, and J. Pickard, 1994. Evaluating expatriate training, *International Studies of Management and Organization*, vol. 24, no. 3, pp. 18–35.

24. C. Wright, and S. Wright, 1994. Do languages really matter? The relationship between international business success and a commitment to foreign language use, *Journal of Industrial Affairs*, vol. 3, no. 1, pp. 3–14. These authors suggest that "international English" is perhaps a better term than "poor" or "broken" English.

25. This survey was reported in an article by L.B. Korn, 1989. How the next CEO will be different, *Fortune*, May 22, 1989, pp. 111–113. A similar difference was obtained (United States, 35%; foreign, 70%) in ratings for the attribute "experienced outside home country."

26. C. Fixman, 1990. The foreign language needs of U.S.-based corporations, *Annals, AAPSS*, 511, September, p. 36.

27. V. Pucik, 1985. Strategic human resource management in a multinational firm, in *Strategic Management of Multinational Corporations: The Essentials*, H.V. Wortzel, and L.H. Wortzel, eds. New York: John Wiley.

28. Fixman, The foreign language needs of U.S.-based corporations.

29. Wright and Wright, Do languages really matter?, p. 5.

30. P. Hepner Hall, and W.B. Gudykunst, 1989. The relationship of perceived ethnocentrism in corporate cultures to the selection, training, and success of international employees, *International Journal of Intercultural Relations*, vol. 13, pp. 183–201.

31. Baliga, and Baker, Multinational corporate policies.

32. R.L. Tung, and Arthur Andersen, 1997. *Exploring International Assignees' Viewpoints: A Study of the Expatriation/Repatriation Process*. Chicago IL: Arthur Andersen, International Executive Services.

33. R. Marschan, D. Welch, and L. Welch, 1997. Language: The forgotten factor in multinational management, *European Management Journal*, vol. 15, no. 5, pp. 591–597; see also Fixman, The foreign language needs of U.S.-based corporations.

34. Marschan, Welch, and Welch, Language: The forgotten factor in multinational management.

35. Ibid.

36. See, for example, H. Park, S.D. Hwang, and J.K. Harrison, 1996. Sources and consequences of communication problems in foreign

subsidiaries: The case of United States firms in South Korea, *International Business Review*, vol. 5, no. 1, pp. 79–98; and A. Rao, and K. Hashimoto, 1996. Intercultural influence: A study of Japanese expatriate managers in Canada, *Journal of International Business Studies*, vol. 27, no. 3, pp. 443–466.

37. Interview as part of a study of expatriate management in Australian companies, conducted by D. Welch, 1989.

38. V. Trigo, and E. Khong, 1996. Seeking harmony—training policies in joint ventures China-Guagzhou: An empirical study, Paper presented at the 3rd Workshop in International Business, August, University of Vaasa, Finland.

39. See, for example, S. Beechler, and J.Z. Yang, 1994. The transfer of Japanese-style management to American subsidiaries: Contingencies, constraints, and competencies, *Journal of International Business Studies*, vol. 25, no. 3, pp. 467–491.

40. J.P. Giusti, D.R. Baker, and P.J. Graybash, 1991. Satellites dish out global training, *Personnel Journal*, June, pp. 80–84.

41. Barham and Devine, The quest for the international manager.

42. 1991. The glamour of gaijins, *The Economist*, September 21, p. 78. This example was reproduced in full in the second edition of our textbook.

43. M. Harvey, 1997. "Inpatriation" training: The next challenge for international human resource management, *International Journal of Intercultural Relations*, vol. 21, no. 3, pp. 393–428.

44. Marschan, Welch, and Welch, Language: The forgotten factor in multinational management.

45. D.A. Ondrack, 1985. International transfers of managers in North American and European MNEs, *Journal of International Business Studies*, vol. 16, no. 3, pp. 1–19.

46. J. Main, 1989. How 21 men got global in 35 days, *Fortune*, November 6, pp. 57–60.

47. A number of writers have also made the point that this form of developmental transfer can also function as a coordination and control strategy. See A. Edstrom, and J. Galbraith, 1977. Transfer of managers as a coordination and control strategy in multinational organizations, *Administrative Science Quarterly*, vol. 22, pp. 248–263; and C.K. Prahalad, and Y.L. Doz, 1981. An approach to strategic control in MNCs, *Sloan Management Review*, vol. 22, no. 4, pp. 5–13.

48. See, for example, B.L. Kirkman, and Shapiro, 1997. The impact of cultural values on employee resistance to teams: Toward a model of globalized self-managing work team effectiveness, *Academy of Management Review*, vol. 22, no. 3, pp. 730–757.
49. J. Welch, 1997. Transfer the best ideas from everyone, everywhere, *Financial Times*, October 1, p. 12.
50. This section is based on D. Welch, 1997. Expatriation and career development in the changing global workscape, Paper presented at the 23rd Annual Meeting, EIBA, Stuttgart, December.
51. D.C. Feldman, and D.C. Thomas, 1992. Career issues facing expatriate managers, *Journal of International Business Studies*, vol. 23, no. 2, pp. 271–294; E. Naumann, 1992. A conceptual model of expatriate turnover, *Journal of International Business Studies*, vol. 23, no. 3, pp. 449–531.

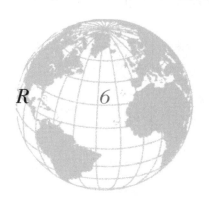

C H A P T E R 6
Compensation

For multinational firms, successful management of compensation and benefits requires knowledge of the employment and taxation laws, customs, environment, and employment practices of many foreign countries. Also needed are familiarity with currency fluctuations and the effect of inflation on compensation, and an understanding of why and when special allowances must be supplied and which allowances are necessary in what countries. All of these needs must be fulfilled within the context of shifting political, economic, and social conditions. The level of local knowledge required in many of these areas requires specialized advice; many multinationals retain the services of consulting firms which may offer a broad range of services or provide highly specialized services relevant to HRM in a multinational context.[1]

Because of their high-cost, HR managers spend a great deal of time developing effective compensation and benefit programs for international employees. A survey by the Conference Board[2] found that 29 percent of firms reported an expatriate cost of 2 to 2.9 times salary, 50 percent reported 3 to 3.9 times salary, and 18 percent reported 4 to 4.9 times salary. A recent report in *Fortune* on doing business in China[3] reported that hiring a local Chinese manager with 15 years of experience would cost less than U.S.$70,000; a U.S. expatriate chief financial officer would cost U.S.$300,000 with the following compensation package (all figures in U.S.$):

Salary	$130,000
Car and driver[4]	12,000
Benefits:	
Medical	3,000
Pension	13,000
Housing	97,000
Flights home	10,000
R and R	10,000
Private school for children	25,000
Total	$300,000

Because of the complexity and expense involved, much of the discussion in this chapter addresses PCN compensation. However, issues relevant to TCNs and HCNs are also described because they are becoming more important to the success of many multinationals.

OBJECTIVES OF INTERNATIONAL COMPENSATION

When developing international compensation policies, a firm seeks to satisfy several objectives. First, the policy should be consistent with the overall strategy, structure, and business needs of the multinational. Second, the policy must work to attract and retain staff in the areas where the multinational has the greatest needs and opportunities. Thus, the policy must be competitive and recognize factors such as incentive for foreign service, tax equalization, and reimbursement for reasonable costs. Third, the policy should facilitate the transfer of international employees in the most cost-effective manner for the firm. Fourth, the policy must give due consideration to equity and ease of administration.

The international employee will also have a number of objectives that need to be achieved from the firm's compensation policy. First, the employee will expect that the policy offers financial protection in terms of benefits, social security, and living costs in the foreign location. Second, the employee will expect that a foreign assignment will offer opportunities for financial advancement through income and/or savings. Third, the employee will expect that issues such as housing, education of children, and recreation will be addressed in the policy. (The employee will also have expectations in terms of career advancement and repatriation, as discussed in Chapters 3, 5, and 7.)

If we contrast the objectives of the multinational and the employee we see the potential for many complexities and possible problems since some of these objectives cannot be maximized on both sides. The "war stories" about problems in international compensation that we read in HR practitioner magazines is testimony to these complexities and problems. Taking away the specialist jargon and allowing for the international context, are the competing objectives of the firm and the employee *fundamentally* different from that which exists in a domestic environment? We think not, and agree with the broad thrust of a challenging article by Milkovich and Bloom,[5] which argues that firms must rethink the traditional view in international compensation, that local conditions dominate compensation strategy. We will return to this issue at the end of the chapter, after we have covered some of the technical aspects and complexities of compensation in an international context.

Key Components of an International Compensation Program

The area of international compensation is complex primarily because multinationals must cater for three categories of employees: PCNs, TCNs, and HCNs. In this section, we discuss key components of international compensation, which include base salary, foreign service inducement/hardship program, allowances, and benefits.

Base Salary

The term *base salary* acquires a somewhat different meaning when employees go abroad. In a domestic context, base salary denotes the amount of cash compensation that serves as a benchmark for other compensation elements (e.g., bonuses and benefits). For expatriates, it is the primary component of a package of allowances, many of which are directly related to base salary (e.g., foreign service premium, cost-of-living allowance, housing allowance) as well as the basis for in-service benefits and pension contributions. It may be paid in home- or local-country currency. The base salary is the foundation block for international compensation whether the employee is a PCN or TCN. Major differences can occur in the employee's package depending on whether the base salary is linked to the home country of the PCN or TCN or whether an international rate is paid. (We will return to this issue later in the chapter.)

Foreign Service Inducement/Hardship Premium

Parent-country nationals often receive a salary premium as an inducement to accept a foreign assignment or as compensation for any hardship caused by the transfer. Under such circumstances, the definition of hardship, eligibility for the premium, and amount and timing of payment must be addressed. In cases in which hardship is determined, U.S. firms often refer to the U.S. Department of State's Hardship Post Differentials Guidelines to determine an appropriate level of payment. As Ruff and Jackson[6] have noted, however, making international comparisons of the cost of living is problematic. It is important to note that these payments are more commonly paid to PCNs than TCNs. Foreign service inducements, if used, are usually made in the form of a percentage of salary, usually 5 to 40 percent of base pay. Such payments vary, depending upon the assignment, actual hardship, tax consequences, and length of assignment. In addition, differentials may be considered; for example, a host-country's work week may be longer than that of the home country, and a differential payment may be made in lieu of overtime, which is not normally paid to PCNs or TCNs.

Allowances

Issues concerning allowances can be very challenging to a firm establishing an overall compensation policy, partly because of the various forms of allowances that exist. The *cost-of-living allowance (COLA)*, which typically receives the most attention, involves a payment to compensate for differences in expenditures between the home country and the foreign country (e.g., to account for inflation differentials). Often this allowance is difficult to determine, so companies may use the services of organizations such as Organization Resource Counselors, Inc., (a U.S.-based firm) or Employment Conditions Abroad (based in Britain) who specialize in providing regularly updated COLA information on a global basis to their clients; the COLA may also include payments for housing and utilities, personal income tax, or discretionary items.[7]

The provision of a *housing allowance* implies that employees should be entitled to maintain their home-country living standards (or, in some cases, receive accommodations that are equivalent to that provided for similar foreign employees and peers). Such allowances are often paid on either an assessed or an actual basis. Other alternatives include company-provided housing, either mandatory or optional; a fixed housing allowance; or assessment of a portion of income, out of which actual housing costs are paid. Housing issues are often addressed on a case-by-case basis, but as a firm internationalizes, formal policies become more necessary and efficient. Financial assistance and/or protection in connection with the sale or leasing of an expatriate's former residence are offered by many multinationals. Those in the banking and finance industry tend to be the most generous, offering assistance in sale or leasing, payment of closing costs, payment of leasing management fees, rent protection, and equity protection. Again, TCNs receive these benefits less frequently than PCNs.

There is also a provision for *home leave allowances*. Many employers cover the expense of one or more trips back to the home country each year. The purpose of paying for such trips is to give expatriates the opportunity to renew family and business ties, thereby helping them to avoid adjustment problems when they are repatriated. Although firms traditionally have restricted the use of leave allowances to travel home, some firms give expatriates the option of applying the allowances to foreign travel rather than returning home. Firms allowing use of home leave allowances for foreign travel need to be aware that expatriate employees with limited international experience who opt for foreign travel rather than returning home may become more homesick than other expatriates who return home for a "reality check" with fellow employees and friends.[8]

Education allowances for expatriates' children are also an integral part of any international compensation policy. Allowances for education can cover items such as tuition, language class tuition, enrollment fees, books and supplies, transportation, room and board, and uniforms (outside of the United States, it is quite common for high school students to wear uniforms). The level of education provided for, the adequacy of local schools, and transportation of dependents who are being educated in other locations may present problems for multinationals. PCNs and TCNs usually receive the same treatment concerning educational expenses. The employer typically covers the cost of local or boarding school for dependent children, although there may be restrictions, depending on the availability of good local schools and on their fees. Attendance at a university may also be provided for when deemed necessary.

Relocation allowances usually cover moving, shipping, and storage charges, temporary living expenses, subsidies regarding appliance or car purchases (or sales), and down payments or lease-related charges. Allowances regarding perquisites (cars, club memberships, servants,[9] etc.)

may also need to be considered (usually for more senior positions, but this varies according to location). These allowances are often contingent upon tax-equalization policies and practices in both the home and the host countries.

Increasingly, as indicated in Chapter 3, many multinational firms are also offering *spouse assistance* to help guard against or offset income lost by an expatriate's spouse as a result of relocating abroad. Although some firms may pay an allowance to make up for a spouse's lost income, U.S. firms are beginning to focus on providing spouses with employment opportunities abroad, either by offering job-search assistance or employment in the firm's foreign unit (subject to a work visa being available).

To summarize, multinationals generally pay allowances in order to encourage employees to take international assignments and to keep employees "whole" relative to home standards. In terms of housing, companies usually pay a tax-equalized housing allowance in order to discourage the purchase of housing and/or to compensate for higher housing costs; this allowance is adjusted periodically, based on estimates of both local and foreign housing costs.

Benefits

The complexity inherent in international benefits often brings more difficulties than when dealing with compensation. Pension plans are very difficult to deal with country to country because national practices vary considerably. Transportability of pension plans, medical coverage, and social security benefits are very difficult to normalize. Therefore, firms need to address many issues when considering benefits, including:

- Whether to maintain expatriates in home-country programs, particularly if the firm does not receive a tax deduction for it.
- Whether firms have the option of enrolling expatriates in host-country benefit programs and/or making up any difference in coverage.
- Whether expatriates should receive home-country or host-country social security benefits.

Most U.S. PCNs typically remain under their home-country's benefit plan. In some countries, expatriates cannot opt out of local social security programs; in such circumstances, the firm normally pays for these additional costs. European PCNs and TCNs enjoy portable social security benefits within the European Union. Laws governing private benefit practices differ from country to country; firm practices also vary. Not surprisingly, multinationals have generally done a good job of planning for the retirement needs of their PCN employees, but this is generally less the case for TCNs.[10] There are many reasons for this: TCNs may have little or no home-country social security coverage, they may have spent many years in countries that do not permit currency transfers of accrued benefit payments, or they may spend their final year or two of employment in a country where final average salary is in a currency that relates unfavorably to their home-country currency. How their benefits are calculated and what type of retirement plan applies to them may make the difference between a comfortable retirement in a country of their choice and a forced penurious retirement elsewhere.

In addition to the already discussed benefits, multinationals also provide vacations and special leave. Included as part of the employee's regular vacation, annual home leave usually provides airfares for families to return to their home countries. Rest and rehabilitation leave, based on the conditions of the host country, also provides the employee's family with free airfares to a more comfortable location near the host country. In addition to rest and rehabilitation leave, emergency provisions are available in case of a death or illness in the family. Employees in hardship locations often receive additional leave expense payments and rest and rehabilitation periods.

APPROACHES TO INTERNATIONAL COMPENSATION

There are two main options in the area of international compensation—the *Going Rate approach* (also referred to as the market rate approach) and the *Balance Sheet approach* (sometimes known as the build-up approach). In this section we describe each approach and discuss the advantages and disadvantages inherent in each approach.[11]

The Going Rate Approach

The key characteristics of this approach are summarized in Exhibit 6–1. With this approach, the base salary for international transfer is linked to the salary structure in the host country. The multinational usually obtains information from local compensation surveys and must decide whether local nationals (HCNs), expatriates of the same nationality, or expatriates of all nationalities will be the reference point in terms of

EXHIBIT 6-1   *Going Rate Approach*

- Based on local market rates

- Relies on survey comparisons
- – Local nationals (HCNs)
- – Expatriates of same nationality
- – Expatriates of all nationalities

- Compensation based on the selected survey comparison

- Base pay and benefits may be supplemented by additional payments for low-pay countries

benchmarking. For example, a Japanese bank operating in New York would need to decide whether its reference point would be local U.S. salaries, other Japanese competitors in New York, or all foreign banks operating in New York. With the Going Rate approach, if the location is in a low-pay country, the multinational usually supplements base pay with additional benefits and payments.

There are advantages and disadvantages of the Going Rate approach that are summarized in Exhibit 6–2. Advantages include: equality with local nationals (very effective in attracting PCNs or TCNs to a location that pays higher salaries than those received in the home country), approach is simple and easy for expatriates to understand, expatriates are

EXHIBIT 6-2   *Advantages and Disadvantages of the Going Rate Approach*

Advantages	Disadvantages
• Equality with local nationals	• Variation between assignments for same employee
• Simplicity	
• Identification with host country	• Variation between expatriates of same nationality in different countries
• Equity amongst different nationalities	
	• Potential re-entry problems

able to identify with the host country, and there is often equity among expatriates of different nationalities.

There are also disadvantages with the Going Rate approach. First, there can be variation between assignments for the same employee—most obviously when we compare an assignment in an advanced economy with one in a developing country, but also between assignments in various advanced economies where differences in managerial salaries and the effect of local taxation can significantly influence an employee's compensation level using the Going Rate approach. Not surprisingly, individual employees are very sensitive to this issue. Second, there can be variation between expatriates of the same nationality in different locations. A strict interpretation of the Going Rate approach can lead to rivalry for assignments to locations that are financially attractive and little interest in locations considered to be financially unattractive. Finally, the Going Rate approach can pose problems upon repatriation when the employee's salary reverts to a home-country level that is below that of the host country. This is not only a problem for firms in developing countries, but also for firms from many countries where local managerial salaries are well below that of the United States, which is the world market leader in managerial salaries.[12] For example, a survey by Towers Perrin[13] of total compensation for CEOs around the world reported the following results:

Country	CEO Compensation (in U.S.$)
United States	$901,181
Hong Kong	$672,877
Singapore	$572,414
France	$523,511
Britain	$489,710
Australia	$476,700
Switzerland	$465,180
Canada	$440,886
Germany	$423,898
Malaysia	$342,151

The Balance Sheet Approach

The key characteristics of this approach (the most widely used approach for international compensation) are summarized in Exhibit 6–3. The

EXHIBIT 6-3   *The Balance Sheet Approach*

- Basic objective is maintenance of home-country living standard, plus financial inducement
- Home-country pay and benefits are the foundations of this approach
- Adjustments to home package to balance additional expenditure in host country
- Financial incentives (expatriate/hardship premium) added to make the package attractive
- Most common system in usage by multinational firms

---

basic objective is to "keep the expatriate whole"[14] (i.e., maintaining relativity to PCN colleagues, and compensating for the costs of an international assignment) through maintenance of home-country living standard, plus a financial inducement to make the package attractive. The approach links the base salary for PCNs and TCNs to the salary structure of the relevant home country. For example, a U.S. executive taking up an international position would have his or her compensation package built on the U.S. base-salary level rather than that applicable to the host country. The key assumption of this approach is that foreign assignees should not suffer a material loss due to their transfer, and this is accomplished through the utilization of what is generally referred to as the *balance sheet approach*. According to Reynolds:[15]

> The balance-sheet approach to international compensation is a system designed to equalize the purchasing power of employees at comparable position levels living abroad and in the home-country, and to provide incentives to offset qualitative differences between assignment locations.

There are four major categories of outlays incurred by expatriates that are incorporated in the balance sheet approach:

1. *Goods and services*—home-country outlays for items such as food, personal care, clothing, household furnishings, recreation, transportation, and medical care.
2. *Housing*—major costs associated with housing in the host country.
3. *Income taxes*—parent-country and host-country income taxes.
4. *Reserve*—contributions to savings, payments for benefits, pension contributions, investments, education expenses, social security taxes, and so on.

Where costs associated with the host-country assignment exceed equivalent costs in the parent country, these costs are met by both the firm and the expatriate to ensure that parent-country equivalent purchasing power is achieved.

Exhibit 6–4 shows a typical spreadsheet for an expatriate assignment using the balance sheet approach. In this example, an Australian expatriate is assigned to a country called New Euphoria which has a COLA index of 150 relative to Australia, and an exchange rate of 1.5 relative to the A\$. In addition to a foreign service premium, a hardship allowance is also payable for this location. Housing is provided by the firm, and a notional cost for this is recognized by a 7 percent deduction from the

EXHIBIT 6–4 *Expatriate Compensation Worksheet*

Employee:	Brian Smith
Position:	Marketing Manager
Country:	New Euphoria
Reason for change:	New Assignment
Effective date of change:	1 February 1998

Item	Amount A\$ PA	Paid in Australian dollars A\$ PA	Paid in local currency NE\$ PA
Base salary	135,000	67,500	101,250
Cost of living allowance	33,750		50,625
Overseas service premium (20%)	27,000	27,000	
Hardship allowance (20%)	27,000	27,000	
Housing deduction (7%)	–9,450	–9,450	
Tax deduction	–51,079	–51,079	
TOTAL	162,221	60,971	151,875

COLA Index = 150

Exchange Rate = 1.5   Authorized/Date

package, along with a notional tax deduction (we discuss taxation later in the chapter). The expatriate can see from this spreadsheet what components are offered in the package and how the package will be split between Australian currency and New Euphoria currency.

There are advantages and disadvantages of the balance sheet approach, which are summarized in Exhibit 6–5. There are three main advantages. First, the balance sheet approach provides equity between foreign assignments and between expatriates of the same nationality. Second, as will be discussed further in Chapter 7, repatriation of expatriates is facilitated by this emphasis on equity with the parent country since expatriate compensation remains anchored to the compensation system in the parent country. Third, this approach is easy to communicate, as Exhibit 6–4 illustrates.

There are two main disadvantages of the balance sheet approach. First, this approach can result in considerable disparities—both between expatriates of different nationalities and between PCNs and HCNs. Problems arise when international staff are paid different amounts for performing the same (or very similar) job in the host location, according to their different home base salary. For example, in the Singapore regional headquarters of a U.S. bank, a U.S. PCN and a New Zealand TCN may perform the same banking duties but the American will receive a higher salary than the New Zealander because of the differences in U.S. and New Zealand base-salary levels. As noted above, differences in base-salary levels can also cause difficulties between expatriates and HCNs. Traditionally, this has referred to the problem of

EXHIBIT 6–5   *Advantages and Disadvantages of the Balance Sheet Approach*

Advantages	*Disadvantages*
• Equity – between assignments – between expatriates of the same nationality	• Can result in great disparities – between expatriates of different nationalities – between expatriates and local nationals
• Facilitates expatriate re-entry	
• Easy to communicate to employees	• Can be quite complex to administer

highly paid PCNs being resented by local HCN employees because these "foreigners" are perceived as being excessively compensated (and because they are blocking career opportunities for locals).

However, feelings of resentment and inequity can also run in the other direction. For instance, as indicated above, the United States has the highest level of managerial compensation in the world. Thus, a firm that establishes a subsidiary in the United States (or acquires a U.S. business) may find that if it uses a balance sheet approach, its expatriates may be substantially underpaid compared to local American employees. While the logic of the balance sheet states that being tied to the home country assists in repatriation because the expatriate identifies with the home country, research in equity theory[16] suggests that employees do not always assess compensation issues in a detached and rational way.[17] As we discussed in Chapter 4, perceived insufficiency of support may be interpreted as a violation of the psychological contract and have a negative impact on expatriate adjustment and performance.

The issue of base-salary differences is also a concern for U.S. employees working for foreign firms operating in the United States. Many non–U.S. multinationals are reluctant to pay high U.S. salaries to U.S. employees who are offered international assignments (as HCNs in the firm's home-country operations, or as TCNs). U.S. employees are equally reluctant to accept the lower salaries paid in the firm's home country. Thus, the balance sheet approach not only can produce disparities, but also may act as a barrier to staff acceptance of international assignments.

A second problem with the balance sheet approach is that while this approach is both elegant and simple as a concept, it can become quite complex to administer. Complexities arise in the areas of taxation, living costs, and differentiating between PCNs and TCNs.

Taxation

Taxation probably causes the most concern to HR practitioners and expatriates (both PCNs and TCNs) since it generally evokes emotional responses. No one enjoys paying taxes and this issue can be very time-consuming for both the firm and the expatriate. To illustrate the potential problems, for the U.S. expatriate an assignment abroad can mean being double-taxed—both in the country of assignment and in the United States. This tax cost, combined with all the other expatriate costs, makes some U.S. multinationals think twice about making use of expatriates. It is important to note that Section 911 of the U.S. Internal

Revenue Service Code contains provisions permitting a substantial deduction on foreign-earned income, but U.S. expatriates must file with the IRS and usually also with the host-country tax office during their period of foreign service—a requirement more onerous than for some other nationalities who may not be required to declare their total global income to their home-country taxation authority.

Multinationals generally select one of the following approaches to handle international taxation:

- *Tax equalization*—firms withhold an amount equal to the home-country tax obligation of the PCN, and pay all taxes in the host country.
- *Tax protection*—the employee pays up to the amount of taxes he or she would pay on compensation in the home country. In such a situation, the employee is entitled to any windfall received if total taxes are less in the foreign country than in the home country.

In her review of global compensation, Stuart[18] adds two other approaches: *ad hoc* (each expatriate is handled differently, depending on the individual package agreed to with the firm), and *laissez-faire* (employees are "on their own" in conforming to host-country and home-country taxation laws and practices). However, neither of these approaches are recommended. We will focus on tax equalization and tax protection since these are the most common approaches.

Tax equalization is by far the more common taxation policy used by multinationals.[19] Thus, for a PCN, tax payments equal to the liability of a home-country taxpayer with the same income and family status are imposed on the employee's salary and bonus. The firm typically pays any additional premiums or allowances, tax-free to the employee. As multinationals operate in more and more countries, they are subject to widely discrepant income tax rates. It is important to note that just focussing on income tax can be misleading because the shares of both social security contributions and consumption taxes are rising in the OECD countries.[20] For example, if we look at total tax revenues as a percentage of GDP, the "top five" highest taxation countries are Denmark, Sweden, Finland, Belgium, and France. The United States is 20th, with the other large advanced economies towards the bottom of the list (Japan, 19th; Britain, 14th; and Germany, 11th).[21]

Many multinationals have responded to this complexity and diversity across countries by retaining the services of an international accounting firm to provide advice and prepare host-country and home-country tax returns for their expatriates. When multinationals plan compensation packages, they need to consider to what extent specific practices can be modified in each country to provide the most tax-effective, appropriate rewards for PCNs, HCNs, and TCNs within the framework of the overall compensation policy of the firm.

International Living Costs Data

Obtaining up-to-date information on international living costs is a constant issue for multinationals. As we noted at the beginning of this chapter, the level of local knowledge required in many areas of international HRM requires specialized advice. Consequently, many multinationals retain the services of consulting firms that may offer a broad range of services or provide highly specialized services relevant to HRM in a multinational context. A number of consulting firms offer regular surveys that calculate the COLA index and are updated in terms of currency exchange rates. A recent survey of living costs[22] in selected cities ranked the ten most expensive cities as Tokyo, Reykjavik (Iceland), Geneva, Oslo, Libreville (Gabon), Copenhagen, Berlin, Helsinki, Stockholm, and Munich. The first U.S. city in the index was New York, ranked as the 28th most expensive city; the least expensive city was La Paz (Bolivia), ranked at 90th.

Multinationals using the balance sheet approach must constantly update compensation packages with new data on living costs, an on-going administrative requirement. This is an issue to which expatriate employees pay great attention, and forms the basis of many complaints if updating substantially lags behind any rise in living costs. Multinationals must also be able to respond to unexpected events, such as the currency and stock market crash that suddenly unfolded in a number of Asian countries in late 1997. Some countries, such as Indonesia, faced a devaluation of their currency (the Indonesian ruphiah) by over 50 percent against the U.S. dollar in a matter of weeks, which had a dramatic impact on prices and the cost of living. There is also much debate about what should be in the "basket of goods" that consulting firms use as the basis for calculating living costs around the world. For example, the British magazine *The Economist* has developed its own benchmark of living costs based on the cost of a McDonald's "Big Mac" around the world.

There are also considerable disparities in purchasing power around the world. Exhibit 6–6 shows a range of data to illustrate this point with the purchasing power of working time shown for a range of factors. For example, while U.S. workers do not have the highest hourly earnings, the purchasing power of their working time is high in terms of less working time required to pay for items such as petrol (gasoline in the U.S.), income tax liability, consumer durables (e.g., a TV set), and food items (e.g., bread and coffee).

It is also possible to take a wider view and focus on *business costs* rather than living costs for expatriates, because the multinational firm is interested in the overall cost of doing business in a particular country as well as the more micro issue of expatriate living costs. A recent study by the Economist Intelligence Unit[23] calculated an index that measures the relative costs of doing business in 27 economies by compiling statistics relating to wages, costs for expatriate staff, air travel and subsistence, corporation taxes, perceived corruption levels, office and industrial rents, and road transport. The "top ten" most expensive countries in terms of business costs in 1997 were:

1. Germany
2. United States
3. Belgium
4. Britain
5. France
6. The Netherlands
7. Sweden
8. Australia
9. Italy
10. Singapore

Germany is the most expensive country overall because of its very high basic wages, while the second most expensive rank for the United States is in large part because of high executive salaries. In general, developed countries rank as more expensive than developing countries because their wage costs are higher.

Differentiating Between PCNs and TCNs

As we have indicated, one of the outcomes of the balance sheet approach is to produce differentiation between expatriate employees of different nationalities because of the use of nationality to determine the relevant home-country base salary. In effect, this is a differentiation between PCNs and TCNs. Many TCNs have a great deal of international experience because they often move from country to country in the employ of

EXHIBIT 6-6 *The Purchasing Power of Working Time*

	Bread (per kg)	Coffee (per kg)		Men's shoes (per pair)		1 litre petrol (super)	Rent 4 rooms[a]		Colour TV (50 cm screen)		Income tax[b] (annual)		Net earnings (hourly) in 1995
	mins	hrs	mins	hrs	mins	mins	hrs	mins	hrs	mins	hrs	mins	$US
Australia	6.5	2	11	4	10	2.5	26	47.5	22	34	265	30.5	12.53
Canada[c]	6.5		47.5	3	4.5	1.5	28	32	14	16	481	3	16.73
France[c]	11.5		25	9	59	6	59	43.5	51	11.5	119[d]	26.5[d]	10.18
Germany[f]	5		20	2	38	2	15	25.5	35		135	42	27.06
Italy	10		42.5	4	56	5.5	54	46	43	49	260	35.5	13.80
Japan	12.5	4	1.5	6		4.5	78	41.5	32	48.5	82	23.5	18.39
Korea	18		15.5	10	8	7.5	69	46[e]	101	20	95	11.5	6.17
Sweden	12	4	34.5	4	12.5	4.5	52	17.5	72	34	974	29.5	12.68
UK	6		55	3	3	5.5	91	26.5	38	6	345	16.5	10.00
USA	3.5		36.5	4	56.5	1	54	56.5	16	29	122	24	18.2

Notes: a Four rooms including kitchen
        b Metalworkers' family of four with one income
        c 1994 data
        d Unmarried metalworker
        e Three rooms including kitchen
        f Former West Germany only

Source: IMF (1996) using 1995 data

Source: G.J. Bamber, P. Ross, and G. Whitehouse, 1998. Employment relations and labour market indicators in ten industrialized market economies: Comparative statistics, *International Journal of Human Resource Management*, vol. 9, no. 2, p. 415. Reprinted with permission.

one multinational (or several) headquartered in a country other than their own (e.g., an Indian banker may work in the Singapore branch of a U.S. bank). As Reynolds[24] has observed, there is no doubt that paying TCNs according to their home-country base salary can be less expensive than paying all expatriates on a PCN scale (particularly if the multinational is headquartered in a country such as the United States or Germany, which has both high managerial salaries and a strong currency), but justifying these differences can be very difficult. Nonetheless, it is common practice for multinationals to use a home-country balance sheet approach for TCNs. Evidently, the reduction in expenses outweighs the difficulty of justifying any pay differentials. However, as firms expand internationally, it is likely that TCN employees will become more valuable and firms may need to rethink their approach to compensating TCNs.

As a starting point, multinational firms need to match their compensation policies with their staffing policies and general HR philosophy. If, for example, a firm has an ethnocentric staffing policy, its compensation policy should be one of keeping the expatriate whole (i.e., maintaining relativity to PCN colleagues plus compensating for the costs of international service). If, however, the staffing policy follows a geocentric approach (i.e., staffing a position with the "best person" regardless of nationality) there may be no clear "home" for the TCN, and the firm will need to consider establishing a system of international base pay for key managers paid in a major reserve currency, such as the U.S. dollar or the Deutsche Mark. This system allows firms to deal with considerable variations in base salaries for managers.

SUMMARY

In this chapter we have examined the complexities which arise when firms move from compensation at the domestic level to compensation in an international context. Compensation policy becomes a much less precise process than is the case in the domestic HR context. We have detailed the key components of an international compensation program and outlined the two main approaches to international compensation (the Going Rate and the balance sheet) and the advantages and disadvantages of each approach. Special problem areas such as taxation, obtaining valid international living costs data, and the problems of managing TCN compensation were also outlined.

In the introduction to this chapter we posed the following question: If we take away the specialist jargon and allow for the international context, are the competing objectives of the firm and the employee *fundamentally* different from that which exists in a domestic environment? We indicated that we thought this was not the case and cited the work of Milkovich and Bloom[25] who have argued that strategic flexibility is necessary in international compensation. Along with researchers such as Roth and O'Donnell[26] and Gomez-Mejia and Wiseman,[27] Milkovich and Bloom argue that nationality or "national systems thinking" has had an excessive influence on managing compensation and reward systems internationally, and propose a strategic flexibility model, shown in Exhibit 6–7.

This model groups forms of total compensation into three sets: core, crafted, and choice. Specific practices in the *core* section may vary according to market and local conditions but must be consistent with the core policies. The *crafted* set of compensation elements assumes that regional managers have discretion to choose from a menu of compensation forms, while alternatives in the *choice* set offer flexibility for employees to select among various forms of compensation. The model also supports

EXHIBIT 6–7 *Strategic Flexibility Model of International Compensation*

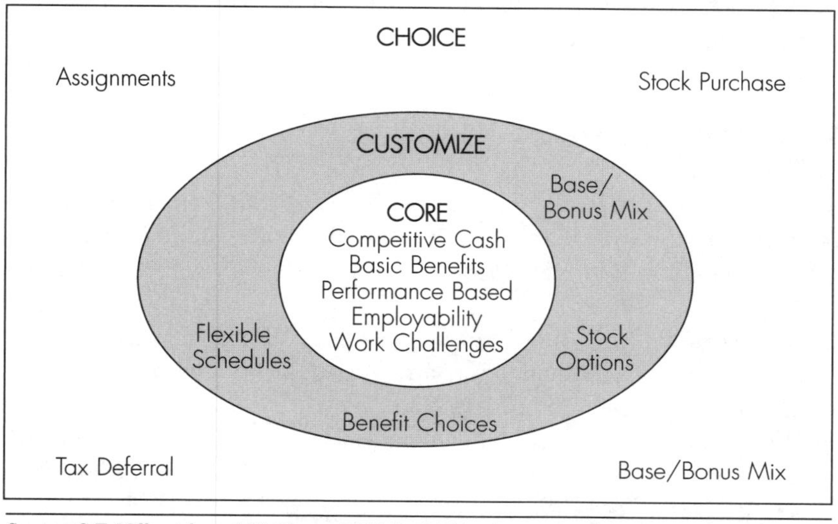

Source: G.T. Milkovich, and M. Bloom, 1998. Rethinking international compensation, *Compensation and Benefits Review*, vol. 30, no. 1, p. 22. Reprinted by permission of the publishers from *Compensation and Benefits Review*, © 1998. American Management Association, New York. All rights reserved.

the performance management approach taken in Chapter 4 (see, for example, Exhibit 4–7). It is clear that such a strategic flexibility model has the potential to overcome some of the problems we have identified in both the Going Rate and Balance Sheet approaches to international compensation because firms may be able to utilize aspects of both approaches that suit their particular circumstances. Future research could test the extent to which this model describes how multinational firms are reacting to the complexities they face in dealing with international compensation.

QUESTIONS

1. What should be the main objectives for a multinational firm with regard to its compensation policies?
2. Describe the main differences in the Going Rate and Balance Sheet approaches to international compensation.
3. What are the key differences in salary compensation for PCNs and TCNs? Do these differences matter?
4. What are the main points multinational firms must consider when deciding how to provide benefits?
5. Why is it important for multinational firms to understand the compensation practices of other countries?

FURTHER READING

1. Bonache, J., and Z. Fernandez, 1997. Expatriate compensation and its link to the subsidiary strategic role: A theoretical analysis, *International Journal of Human Resource Management*, vol. 8, no. 4, pp. 457–475.
2. Gomez-Mejia, L.R., and L.E. Palich, 1997. Cultural diversity and the performance of multinational firms, *Journal of International Business Studies*, vol. 28, no. 2, pp. 309–335.
3. Harvey, M., 1993. Empirical evidence of recurring international compensation problems, *Journal of International Business Studies*, vol. 24, no. 4, pp. 785–799.
4. Rayman, J., and B. Twinn, 1983. *Expatriate Compensation and Benefits: An Employer's Handbook*, London: Kogan Page.

5. Schuler, R.S., and N. Rogovsky, 1998. Understanding compensation practice variations across firms: The impact of national culture, *Journal of International Business Studies*, vol. 29, no. 1, pp. 159–177.

6. Solomon, C.M., 1995. Global compensation: Learn the ABCs, *Personnel Journal*, July, pp. 71–76.

ENDNOTES

1. For example, specialized firms such as P-E International in Britain provide a survey of Worldwide Living Costs, while Price Waterhouse offers a worldwide consulting service called "Global Human Resource Solutions" which covers a broad range of international HR issues.

2. The Conference Board, 1996. Managing expatriates' return: A research report, Report # 1148-96-RR, New York.

3. Richard Tomlinson, 1997. You get what you pay for, corporate recruiters in China find, *Fortune*, April 28, pp. 218–219.

4. While a driver may be considered a luxury in most Western countries, available only to CEOs, in developing economies a driver is both economical in terms of cost and it is in the interests of the multinational to provide this benefit. Apart from the practical realities that managers are expected to have a driver, parking is frequently chaotic in developing countries (especially in large cities) and the driver also performs the function of a parking attendant. It can also be quite dangerous for expatriates to drive in some developing countries. For example, in some developing countries it is quite common for the police to arrest drivers involved in traffic accidents and leave them in detention while the matter is sorted out in terms of responsibility and damages. Such a risk is unacceptable to most firms and many multinationals do not allow their expatriate employees to drive at all in some developing countries and provide local drivers for both the expatriate and spouse.

5. G.T. Milkovich, and M. Bloom, 1998. Rethinking international compensation, *Compensation and Benefits Review*, vol. 30, no. 1, pp. 15–23.

6. H.J. Ruff, and G.I. Jackson, 1974. Methodological problems in international comparisons of the cost of living, *Journal of International Business Studies*, vol. 5, no. 2, pp. 57–67.

7. Ibid.
8. The experience of the first two authors in their research on expatriates and their families is that, for some expatriates (particularly expatriates with little international experience), using home leave allowances for foreign travel can intensify feelings of homesickness. Without the benefit of returning home to mix with employees and friends, it is possible to idealize what they remember of their experience at work and home and fail to come to a measured judgement of what is good and bad in both their host and home environments. Some spouses commented that their first home leave was beneficial in helping them to adjust to the host location. Being treated by family and friends as a visitor in their hometown made them identify with the host location as "home," and they returned with a more positive attitude. Thus, in general, we would take the view that home leave allowances should normally be used for the purpose for which they are intended—to give employees and their families the opportunity to renew family and business ties, thereby helping them to avoid adjustment problems when they are repatriated.
9. It is common in Asia and many developing countries in other regions for expatriates and local business people to employ maids and cooks in their houses. As stated in an earlier endnote when discussing employment of drivers, it may be expected that an expatriate would employ servants and to not do so would be judged negatively since this would be depriving people of employment. Not surprisingly, this is one benefit that expatriate spouses miss when they return to their home country.
10. 1990. Trends in expatriate compensation. *Bulletin to Management*, October 18, p. 336.
11. The material in the exhibits describing the two main approaches to international compensation are based on various sources—the research and consulting experience of the first author and various discussions on this topic with a range of HR managers and consultants in Australia and the United States.
12. In interviews conducted by the first author with senior management of Australian firms operating internationally, repatriation difficulties was one of the major reasons cited for not following a Going Rate approach with Australian expatriates.
13. Towers Perrin, *Worldwide Total Remuneration 1997*. Total compensation included basic salary, variable bonus, compulsory company contributions, voluntary company contributions, perquisites, and

long-term incentives. See also the Towers Perrin website (www.towers.com) for further information.

14. See B.W. Teague, 1972. *Compensating Key Personnel Overseas*, New York: The Conference Board, for a discussion of the concept of keeping the expatriate "whole."

15. This discussion of the balance sheet approach is based on C. Reynolds, 1986. Compensation of overseas personnel, in *Handbook of Human Resources Administration*, 2d ed. J.J. Famularo, ed. New York: McGraw-Hill.

16. See Chapter 3 of T.J. Bergmann, V.G. Scarpello, and F.S. Hills, 1998. *Compensation Decision Making*, 3d ed. Fort Worth, TX: Dryden Press, for a recent review of equity theory applied to compensation.

17. For example, the first author has interviewed a number of Australian expatriates working in the United States. In all cases they were compensated using a balance sheet approach and in all cases each expatriate commented on the effect that a lower Australian base salary had on the overall level of their salary package relative to local U.S. employees. Most were earning substantially less than local senior managers and some were earning less than their local subordinates.

18. P. Stuart, 1991. Global payroll—A taxing problem, *Personnel Journal*, October, pp. 80–90.

19. Ibid.

20. 1997. Taxes, *The Economist*, September 13, p. 123.

21. Ibid.

22. "International living costs index" by Worldwide Living Cost P-E, Britain, as reported in the *Financial Times*, April 4, 1997.

23. Reported in *The Economist*, January 24, 1998, p. 110.

24. C. Reynolds, Cost-effective compensation, p. 320.

25. G.T. Milkovich, and M. Bloom, Rethinking international compensation.

26. K. Roth, and S. O'Donnell, 1996. Foreign subsidiary compensation strategy: An agency theory perspective, *Academy of Management Journal*, vol. 39, no. 3, pp. 678–703.

27. L. Gomez-Mejia, and R.M. Wiseman, 1997. Reframing executive compensation: An assessment and outlook, *Journal of Management*, vol. 23, no. 3, pp. 291–374.

C H A P T E R 7
Repatriation

I t is evident from the preceding chapters that there have been considerable advances in our understanding and knowledge of the issues surrounding the management of expatriates in terms of
recruitment and selection, predeparture training, and on-assignment
support. However, as Exhibit 7–1 indicates, the expatriation process
also includes repatriation: the activity of bringing the expatriate back to
the home country.

It has become more widely recognized by practitioners and academics
that repatriation needs careful managing, although this increased attention is somewhat belated. The mounting empirical and anecdotal evidence shows that re-entry into the home country presents new
challenges as the repatriate (returning person) copes with what has been
termed **re-entry shock,** or reverse culture shock. While people frequently expect life in a new country to be different, they may be less
prepared for homecoming to present problems of adjustment. As a

EXHIBIT 7-1 *Expatriation Includes Repatriation*

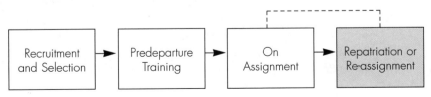

consequence, it can be a traumatic experience for some,[1] even more than what was encountered in the foreign location. From the multinational's perspective, repatriation is frequently considered as the final stage in the expatriation process (as indicated in Exhibit 7–1), but the multinational's ability to attract future expatriates is affected by the manner in which it handles repatriation.[2]

In this chapter, we focus on the key factors associated with re-entry, including how the individual and the receiving work unit handle the repatriation process as well as family adjustment. We also explore how repatriation affects the successful "closure" of the foreign assignment, future career paths within the multinational and staff availability for international assignments, and family readjustment.

THE REPATRIATION PROCESS

Typically, on completion of the foreign assignment, the multinational brings the expatriate back to the home country, although it should be noted that not all international assignments end with a transfer home— rather, the expatriate is re-assigned to another international post (shown by the dotted line in Exhibit 7–1). Some expatriates may agree to become part of the multinational's international team of managers, and thus have consecutive international assignments, as we discussed in Chapter 5. Should one of these assignments be with the home-country operations, it will be treated as "just another posting." At some point, members of this international team, or "cadre," will face repatriation, and since this may occur at the retirement-from-work life stage, there are different concerns that need to be addressed, which are discussed later in this chapter.

It is possible to divide repatriation into four related phases, as illustrated in Exhibit 7–2.

1. *Preparation* involves developing plans for the future and gathering information about the new position. The firm may provide a checklist of items to be considered before the return home (e.g., closure of bank accounts and settling bills) or a thorough preparation of employee and family for the transfer home. However, there is little evidence in the literature that preparation for repatriation is seen by the multinational to be as important as predeparture training;[3] at best, there may be some inclusion of repatriation issues in the predeparture training provided to the expatriate.

EXHIBIT 7–2   *The Repatriation Process*

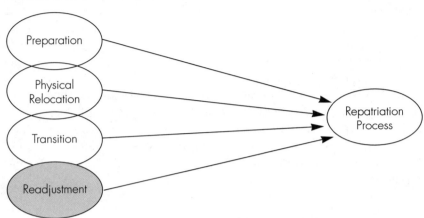

Source: Adapted from D. Welch, T. Adams, B. Betchley, and M. Howard, 1992. The view from the other side: The handling of repatriation and other expatriation activities by the Royal Australian Airforce, in *Proceedings of the Academy of International Business Southeast Asia Conference*, O. Yau, and B. Stening, eds. June, Brisbane.

2. *Physical relocation* refers to removing personal effects, breaking ties with colleagues and friends, and travelling to the next posting, usually the home country. Most multinationals use removal firms or relocation consultants to handle the physical relocation, both for the movement out and the return home of the employee and family, and this may be formalized in their HR policies. According to Forster,[4] comprehensive and personalized relocation assistance reduces the amount of uncertainty, stress, and disruption experienced by the repatriate and family.

3. *Transition* means settling into temporary accommodation where necessary, making arrangements for housing and schooling, and carrying out other administrative tasks (e.g., renewing driver's license, applying for medical insurance, opening bank account). Some companies hire relocation consultants to assist in this phase also.

4. *Readjustment* involves coping with reverse culture shock and career demands.[5]

Of the four phases identified in Exhibit 7–2, the readjustment phase is the one that seems to be the least understood and most poorly handled (highlighted by shading of that phase). For example, in 1996 Harzing conducted a comprehensive survey of 287 subsidiaries of nearly 100 different multinationals. She reports that 52 percent of sampled firms experienced repatriate re-entry problems.[6]

As with crosscultural adjustment, the re-entry process is a complex interaction of several factors. For the convenience of the following discussion, we have grouped the major factors under two headings: Job-Related Factors and Social Factors.

Job-Related Factors

The re-entry phase may include a number of problems that are related directly to the repatriate's attitude about the effect that an international assignment has on future employment prospects.

Career Anxiety

Perhaps for the majority of repatriates, the overriding concern is the effect of the international assignment on the person's subsequent career path. The limited research on repatriation indicates that for most expatriates a major reason for accepting the international assignment is its value in terms of career progression.[7] This expectation may be based on:

- Clear messages sent by top management to the effect that an international assignment is a condition for career progression; that is, verbal or written statements such as: "We are an international company and we need internationally-oriented people who have worked in our international facilities."
- Comments made by HR or line managers during the recruitment and selection stage; for example, the line manager may suggest to a younger employee: "You should volunteer for that international assignment. It would be a smart career move at this stage in your life."
- Perceptions of the career potential of the international assignment given the career paths of former expatriates—other people have been promoted upon repatriation so this is perceived to be the norm.

As a consequence, the re-entry position frequently is judged by whether it matches the repatriate's career expectation, particularly when the international assignment has caused considerable family disruption such as a forced break in the career of the accompanying partner or difficulties experienced with the education of the children involved. Put simply, the repatriate wants the "end to justify the means," so that the family unit is fully compensated for the sacrifices it has made in expectation of career advancement.

Anxiety over the re-entry position may begin long before repatriation occurs. The expatriate may fear that the period abroad has caused a loss of visibility and isolation from the parent company—as captured in the phrase: "Out of sight, out of mind."[8] The perception may be a function of the degree of autonomy and independence the expatriate and the subsidiary are given by the multinational and the amount of contact that the person has with the home work unit. A recent survey by Harzing[9] found that expatriates sent to independent subsidiaries are more likely to experience this feeling. As a consequence, the person fears he or she has been forgotten when decisions about promotion are made back at headquarters. The expatriate can also become anxious that the company has not planned adequately, so she or he will be placed in a mediocre or makeshift job.[10] It may be that the multinational is in the process of change—such as restructuring accompanied by job shedding, or in the aftermath of a merger or acquisition. Knowledge of these changes will add to the level of anxiety, particularly if the expatriate does not have a guaranteed job upon repatriation. Such concerns may affect productivity during the last couple of months of the international assignment as the person contemplates the re-entry process.

Upon repatriation, the manager may find that these fears have materialized. Peers have been promoted ahead of the repatriated manager, and the repatriate is placed in a position that is, in effect, a demotion. For example, one U.S. repatriate is quoted as saying: "I believe I would have moved much higher had I not gone overseas."[11] The situation may be exacerbated if the repatriate had held a senior position in the foreign location and now finds himself (or herself) at a less senior level. Worse, the repatriate may find that, since there is no suitable position available, she or he is retrenched. This has become of greater concern in the aftermath of the recent restructuring undertaken by many multinationals, and more companies alter their policies regarding the guarantee of a re-entry position. As a 1997 survey by The Conference Board of 152 HR expatriate managers from U.S., European, and Asian multinationals found, re-entry into now-smaller home operations is more problematical:

> Through the mid-1980s, most companies offered a return guarantee to expatriates, ensuring a position at the same level within the organization. Since then, however, the trend has been for companies to offer a general guarantee without specifying the level of the position upon repatriation.[12]

It should be noted that the Conference Board survey found a difference between continental European multinationals and those from the United States and United Kingdom. Twenty-three continental European companies (74 percent) provided written guarantees of a return position, compared with 8 (50 percent) of the U.K. companies and 95 (38 percent) of the U.S. companies in the sample. This difference is supported by other studies. The Tung–Arthur Andersen 1997 survey of 49 North American firms reports that the majority (almost 60 percent) did not guarantee a position at home upon successful completion of the international assignment.[13] In her study of international HR practices in German and U.K. firms, Marx[14] found that the major country difference was the "guaranteed job on return category." The majority of German firms offered a guaranteed job upon return from the foreign assignment, whereas the converse was reported by the U.K. firms—that is, the majority of U.K. firms admitted that they were not able to offer jobs upon repatriation. Marx suggests that continental European firms may have to provide such guarantees in order to attract expatriates. She explains the differences found between German and U.K. multinationals may be due to a lower German tolerance of ambiguity and job insecurity.

Another explanation for these differences may be that U.S. and U.K. multinationals have been through large-scale restructurings. Downsizing has resulted in slimmer and flatter organizations with fewer openings for repatriates; continental European firms have perhaps found it more difficult to implement, or are just embarking on such restructuring. The 1997–98 Price Waterhouse survey[15] reports that the number of multinationals giving written or unwritten guarantees has decreased from 69 percent in the 1995 survey to 46 percent. Of course, the sample included European subsidiaries of U.S. multinationals, as well as U.K. multinationals, which may distort the picture a little but, nevertheless, more European firms are expanding into non-European markets and closing facilities in Europe, which means fewer positions for repatriates.

Should this trend of not guaranteeing re-entry positions continue, it is likely to have an adverse impact on staff availability. The implicit message being sent to personnel is that an international assignment is a high-risk career strategy,[16] which is a powerful deterrent for potential, high caliber expatriates. There is the added danger that the policy of non-guarantee of a re-entry position may serve to reinforce the career anxiety of expatriates currently on foreign assignments, thus affecting their adjustment, productivity, and commitment to the multinational. Marx found that for the German firms in her sample, "attracting people to go abroad" was the fourth most frequently reported problem. German HRM managers included "worry about missing out on career prospects whilst working abroad" as one of the barriers to mobility.[17] Other European firms are reporting similar difficulties: Forty-eight percent of the European firms in the Price Waterhouse survey referred to above reported experiencing problems with attracting employees for international assignments. Among the reasons cited for this situation was "job security/availability upon repatriation."

Devaluing the International Experience

Career anxiety is compounded if the re-entry position does not appear to be connected with the person's international experience. Often, repatriates find themselves in "holding" positions, such as a task force or project team, in temporary positions, engaged in duties that do not appear to exploit their newly gained, international expertise.[18] The feeling voiced by many repatriates is echoed in the following comment by an Australian repatriate: "You gain a lot of experience, but it is dismissed here."[19] A similar view was related by a Norwegian repatriate: "The job I returned to was not satisfactory.... I felt strongly overqualified and it took three-quarters of a year before I got a relevant job."[20] In these situations, repatriates become an underutilized resource, programs that exploit the international experience and cosmopolitan view that the expatriate has gained while abroad do not exist, and the return position is frequently a lateral move rather than a promotion.[21] Such treatment was highlighted by Tung's earlier study.[22] It remains evident in the recent Conference Board, Tung–Arthur Andersen, and Price Waterhouse surveys referred to above.

The perceived degrading of the repatriate's recent experience may be coupled with negative career progression; that is, the re-entry position is a less challenging job with reduced responsibility and status than that held either during the international assignment or prior to the period abroad. This combination can have a demotivating effect on the repatriate, as well as affect the multinational's ability to attract potential expatriates, as discussed earlier.

The devaluing of the international experience has been linked to repatriate turnover. For example, Stroh[23] found that the best predictors of repatriate turnover were whether the company had a career development plan, and whether the company was undergoing turbulence, such as downsizing. "Organizations that were more likely to plan for the repatriation of their employees and that provided career development planning for them were more likely to have lower rates of repatriate turnover." Black, Gregersen, and Mendenhall[24] argue that work adjustment has an important impact on a person's intent to stay with the organization. Career expectations have been discussed in relation to expatriate adjustment and performance, but it is easy to see how the repatriate may evaluate his or her treatment upon re-entry and interpret his or her treatment as a violation of the psychological contract. This perception may stem from the belief that the person's performance abroad warrants promotion; that signals were given by the organization that effective performance in the international assignment would result in career advancement. When the expected promotion does not eventuate, the repatriate may feel there is no option but to exit the organization.[25]

Coping with New Role Demands

Given the above factors, it is not surprising that re-entry poses a challenge for the repatriate and frequently reveals a mismatch of expectations, which affect the repatriate's perception of the new role, especially if an anticipated promotion does not materialize. As we discussed in Chapter 4, effective role behavior is an interaction between the concept of the role, the interpretation of expectations, the person's ambitions, and the norms inherent in the role. Exhibit 7–3 illustrates the elements of the repatriate's role as a focus for a discussion of the readjustment issues related to role behavior.

The literature suggests that readjustment problems may occur because, although the repatriate is attempting to function back in the home country, his or her role conception remains influenced by that of the foreign assignment. The message being sent (denoted by the direction of the arrow in Exhibit 7–3) by the parent company (the role sender) has crossed the cultural boundary. The person has been operating for some time in the foreign location, and consequently may have made significant changes to his or her role behavior.[26] For example, an American working in Indonesia may have altered his participative managerial style to one more authoritarian based on messages sent by the foreign subsidiary, or it could be that the time in the Indonesian subsidiary has reinforced an authoritarian tendency. Conflict is likely to occur if the repatriate does not resume the managerial behavior appropriate to the U.S. context upon return.

Torbiörn[27] contends that as long as the repatriate's "identity and basic values are still bound up in the culture of the home country, the strain of adjusting to conditions at home will be slight." However, while the

EXHIBIT 7-3 *The Repatriate Role*

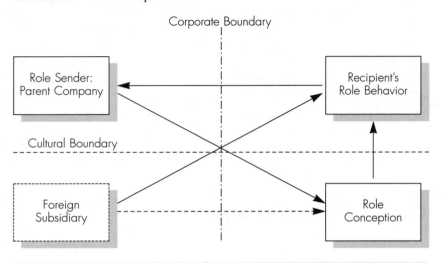

Source: Adapted from I. Torbiörn, 1985. The structure of managerial roles in cross-cultural settings, *International Studies of Management & Organization*, vol. 15, no. 1, p. 69.

repatriate may retain the role conception and the cultural norms regarding behavior appropriate to that role, his or her ambitions may color the interpretation of expectations. In this sense, the foreign subsidiary's influence may linger (indicated by the dotted arrow in Exhibit 7–3) and what is communicated to the parent company, in the form of role behavior, will not conform to the parent's expectations. As shown by the broken line between the role sender and role recipient boxes at the top of Exhibit 7–3, there is a "corporate boundary" to be crossed in the communication of the role conception between the role recipient (the repatriate) and the role sender (the parent company). The role sender, however, may not recognize the cultural and corporate boundaries that affect the repatriate's role conception and role behavior, thus unwittingly contributing to readjustment problems.

While research in this area is limited, in their study of 125 repatriated managers from four large U.S. multinationals, Black and Gregersen[28] found that role clarity, rather than role conflict, was significantly related to work adjustment. Discussing these findings, the authors explain that role conflict may be an important factor in expatriate assignments due to conflicting role signals between home office and the foreign subsidiary, whereas role conflict upon return most likely stems from conflicting job signals from different individuals within the home operation. They add, "While there are advantages in providing jobs that are clear and free from role conflicts, it is perhaps more important for firms to provide clear jobs upon repatriation." In other words, role clarity emerges as an aspect of healthy readjustment.

A further contribution to our understanding of repatriate readjustment comes from Black and Gregersen's finding regarding role discretion. Role discretion refers to the freedom to adjust the work role to fit the individual, making it easier for the person to utilize past, familiar behavior, thus reducing the level of uncertainty in the new job that assists adjustment. They found from their sample that role discretion had a positive impact on adjustment—a finding that appears to confirm earlier studies on the relationship between role discretion, role clarity, and work adjustment.[29] In a later survey of Finnish repatriates, Gregersen found fairly consistent results in terms of role clarity and role discretion with those of American repatriates. He comments:

> The consistent results between American and Finnish managers suggest that greater role discretion upon repatriation seems to facilitate repatriation adjustment. In addition, the importance of role clarity to work adjustment suggests that Finnish and American firms may want to provide clearer jobs upon repatriation.[30]

However, it would appear that, for North American companies at least, role clarity and role discretion remains a repatriation issue. It emerged as important in Baughn's[31] survey of U.S. repatriates. The category "reduced responsibility and autonomy on the job" was ranked second, after "career advancement," as a major concern upon repatriation for respondents in the Tung–Arthur Andersen survey. These findings lend added support to the combining of role clarity, role conflict, and role discretion into a category 'Job Variables' in the theoretical model of repatriation developed by Black, Gregersen, and Mendenhall.[32]

The above studies suggest that the corporate boundary in Exhibit 7–3 may be stronger than the "cultural boundary," in terms of the repatriate role. Limited support for this conclusion also may be drawn from the results of a recent U.K. study. Forster[33] surveyed 124 expatriates who had returned to the United Kingdom in the preceding twelve months. Analysis of the responses indicated five predictors for repatriation maladjustment (in ranked order): length of time abroad, unrealistic expectations of job opportunities in the home company, downward job mobility, reduced work status, and negative perceptions of the help and support provided by employers during and after repatriation. Job-related factors were found to be more important than non-work and family factors.

A point found significant in the above studies, which is not directly addressed but may help to explain the interrelationships between the variables, is that the period abroad does alter the person. The experiences of living and working in another country can affect the person's self-efficacy (the degree to which an individual believes that she or he can execute a set of behaviors). As well, the expatriate position commonly involves a more demanding job position. Learning how to successfully cope with the various challenges encountered during the foreign assignment may give the person more self-confidence, along with a broader perspective.[34] These changes may be subtle for some people; for others they can be profound—and may be influenced by factors such as length of time spent abroad, country of assignment, and individual differences such as age and personality. As a result, the re-entry shock experienced by the repatriate may be as much a function of the degree to which the person has altered, as to the changes that have occurred in the home country, as indicated in Exhibit 7–4.

The period of time spent abroad is an important aspect. The longer the person is away from the home country, the more likely there will be readjustment problems upon return.[35] Another contributing factor may be the length of time that the repatriate is kept in a so-called "holding pattern,"

EXHIBIT 7–4   *Repatriate Readjustment*

as mentioned earlier. This may be acceptable as an interim measure, but the longer the repatriate is treated as temporary, the more likely he or she is to become anxious about the future, and have less commitment to the home work unit and the parent organization.[36]

Other workplace changes may affect readjustment. The repatriate often encounters changes in the formal and informal information channels in the home organization, particularly if there has been widespread restructuring and downsizing. Technological advances in the multinational may render the repatriate's functional skills and knowledge outdated. A Norwegian repatriate described his reaction: "Everything had changed.... I had inadequate technological knowledge on, for instance, PC systems."[37] Unless there was sufficient contact with the expatriate during the international assignment, the person will be unprepared for these changes. When coupled with other job-related problems, these changes make work adjustment a difficult process.

Loss of Status and Pay

Usually, the international assignment is a form of promotion. It carries greater autonomy, a broader area of responsibility (because of the smaller size of the international subsidiary) and, at the top management level, a prominent role in the local community. The result is higher status. Some expatriates use the term *kingpin* to describe their positions abroad. Upon return, the repatriate is expected to resume her or his position within the home company—with the loss of status and autonomy. In effect, the repatriate is treated as just another company executive. This shift may cause readjustment problems. For example, a repatriate can find that, whereas in the foreign operation he or she was the key decision maker, now he or she has to seek permission from a superior. One Australian repatriate described this feeling: "Over there, you are the big fish in the small pond. Back home, you return to being the small fish in a big pond."[38]

Compounding the problem is the loss of expatriate premiums. As Conway states, "More commonly, employees are brought home to resume life on a scale that may be significantly less comfortable than what they had grown used to abroad. Pay is usually lower in absolute terms."[39] A similar finding is reported by the Tung–Arthur Andersen survey referred to earlier. However, in their study of 21 U.S. firms, Napier and Petersen[40] found that most of the repatriates in their sample felt that their personal finances were better *after* the assignment than before, even though they were not as favorable as before the international assignment. Napier and

Petersen explain that the total compensation package received while on assignment was greater than before, thus allowing the person to return to the United States with increased savings.

Another contributing factor is that the returning manager may no longer be able to afford to buy a home similar to the one sold a few years before. A U.S. study suggests that the current practice of providing expatriates with better housing than they had at home may contribute to repatriation problems; that is, a drop in the standard of housing conditions has a negative impact on the adjustment of U.S. repatriates.[41] This creates somewhat of a dilemma for U.S. HR managers. As discussed previously, the amount of support provided for the expatriate and family is critical to adjustment and intent to stay, but may have a negative effect on re-entry.

Social Factors

The familiar surrounds of the home environment may ease the transition, or at least the cultural adjustment will not be as demanding as that confronted in the foreign country. However, the international experience can distance the repatriate, and his or her family, socially and psychologically. If the expatriate position gave the person a high profile, involving interaction with the social and economic elite, the return home may bring with it some measure of social disappointment, thus reinforcing the *kingpin* syndrome. The financial loss of the compensation premium, housing subsidy, and related benefits can exacerbate these feelings.

It must be stressed here that where spouses, partners, and children are involved each family member is experiencing his or her own readjustment problems. For some returnees re-entry is a shock. It is as if they had pressed the "pause" button as they flew out of the country and expected life at home to remain in the "freeze frame." Re-entry reminds them that life is not static. As a coping behavior in the foreign location, others may have glamorized life back home and now have to come to terms with reality—to accept the negative as well as the positive aspects of home. For example, the foreign country may have appeared more expensive in relative terms, but upon repatriation, the family is confronted with a higher level of inflation in the home country than was previously the case. Conversely, life at home may now seem dull and unexciting, and the family may begin to glamorize the life they left behind in the foreign location. These reactions can be compounded if the family income has been reduced upon repatriation. Forty-five percent of the HR professionals responding to the Conference Board survey mentioned earlier reported that the majority of expatriates experienced a fall in income with the removal of the compensation benefits received while abroad. Of course, the income level depends on whether the spouse or partner has been able to work while in the foreign location, and how quickly she or he is able to find a suitable job upon repatriation.

Naturally, impressions generated about changes in the home country may depend on how effectively the family has been able to keep up-to-date with events back home. One could expect that the coverage by satellite television news channels such as CNN and BBC World, and global-oriented newspapers, make it easier for U.S. and U.K. expatriates to follow their home events than those coming from smaller countries (e.g., Australia or Norway). The Internet has the potential to provide an avenue for expatriates to stay in touch. Of course, the usefulness of media services depends on the availability of, and access to, television cable networks and computer facilities in the foreign location.

Reestablishing social networks can also be difficult, especially if the family has been repatriated to a different state or town in the home country. Families who return to their previous domestic locations often find that friends have moved away; repatriated spouses or partners may find their friends have re-entered the workforce and are no longer available for social activities. There can be a sense of loss as the level of attention and support from the multinational is withdrawn: "The phone does not ring. We went from a very close [expatriate] community to here where everyone is very busy with their own lives."[42] Many repatriates report that people show little interest in hearing about their expatriate experiences, which can make conversation uncomfortable.[43] As one U.S. repatriate relates: "It was very difficult discussing my experiences with my co-workers and friends because Americans refuse to accept that life somewhere else could be as good or better than in the U.S.A."[44]

Children may also find re-entry difficult. Coming back to school, attempting to regain acceptance into peer groups, and being out-of-touch with current slang, sports, and fashion can cause problems. However, there are few reported studies in the literature that focus on children's repatriation. An exception is a study of 40 Japanese children that found that the children faced difficulties reintegrating into both their peer groups and the Japanese educational system.[45] One can speculate though that the more difficult the re-entry process for the children, the greater the "spill-over" effect for the repatriate.

Effect on Partner's Career

Partners encounter difficulties in re-entering the workforce, particularly if the partner has not been able to work outside the home prior to, or during, the foreign assignment, but now desires to find outside employment—either as part of a re-entry coping strategy or due to altered family circumstances. Negative experiences during the job search may affect the partner's self-worth, compounding the readjustment process, and even causing tension in the relationship. For those who held positions prior to the international assignment, difficulties in re-entering the workforce may depend on occupation,[46] length of time abroad, unemployment levels in the home country, and personal characteristics such as age and gender.[47]

There is a dearth of research into the effects of the foreign assignment and repatriation upon the partner's career, and many questions surrounding this issue remain unexplored. For instance,

- Do new employers consider the value of the time abroad to "compensate" for the forced career disruption? The Conference Board survey reports "That being a 'trailing' spouse during the expatriate's international assignment constitutes a damaging gap in their employment history."[48]
- Have those partners who were able to work during the foreign assignment found employment in career-related jobs and been able to progress upon repatriation?
- Do male "trailing" partners face different challenges upon repatriation than do females? In one of the few reported studies into dual-career expatriates, Harvey[49] found a difference between female expatriate managers' expectations prior to and after expatriation, exposing the need for support for the male "trailing" partner. The international assignment was the focus of Harvey's study, but one could assume that the same results would hold true upon repatriation.

Readjustment of the expatriate, whether male-led or female-led, may be linked with concerns that the foreign assignment might have on the partner's career. Given that dual-career couples are on the increase and that more females expect international assignments, the issue of the partner's career is likely to become a major factor determining staff availability for future international assignments. The 1997–98 Price Waterhouse survey indicates that some companies are providing accompanying partners with job-finding assistance upon repatriation (21 percent indicated job finding assistance, 9.8 percent counseling, and 6 percent financial assistance for retraining).

In summary, re-entry shock can produce a U-Curve similar to that examined in Chapter 3 in terms of adjustment to the host location. Indeed, it is sometimes referred to as the W-Curve to include re-entry shock upon repatriation. As can be seen from the case in Exhibit 7–5, job-related and social factors may combine to create a somewhat volatile situation that may lead to the repatriate's exit from the multinational.

EXHIBIT 7–5 *Re-Entry Problems*[50]

John Handel had been back in his hometown for two months after an exciting three years working in the Japanese subsidiary of a U.S. multinational. As he sat in his empty office looking out at the city skyline, John reviewed his situation. Well, he had to admit, for him it had been an exciting and challenging time since his position there as finance manager had been a promotion. More importantly, it had brought him in contact with different work approaches and procedures and he had interacted with American expatriates from headquarters as well as local Japanese. Even though his previous position had been in the Asia Pacific Regional Office, it had not provided him with the same exposure as he enjoyed in Japan. John knew that he had gained valuable experience and self-confidence as a result.

It had not been all excitement though for the family. Anne, his wife, did not complain but John knew that she faced a difficult time because of his international assignment. One reason was because his two teenage children had to attend the International School located at a considerable distance from the Japanese subsidiary, which meant they only came "home" on weekends. It made life particularly lonely for Anne, who was not working in Japan. She did admit that she often missed her work as a pathologist. Anne was having trouble back home finding employment—her previous department in a local medical school had been closed down due to reduced government funding.

Both children enjoyed the international environment at the school, and had adjusted better than John had hoped. Coming back to Australia though was proving to be traumatic. His elder son had not been accepted into his chosen university course due to nonrecognition of the accreditation of the International School—or at least that was what Peter claimed. His younger son, Jason, wasn't adjusting easily either.

Dinner last night had not been a happy occasion, but tonight would be worse, John knew. How was he going to explain that the family had made such sacrifices to further his career that was now going nowhere? His

(continued)

EXHIBIT 7-5 *Continued*

repatriated position back to the Regional Office was badly timed, to say the least. Headquarters in the States had decided to reorganize the entire global operation and, as a result, the Regional Office was to be upgraded to a Regional Headquarters, and relocated in Japan. John knew that it made sound business sense—most of the Asian-Pacific activity was centered around the Japanese facility and its South-East Asian and Chinese markets. To retain its regional headquarters in Australia on the grounds of sentiment was unthinkable in such a highly competitive industry. "But where does that leave me? All the work is being transferred northwards. My position will now be filled by someone from either headquarters or, more probably, from Japan. My boss made that quite clear. I could not have asked the family to move back anyway," thought John. The situation was compounded by the news today that several of his colleagues in the regional office had been made redundant. "My acceptance of the international assignment has been career suicide—and not just for me," John thought. "I will have to see if there are positions available elsewhere if I am going to be able to face Anne and the boys tonight. Surely another company will value my international experience."

Multinational Responses

Early studies into the issue of repatriation indicated that it was somewhat neglected by multinationals. For example, Mendenhall, Dunbar, and Oddou[51] concluded that U.S. human resource professionals might be unaware of the challenges facing repatriated managers. Commenting on the results of his 1989 study Harvey[52] noted that:

> Even though many executives have experienced difficulties upon repatriation, [U.S.] multinational companies have seemingly not addressed the issues related to repatriation with the same level of interest as preparing executives for expatriation.

While there appears to have been some increase in the level of awareness, the 1997 Conference Board survey reported that only 27 percent of responding firms indicated they held re-entry sessions to discuss issues such as career objectives, performance, and plan for re-entry; the majority of these firms indicated that they waited until 90 days or less before initiating such sessions.[53]

In 1989 Harvey[54] surveyed members of the Institute for International HRM of the U.S. Society for Human Resource Management to ascertain

U.S. firms' current approaches to repatriation. He found that 31 percent of U.S. firms offered some form of repatriation program. Harvey's findings are comparable with those of the 1997 Conference Board survey with 22 percent of the U.S. multinationals, 25 percent of U.K. multinationals, and 5 percent of continental European multinationals offering formal repatriation programs. Harvey's survey found that 35 percent of the programs included the spouse, whereas only 19 percent of firms in the Conference Board survey indicated spouse programs. One must add a note of caution here. The Conference Board report does not break down the figures by country so it is not possible to compare the U.S. data on spouse and family inclusion with that of Harvey's earlier study.

Harvey asked those firms that indicated they did not have a repatriation training program to give reasons for the lack of such a program. The most frequently mentioned reasons were:

- Lack of expertise in establishing a program (47 percent);
- Cost of program to train repatriates (36 percent); and
- No perceived need for repatriation training by top management (35 percent).

Harvey concluded:

> The lack of acceptance of repatriation programs among the survey respondents tends to illustrate the absence of organized efforts by large sophisticated multinationals to assist expatriated personnel.... The almost total lack of attention to family members would appear to be one of the most egregious errors being made.

One reason for this oversight may be that repatriation problems are not dramatic, or visible, or readily identifiable as expensive. By its very nature, an incidence of so-called expatriate failure is likely to attract attention within the home work unit; whereas a repatriate exiting the organization can become just another statistic, unless the multinational has a policy of separating out repatriates from the general employee turnover numbers. Black and Gregersen calculate that a U.S. multinational spends around $1 million on each expatriate over the duration of a foreign assignment. They argue that if approximately 25 percent of employees exit the firm within a year of repatriation it "represents a substantial financial and human capital loss to the firm, especially if the skills, knowledge, and experience that the individual gains are important to the firm and scarce in the internal or external labor markets."[55]

While there is no simple, quick solution, preparing the repatriate and family for re-entry appears to have some value. The potential for mismatch of expectations regarding the future may be addressed as part of pre-repatriation training before the return, and discussed during re-entry counseling sessions (sometimes referred to as debriefing) between the receiving organization in the home country and the repatriate. In today's parlance, such sessions would enable both parties to "take a reality check."

What should be covered in formal repatriation programs? Exhibit 7–6 is an amalgam of the lists suggested by respondents in the various surveys referred to above.

Some companies assign the expatriate a **mentor** (also referred to as a company contact, sponsor, or "godfather"). The mentor is usually in a more senior position than the expatriate, from the sending work unit, and knows the expatriate personally. The rationale behind the use of a mentor is to alleviate the "out-of-sight, out-of-mind" feeling discussed earlier through the provision of information (e.g., workplace changes) on a regular basis, so that the expatriate is more prepared for conditions faced upon re-entry. A mentor should also ensure that the expatriate is not forgotten when important decisions are made regarding positions, promotions, and so on.

EXHIBIT 7–6 *Topics Covered by a Repatriation Program*

- Preparation, physical relocation, and transition information (what the company will help with)
- Financial and tax assistance (including benefit and tax changes, loss of overseas allowance)
- Re-entry position and career path assistance
- Reverse culture shock (including family disorientation)
- School systems and children's education (including adaptation)
- Workplace changes (such as corporate culture, structure, decentralization)
- Stress management, communication-related training
- Establishing networking opportunities
- Help in forming new social contacts

The Conference Board survey[56] found that 26 percent of respondents provided mentors for their expatriates, although this was related to various organizational factors:

1. *Size of expatriate workforce.* Firms with more than 250 expatriates were more likely to assign mentors (43 percent) than those with 55–100 expatriates (15 percent).
2. *Work unit responsible for the expatriate.* Mentors are more likely if corporate HR formulates expatriate policy (in 35 percent of cases), and when the expatriate is managed by a separate international assignments unit (in 41 percent of cases) rather than at the divisional level (18 percent).
3. *Nationality of responding company.* Thirty-five percent of continental European firms reported the use of mentors compared to 20 percent in U.S. firms. Over a quarter of the European-based firms in the 1997–98 Price Waterhouse survey use a career mentor/sponsor system, with a further 19 percent indicating that such a scheme would be introduced in the future.

It is reasonable to suggest that the practice of mentoring has to be managed to be effective. For example, what happens when the mentor retires or leaves the firm (two likely events in a multinational undergoing radical restructuring)? Who monitors the mentor's performance? It may be that having a mentor assists the expatriate adjust during the foreign assignment but, by itself, does not necessarily help in re-entry. Stroh[57] concludes that her study "did not show that having a mentoring program would make an independent contribution to repatriate retention rate," although there was a suggested link between assignment of a mentor, career development, and repatriate retention. In other words, an effective mentor is likely to alert the firm of the eminent return of the repatriate and thus affect the re-entry position, or the practice is part of a managed repatriation program.

An interesting finding of the Price Waterhouse survey is that, where a mentoring system is in place, there has been a significant increase in the number of firms that clearly define mentor duties (69 percent in contrast to 46 percent in 1995). The duties reported include:

- Maintaining contact with the expatriate throughout the assignment;
- Ensuring expatriates are kept up-to-date with developments in the home country;
- Ensuring expatriates are retained in existing management development programs; and
- Assisting expatriates with the repatriation process, including helping them with a repatriation position.

The survey, however, does not report how these mentors were monitored.[58]

Concluding Remarks

This chapter has been concerned with the repatriation process. One may conclude that in re-entry readjustment, the broader sociocultural context of the home country takes a backstage position—unlike in the expatriation adjustment phase, where the foreign culture can be overwhelming.[59] Cultural novelty has been found to affect adjustment and, for the majority of repatriates, coming home to the familiar culture may assist in readjustment. Gregersen,[60] for example, argues that expatriates with more extensive international experience, in more significantly different cultures, are the group most likely to experience reverse culture shock. Indeed, given the more profound effect that job-related factors appear to have, **re-entry shock** is perhaps a more accurate term to describe the readjustment process experienced upon repatriation.

It is evident that the way the multinational handles repatriation has an impact on staff availability for international assignments. Re-entry positions signal the importance given to international experience. If the repatriate is promoted or given a position that obviously capitalizes on international experience, other members of the multinational interpret international assignments as a positive career move. On the other hand, if the multinational does not reward expatriate performance, tolerates high turnover among repatriates, or is seen to terminate a repatriate's employment on re-entry, it sends a clear message—its workforce may interpret the acceptance of an international assignment as a high-risk decision in terms of future career progression within the organization. The multinational's ability to attract high-caliber staff for international assignments is thereby lessened and can have a long-term negative effect on its activities.

Viewing repatriation as part of the expatriation process, as suggested in Exhibit 7–1, should remind those responsible for expatriation management of the need to prepare repatriates for re-entry. While recognition of the importance of repatriation programs is increasing, and companies are experimenting with other measures such as mentors, other avenues could be explored (e.g., using repatriates as an important information source). Inviting repatriates to assist in developing repatriation programs may contribute to relevant and effective policies. It may also have a desirable side-effect upon readjustment, simply by giving participants a sense that they are not an underutilized resource, and that the firm recognizes they can make a valuable contribution to the expatriation process. Conway[61] makes a further point that the trend towards using external consultants to handle relocation may preclude the multinational from obtaining relevant feedback, particularly from repatriates. It is, naturally, important that wherever possible the multinational ensures equity of treatment between PCNs, TCNs, and HCNs.

While the focus of this chapter has been repatriation in the general sense, the issue of career expatriates should be raised. The repatriation literature reviewed in preparation for this chapter makes little mention of the process of managing the return of those who have worked outside their home countries for lengthy periods of time. For this strategically important group of employees, at some point repatriation may coincide with retirement. One is left with the impression that those who return to retire in their home country are no longer of concern to their firms. However, one could expect that these individuals would require special counseling to assist not only the transition back to the home country, but from work to retirement as well.

QUESTIONS

1. What factors contribute to re-entry shock?
2. How can multinationals assist dual-career couples' repatriation?
3. What are the elements of a good mentoring system?
4. What aspects would you include in a pre-repatriation program?
5. Discuss the case presented in Exhibit 7–5. What steps should the HR department concerned have taken to assist in John's repatriation?

FURTHER READING

1. Black, J.S., H.B. Gregersen, and M.E. Mendenhall, 1992. Toward a theoretical framework of repatriation adjustment, *Journal of International Business*, vol. 23, no. 4, pp. 737–760.
2. Enloe, W., and P. Lewin, 1987. Issues of integration abroad and readjustment to Japan of Japanese returnees, *International Journal of Intercultural Relations*, vol. 11, pp. 223–248.
3. Hammer, M.R., W. Hart, and Randall Rogan, 1998. Can you go home again? An analysis of the repatriation of corporate managers and spouses, *Management International Review*, vol. 38, no. 1, pp. 67–86.

4. Harvey, M.G., 1989. Repatriation of corporate executives: An empirical study, *Journal of International Business Studies*, vol. 20, no. 1, pp. 131–144.
5. Peltonen, T., 1997. Facing the rankings from the past: A tournament perspective on repatriate career mobility, *International Journal of Human Resource Management*, vol. 8, no. 1, pp. 106–123.
6. Stroh, L.K., 1995. Predicting turnover among repatriates: Can organizations affect retention rates? *International Journal of Human Resource Management*, vol. 6, no. 2, pp. 443–456.

ENDNOTES

1. M. Conway, 1984. Reducing expatriate failure rates, *Personnel Administrator*, vol. 29, no. 7, pp. 31–38; R. Moran, 1989. Coping with re-entry shock, *International Management*, December, p. 67; M.G. Harvey, 1989. Repatriation of corporate executives: An empirical study, *Journal of International Business Studies*, vol. 20, no. 1, Spring, pp. 131–144.
2. D. Welch, 1994. Determinants of international human resource management approaches and activities: A suggested framework, *Journal of Management Studies*, vol. 31, no. 2, pp. 139–164; Harvey, Repatriation of corporate executives.
3. Harvey, Repatriation of corporate executives.
4. N. Forster, 1994. The forgotten employees? The experiences of expatriate staff returning to the UK, *International Journal of Human Resource Management*, vol. 5, no. 2, p. 408.
5. D. Welch, T. Adams, B. Betchley, and M. Howard, 1992. The view from the other side: The handling of repatriation and other expatriation activities by the Royal Australian Airforce, in *Proceedings of the AIR Southeast Asia Conference*, O. Yau, and B. Stening, eds. June, Brisbane.
6. A.W. Harzing, 1996. *Environment, Strategy, Structure, Control Mechanisms, and Human Resource Management in Multinational Companies*, Company Report: University of Limburg.
7. R.L. Tung, and Arthur Andersen, 1997. *Exploring International Assignees' Viewpoints: A Study of the Expatriation/Repatriation Process*, Chicago, IL: Arthur Andersen, International Executive Services; D. Welch, 1997. Expatriation and career development in the changing global workscape, Paper presented at the 23rd Annual

EIBA Conference, December, Stuttgart; D.C. Feldman, and D.C. Thomas, 1992. Career issues facing expatriate managers, *Journal of International Business Studies*, vol. 23, no. 2, pp. 271–294.

8. Harzing, *Environment, Strategy, Structure, Control Mechanisms*; D. Osborn, 1997. The international mobility of French managers, *European Management Journal*, vol. 15, no. 5, pp. 584–590.

9. Harzing, *Environment, Strategy, Structure, Control Mechanisms*.

10. D.E. Welch, 1990. The personnel variable in international operations: A study of expatriate management in Australian companies, unpublished Ph.D. thesis, Monash University, Australia; S. Black, and H.B. Gregersen, 1991. When Yankee comes home: Factors related to expatriate and spouse repatriation adjustment, *Journal of International Business Studies*, vol. 22, no. 4, pp. 671–694. See also N.K. Napier, and R.B. Peterson, 1991. Expatriate re-entry: What do expatriates have to say?, *Human Resource Planning*, vol. 14, no. 1, pp. 19–28.

11. Feldman, and Thomas, Career issues facing expatriate managers.

12. The Conference Board, 1997. *Managing Expatriates' Return: A Research Report*, New York: Report No. 1148-96-RR, p. 16.

13. Tung, and Arthur Andersen, *Exploring International Assignees' Viewpoints*.

14. E. Marx, 1996. *International Human Resource Practices in Britain and Germany*, London: Anglo-German Foundation for the Study of Industrial Society.

15. Price Waterhouse Europe, 1997. International assignments: European policy and practice, Price Waterhouse International Assignment Services Europe.

16. Welch, Determinants of international human resource management. See also N.J. Adler, 1997. *International Dimensions of Organizational Behavior*, 3rd ed. Cincinnati, OH: South-Western.

17. Marx, *International Human Resource Practices in Britain and Germany*.

18. J.E. Beck, 1988. Expatriate management development: Realizing the learning potential of the overseas assignment, in *Best Papers Proceedings, Academy of Management 48th Annual Meeting*, F. Hoy, ed. August, Anaheim, CA, pp. 112–116; R.L. Tung, 1988. Career issues in international assignments, *Academy of Management Executive*, vol. 2, no. 3, pp. 241–244; and H.B. Gregersen, 1992. Commitments to a parent company and a local work unit during repatriation, *Personnel Psychology*, vol. 45, no. 1, Spring, pp. 29–54.

19. Welch, Determinants of international human resource management, p. 148.
20. A.J. Jensen, and J. Attunes, 1996. International human resource management in Norwegian companies, Siviløkonom thesis, Norwegian School of Management, Oslo, p. 92.
21. Moran, Coping with re-entry shock; R.L. Tung, and E.L. Miller, 1990. Managing in the twenty-first century: The need for global orientation, *Management International Review*, vol. 30, no. 1, pp. 5–18; and Adler, *International Dimensions of Organizational Behavior.*
22. Tung, Career issues in international assignments. The devaluing of the international experience may be explained by the fact that U.S. companies tend to focus more readily on the domestic market, while companies operating from countries with smaller domestic markets must rely more heavily on international markets for revenue. (I. Björkman, and M. Gersten, 1993. Selecting and training Scandinavian expatriates: Determinants of corporate practice, *Scandinavian Journal of Management*, vol. 9, no. 2, pp.145–161.) It should also be noted that, while this might be the case for multinationals, a Finnish study of 180 repatriates from international assignments involving government-sponsored foreign aid projects found that, for 63 percent of respondents, the period abroad had a neutral affect on their careers. T. Peltonen, 1992. A study of the foreign development assignments immediate impact on professional careers, Master's thesis, Helsinki School of Economics and Business Administration, February, Helsinki, Finland.
23. L.K. Stroh, 1995. Predicting turnover among repatriates: Can organizations affect retention rates?, *International Journal of Human Resource Management*, vol. 6, no. 2, p. 450.
24. J.S. Black, H.B. Gregersen, and M.E. Mendenhall, 1992. Toward a theoretical framework of repatriation adjustment, *Journal of International Business*, vol. 23, no. 4, pp. 737–760.
25. Welch, Expatriation and career development.
26. L. Gomez-Mejia, and D.B. Balkin, 1987. The determinants of managerial satisfaction with the expatriation and repatriation process, *Journal of Management Development*, vol. 6, no. 1, pp. 7–17.
27. I. Torbiörn, 1985. The structure of managerial roles in cross-cultural settings, *International Studies of Management & Organization*, vol. 15, no. 1, p. 69.

28. Black, and Gregersen, When Yankee comes home, p. 688. In his separate study, Gregersen (Commitments to a parent company) found role clarity an important component of commitment to both the parent company and the local work unit after repatriation.

29. H.B. Gregersen, and J.S. Black, 1990. A multifaceted approach to expatriate retention in international assignments, *Group and Organization Studies*, vol. 15, no. 4, pp. 461–485; also Torbiörn, 1985.

30. H.B. Gregersen, 1992. Coming home to the Arctic cold: Finnish expatriate and spouse repatriation adjustment and work-related outcomes, Paper presented at the Academy of International Business Meeting, November, Brussels, p. 23.

31. C. Baughn, 1995. Personal and organizational factors associated with effective repatriation, in *Expatriate Management: New Ideas for International Business*, J. Selmar, ed. Westport CT: Quorum Books.

32. Black, Gregersen, and Mendenhall, Toward a theoretical framework of repatriation.

33. Forster, The forgotten employees?

34. Napier, and Peterson, Expatriate re-entry.

35. Black, and Gregersen, When Yankee comes home, p. 686; Baughn, Personal and organizational factors.

36. Harvey, Repatriation of corporate executives; and Stroh, Predicting turnover among repatriates.

37. Jensen, and Ottesen, International human resource management in Norwegian companies.

38. Welch, The personnel variable in international operations.

39. Conway, Reducing expatriate failure rates, p. 38.

40. Napier, and Petersen, Expatriate re-entry, p. 24.

41. Black, and Gregersen, When Yankee comes home.

42. H. De Cieri, P.J. Dowling, and K.F. Taylor, 1991. The psychological impact of expatriate relocation on partners, *International Journal of Human Resource Management*, vol. 2, no. 3, p. 403.

43. M.G. Harvey, 1982. The other side of foreign assignments: Dealing with the repatriation dilemma, *Columbia Journal of World Business*, vol. 17, no. 1, pp. 52–59; R. Savich, and W. Rodgers, 1988. Assignment overseas: Easing the transition before and after, *Personnel*, August, pp. 44–48.

44. Baughn, Personal and organizational factors associated with effective repatriation, p. 224.

45. W. Enloe, and P. Lewin, 1987. Issues of integration abroad and readjustment to Japan of Japanese returnees, *International Journal of Intercultural Relations*, vol. 11, pp. 223–248.
46. G.K. Stevens, and S. Black, 1991. The impact of spouse's career-orientation on managers during international transfers, *Journal of Management Studies*, vol. 28, no. 4, pp. 417–428.
47. Black, and Gregersen, When Yankee comes home.
48. The Conference Board, *Managing Expatriates' Return*, p. 40.
49. M.G. Harvey, 1997. Dual-career expatriates: Expectations, adjustment and satisfaction with international relocation, *Journal of International Business Studies*, vol. 28, no. 3, pp. 627–658.
50. This case was written by D. Welch and is based on a real incident. The names of the people concerned have been changed to respect confidentiality and preserve anonymity.
51. Mendenhall, Dunbar, and Oddou, 1987. Expatriate selection, training and career-pathing: A review and a critique, *Human Resource Planning*, vol. 26, no. 3, pp. 331–345.
52. Harvey, Repatriation of corporate executives, p. 135.
53. The Conference Board, p. 28.
54. Harvey, Repatriation of corporate executives, p. 140.
55. Black, and Gregersen, When Yankee comes home.
56. The Conference Board, *Managing Expatriates' Return*.
57. Stroh, Predicting turnover among repatriates, p. 454.
58. Price Waterhouse Europe, International assignments, p. 32.
59. Black, and Gregersen, When Yankee comes home.
60. Gregersen, Commitments to a parent company.
61. Conway, Reducing expatriate failure rates.

C H A P T E R   8

*Labor Relations**

B efore we examine the key issues in labor relations as they relate to multinational firms, we need to consider some general points about the field of international labor relations.[1] First, it is important to realize that it is difficult to compare industrial relations systems and behavior across national boundaries; a labor relations concept may change considerably when translated from one industrial relations context to another.[2] The concept of collective bargaining, for example, in the United States is understood to mean negotiations between a labor union local and management; in Sweden and Germany the term refers to negotiations between an employers' organization and a trade union at the industry level. Crossnational differences also emerge as to the objectives of the collective bargaining process and the enforceability of collective agreements. Many European unions view the collective bargaining process as an ongoing class struggle between labor and capital, whereas in the United States union leaders tend toward a pragmatic economic view of collective bargaining rather than an ideological view. Second, it is generally recognized in the international labor relations field that no industrial relations system can be understood without an appreciation of its historical origin.[3] As Schregle[4] has observed,

*The significant contribution of Dr. Helen De Cieri (University of Melbourne, Australia) to the writing of this chapter is gratefully acknowledged.

A comparative study of industrial relations shows that industrial relations phenomena are a very faithful expression of the society in which they operate, of its characteristic features and of the power relationships between different interest groups. Industrial relations cannot be understood without an understanding of the way in which rules are established and implemented and decisions are made in the society concerned.

An interesting example of the effect of historical differences may be seen in the structure of trade unions in various countries. Poole[5] has identified several factors that may underlie these historical differences:

- The mode of technology and industrial organization at critical stages of union development;
- Methods of union regulation by government;
- Ideological divisions within the trade union movement;
- The influence of religious organizations on trade union development; and
- Managerial strategies for labor relations in large corporations.

As Exhibit 8–1 shows, union structures differ considerably among Western countries. These include industrial unions, which represent all

EXHIBIT 8–1   *Trade Union Structure in Leading Western Industrial Societies*

Australia	general, craft, industrial, white-collar
Belgium	industrial, professional, religious, public sector
Canada	industrial, craft, conglomerate
Denmark	general, craft, white-collar
Finland	industrial, white-collar, professional and technical
Great Britain	general, craft, industrial, white-collar, public sector
Japan	enterprise
The Netherlands	religious, conglomerate, white-collar
Norway	industrial, craft
Sweden	industrial, craft, white-collar and professional
Switzerland	industrial, craft, religious, white-collar
United States	industrial, craft, conglomerate, white-collar
West Germany	industrial, white-collar

Source: M. Poole, 1986. *Industrial Relations: Origins and Patterns of National Diversity*, London: Routledge & Kegan Paul, p. 79. Reprinted with permission.

grades of employees in an industry; craft unions, which are based on skilled occupational groupings across industries; conglomerate unions, which represent members in more than one industry; and general unions, which are open to almost all employees in a given country. These differences in union structures have had a major influence on the collective bargaining process in Western countries. Some changes in union structure are evident over time; for example, enterprise unions are increasingly evident in industrialized nations. Enterprise unions are common in Asia-Pacific nations, although there are national variations in their functions, and in the proportion of enterprise unions to total unions.[6]

The less one knows about how a structure came to develop in a distinctive way, the less likely one is to understand it. As Prahalad and Doz[7] note, the lack of familiarity of multinational managers with local industrial and political conditions has sometimes needlessly worsened a conflict that a local firm would have been likely to resolve.[8] Increasingly, multinationals are recognizing this shortcoming and admitting that industrial relations policies must be flexible enough to adapt to local requirements. This is evidently an enduring approach, even in firms that follow a nonunion labor relations strategy where possible, as Exhibit 8–2 points out.

KEY ISSUES IN INTERNATIONAL LABOR RELATIONS

The focus of this chapter is on the labor relations strategies adopted by multinationals rather than the more general topic of comparative labor relations.[9] A central question for labor relations in an international context is that of the orientation of multinational firms to organized labor.

Labor Relations Policies and Practices of Multinational Firms

Because national differences in economic, political, and legal systems produce markedly different labor relations systems across countries, multinationals generally delegate the management of labor relations to their foreign subsidiaries. However, a policy of decentralization does not keep corporate headquarters from exercising some coordination over labor relations strategy. Generally, corporate headquarters will become involved in or oversee labor agreements made by foreign subsidiaries because these agreements may affect the international plans of the firm

EXHIBIT 8-2   *IHR in the News*

Advice for Companies Going Global

The key to successfully expanding overseas is to become one with the culture of the location, even if it means unionization of employees, Michael R. Quinlan, chairman and chief executive officer of McDonald's Corp., tells conferees at a meeting of the Human Resources Management Association of Chicago.

After opening fast-food restaurants in 53 nations, McDonald's has learned that it must follow the established practices of a foreign country to succeed there, Quinlan says. For example, a number of European countries and Australia have very strict unionization standards, and operations there are unionized as a condition of doing business. Acknowledging that McDonald's has had some "horrible union fights around the world," Quinlan advises employers considering expansion into other nations to "do it their way, not your way."

The main implication of dealing with unions is the increased cost of wages and benefits, according to Quinlan. Still, he adds that he does not feel unionization has interfered with employees' loyalty to McDonald's, or to the company's philosophy of service and employee motivation. Declaring that unions do not "bring much to the equation" of the employee/employer relationship, Quinlan says McDonald's is "basically a nonunion company" and intends to stay that way.

Another source of difficulty for McDonald's in its expansion overseas lies in the fact that fast-food restaurants are unfamiliar in most nations. Opening the first McDonald's inside the Communist-bloc, in Yugoslavia, took 12 years, Quinlan notes. He also points out that the company's policy is to staff its restaurants, from crew through management, only with nationals—for the 3,300 foreign outlets, the corporation employs only 35 expatriate U.S. citizens, and its goal is to have 100 percent local employees within five years.

Source: Reprinted with permission from Bulletin to Management (BNA Policy and Practice Series), Vol. 42, pp. 66, 71 (March 7, 1991). Copyright 1991 by The Bureau of National Affairs, Inc. (800-372-1033) <http://www.bna.com>

and/or create precedents for negotiations in other countries. Further, Marginson, Armstrong, Edwards, and Purcell[10] found that the majority of the firms in their study monitored labor performance across units in different countries. Comparison of performance data across national units of the firm creates the potential for decisions on issues such as unit location, capital investment, and rationalization of production capacity.

The use of comparisons would be expected to be greatest where units in different countries undertake similar operations.

Much of the literature on the labor relations practices of multinationals tends to be at a more cross-national or comparative level. There is, however, some research on labor relations practices at the firm level. Empirical research has identified a number of differences in multinational approaches to labor relations. For example, a series of studies by Hamill[11] found that U.S. firms were less likely than their British counterparts to recognize trade unions, preferred not to join employer associations, had more highly developed and specialized personnel departments at plant level, and tended to pay higher wages and offer more generous employee fringe benefits than local firms. Marginson, Armstrong, Edwards, and Purcell investigated the potential consequences of firm strategies for the management of labor, using a 1992 survey of multinationals operating in Britain.[12] They found a tendency for strategic decisions that affect the interests of employees to be made beyond national jurisdictions. Indeed, a number of studies have examined differences in the propensity of multinational headquarters to intervene in, or to centralize control over, matters such as industrial relations in host locations. Multinational headquarters involvement in labor relations is influenced by several factors, as detailed below.

The Degree of Inter-Subsidiary Production Integration. According to Hamill,[13] a high degree of integration was found to be the most important factor leading to the centralization of the labor relations function within the firms studied. Labor relations throughout a system become of direct importance to corporate headquarters when transnational sourcing patterns have been developed; that is, when a subsidiary in one country relies on another foreign subsidiary as a source of components or as a user of its output.[14] In this context, a coordinated labor relations policy is one of the key factors in a successful global production strategy.[15] One example of the development of an international policy for labor relations can be seen in the introduction of employee involvement across Ford's operations.[16]

Nationality of Ownership of the Subsidiary. There is evidence of differences between European and U.S. firms in terms of headquarters involvement in labor relations.[17] A number of studies have revealed that U.S. firms tend to exercise greater centralized control over labor relations than do British or other European firms.[18] U.S. firms tend to place greater emphasis on formal management controls and a close reporting system (particularly within the area of financial control) to ensure that planning targets are met. In his review of empirical research of this area, Bean[19] showed that foreign-owned multinationals in Britain prefer single-employer bargaining (rather than involving an employer association), and are more likely than British firms to assert managerial prerogative on matters of labor utilization. Further, Hamill[20] found U.S.-owned subsidiaries to be much more centralized in labor relations decision making than British-owned. Hamill attributed this difference in management procedures to the more integrated nature of U.S. firms, the greater divergence between British and U.S. labor relations systems than between British and other European systems, and the more ethnocentric managerial style of U.S. firms.

International Human Resource Management Approach. In Chapters 2 and 3, we discussed the various international human resource management approaches utilized by multinationals; these have implications for international labor relations. Interestingly, an ethnocentric predisposition is more likely to be associated with various forms of labor relations conflict.[21] Conversely, it has been shown that more geocentric firms will bear more influence on host-country industrial relations systems, due to their greater propensity to participate in local events.[22]

MNE Prior Experience in Labor Relations. European firms have tended to deal with labor unions at industry level (frequently via employer associations) rather than at firm level. The opposite is more typical for U.S. firms. In the United States, employer associations have not played a key role in the industrial relations system, and firm-based labor relations policies are the norm.[23]

Subsidiary Characteristics. Research has identified a number of subsidiary characteristics to be relevant to centralization of labor relations. First, subsidiaries that are formed through acquisition of well-established indigenous firms tend to be given much more autonomy over labor relations than are greenfield sites set up by a multinational firm.[24] Second, according to Enderwick, greater intervention would be expected when the subsidiary is of key strategic importance to the firm and the subsidiary is young.[25] Third, where the parent firm is a significant source of operating or investment funds for the subsidiary, that is, where the subsidiary is more dependent on headquarters for resources, there will tend to be increased corporate involvement in labor relations and human resource management.[26] Finally, poor subsidiary performance tends to be accompanied by increased corporate involvement in labor relations. Where poor performance is due to labor relations problems, multinationals tend to attempt to introduce parent-country labor relations practices aimed at reducing industrial unrest or increasing productivity.[27]

Characteristics of the Home Product Market. An important factor is the extent of the home product market (discussed in some depth in Chapter 1).[28] If domestic sales are large relative to overseas operations (as is the case with many U.S. firms), it is more likely that overseas operations will be regarded by the parent firm as an extension of domestic operations. This is not the case for many European firms, whose international operations represent the major part of their business. Lack of a large home market is a strong incentive to adapt to host-country institutions and norms. There is evidence of recent change in the European context: Since the implementation of the Single European Market in 1993, there has been growth in large European-scale companies (formed via acquisition or joint ventures) that centralize management organization and strategic decision making. However, processes of operational decentralization with regard to labor relations are also evident.[29]

Management Attitudes Towards Unions. An additional important factor is that of management attitudes or ideology concerning unions.[30] Knowledge of management attitudes concerning unions may provide a more complete explanation of multinational labor relations behavior than could be obtained by relying solely on a rational economic model. Thus, management attitudes should also be considered in any explanation of managerial behavior along with such factors as market forces and strategic choices. This is of particular relevance to U.S. firms, since union avoidance appears to be deeply rooted in the value systems of American managers.[31]

As Exhibit 8–3 shows, the United States has one of the lowest union-density rates (the percentage of wage and salary employees who are union members) in the Western world. Hence, U.S. managers are less likely to have extensive experience with unions than managers in many other countries. Worldwide trade union membership has fallen over the past decade, although the decline is not universal. This decline in union density in many countries may be explained by economic factors such as

EXHIBIT 8–3   *Union Membership for Selected Countries*

	Union density		Proportionate changes in union density (%)	Rank order of union density[c]	
	1985	1995	1985–95	1985	1995
Australia[d]	46	33	−28	2	4
Canada[e]	35	35	0	6	3
France[d]	15	11	−27	9	10
Germany[e]	36[a]	30	−16	5	5
Italy[d,e]	42	38	−10	4	2
Japan[d,e]	29	24	−18	7	7
Korea[f]	12	13	+8.3	10	9
Sweden[d]	85	83	−2.2	1	1
UK[d]	45	29	−35	3	6
USA[g]	18	15[b]	−12	8	8

Notes: a   1991.
      b   1993.
      c   Rank order of union density of the ten countries listed.
      d   Replies by governments.
      e   Replies by workers' organizations.
      f   Replies from Korea Labour Statistics Department.
      g   Adjusted density rate.

Source: ILO unpublished data (1996); Australia ABS Cat. No. 6325.0
Korea NSO

Source: G.J. Bamber, P. Ross, and G. Whitehouse, 1998. Employment relations and labour market indicators in ten industrialised market economies: Comparative statistics, *International Journal of Human Resource Management*, vol. 9, no. 2, Table 14. Reprinted with kind permission of the editor.

reduced public sector employment, reduced employment in manufacturing industries as a share in total employment, and increased competition; it is also suggested to be associated with decentralization of labor relations to business unit level, changes in governance, and legislative changes. For example, the sharpest drop in union density (almost 36 percent over the past decade) has been in central and eastern Europe, and may be explained by political and economic changes associated with the dissolution of the Soviet bloc and the end of compulsory union membership. Union membership decline is also linked to the introduction of new forms of work organization, globalization of production, and changes in workforce structure.[32]

Although there are several problems inherent in data collection for a crossnational comparison of union-density rates, several theories have been suggested to explain the variations among countries. Such theories consider economic factors such as wages, prices, and unemployment levels; social factors such as public support for unions; and political factors. In addition, studies indicate that the strategies utilized by labor, management, and governments are particularly important.[33]

Another key issue in international labor relations is industrial disputes. Hamill[34] examined strike-proneness of multinational subsidiaries and indigenous firms in Britain across three industries. Strike-proneness was measured via three variables—strike frequency, strike size, and strike duration. There was no difference across the two groups of firms with regard to strike frequency, but multinational subsidiaries did experience larger and longer strikes than local firms. Hamill suggests that this difference indicates that foreign-owned firms may be under less financial pressure to settle a strike quickly than local firms—possibly because they can switch production out of the country.

Overall, it is evident that international labor relations are influenced by a broad range of factors. Commenting on the overall results of his research, Hamill[35] concluded that:

> general statements cannot be applied to the organization of the labor relations function within MNCs. Rather, different MNCs adopt different labor relations strategies in relation to the environmental factors peculiar to each firm. In other words, it is the type of multinational under consideration which is important rather than multinationality itself.

LABOR UNIONS AND INTERNATIONAL LABOR RELATIONS

Labor unions may limit the strategic choices of multinationals in three ways: by influencing wage levels to the extent that cost structures may become uncompetitive, by constraining the ability of multinationals to vary employment levels at will, and by hindering or preventing global integration of the operations of multinationals.[36] We shall briefly examine each of these potential constraints.

Influencing Wage Levels

Although the importance of labor costs relative to other costs is decreasing, labor costs still play an important part in determining cost competitiveness in most industries. The influence of unions on wage levels is, therefore, important. Multinationals that fail to successfully manage their wage levels will suffer labor cost disadvantages that may narrow their strategic options.

Constraining the Ability of Multinationals to Vary Employment Levels at Will

For many multinationals operating in Western Europe, Japan, and Australia, the inability to vary employment levels at will may be a more serious problem than wage levels. Many countries now have legislation that limits considerably the ability of firms to carry out plant closure, redundancy, or layoff programs unless it can be shown that structural conditions make these employment losses unavoidable. Frequently, the process of showing the need for these programs is long and drawn-out. Plant closure or redundancy legislation in many countries also frequently specifies that firms must compensate redundant employees through specified formulae such as two weeks' pay for each year of service. In many countries, payments for involuntary terminations are rather substantial, especially in comparison to those in the United States.

Labor unions may influence this process in two ways: by lobbying their own national governments to introduce redundancy legislation, and by encouraging regulation of multinationals by international organizations such as the Organization for Economic Cooperation and Development (OECD). (Later in this chapter we describe the *Badger* case, which forced Raytheon to finally accept responsibility for severance payments to employees made redundant by the closing down of its Belgian subsidiary.) Multinational managers who do not take these restrictions into account in their strategic planning may well find their options severely limited. In fact, recent evidence shows that multinationals are beginning to consider the ability to dismiss employees to be one of the priorities when making investment location decisions.[37]

Hindering or Preventing Global Integration of the Operations of Multinationals

In recognition of these constraints, many multinationals make a conscious decision not to integrate and rationalize their operations to the most efficient degree, because to do so could cause industrial and political problems. Prahalad and Doz[38] cite General Motors as an example of this "suboptimization of integration." GM was alleged in the early 1980s to have undertaken substantial investments in Germany (matching its new investments in Austria and Spain) at the demand of the German metalworkers' union (one of the largest industrial unions in the Western world) in order to foster good labor relations in Germany. One observer of the world auto industry suggested that car manufacturers were suboptimizing their manufacturing networks partly to placate trade unions and partly to provide redundancy in sources to prevent localized social strife from paralyzing their network. This suboptimization led to unit manufacturing costs in Europe that were 15 percent higher, on average, than an economically optimal network would have achieved. Prahalad and Doz drew the following conclusion from this example:[39]

> Union influence thus not only delays the rationalization and integration of MNCs' manufacturing networks and increases the cost of such adjustments (not so much in the visible severance payments and 'golden handshake' provisions as through the economic losses incurred in the meantime), but also, at least in such industries as automobiles, permanently reduces the efficiency of the integrated MNC network. Therefore, treating labor relations as incidental and relegating them to the specialists in the various countries is inappropriate. In the same way as government policies need to be integrated into strategic choices, so do labor relations.

THE RESPONSE OF LABOR UNIONS TO MULTINATIONALS

Labor union leaders have long seen the growth of multinationals as a threat to the bargaining power of labor because of the considerable power and influence of large multinational firms. While it is recognized that multinationals are "neither uniformly anti-union nor omnipotent and monolithic bureaucracies,"[40] their potential for lobbying power and flexibility across national borders creates difficulties for employees and trade unions endeavoring to develop countervailing power. There are several ways in which multinationals have an impact on trade union and employee interests. Kennedy[41] has identified the following seven characteristics of MNEs as the source of labor unions' concern about multinationals:

- *Formidable financial resources.* This includes the ability to absorb losses in a particular foreign subsidiary that is in dispute with a national union and still show an overall profit on worldwide operations. Union bargaining power may be threatened or weakened by the broader financial resources of a multinational. This is particularly evident where a multinational has adopted a practice of transnational sourcing and cross-subsidization of products or components across different countries. "The economic pressure which a nationally based union can exert upon a multinational is certainly less than would be the case if the company's operations were confined to one country."[42]
- *Alternative sources of supply.* This may take the form of an explicit "dual sourcing" policy to reduce the vulnerability of the multinational to a strike by any national union. Also, temporary switching of production in order to defeat industrial action has been utilized to some extent, for example, in the automotive industry.[43]
- *The ability to move production facilities to other countries.* A reported concern of employees and trade unions is that job security may be threatened if a multinational seeks to produce abroad what could have, or previously has, been manufactured domestically. National relative advantages provide MNEs with choice as to location of units. Within the EU, for example, evidence suggests that multinational management are locating skill-intensive activities in countries with national policies promoting training and with relatively high labor costs. Conversely, semi-skilled, routine activities are being located in countries with lower labor costs.[44] Threats by multinationals, whether real or perceived, to reorganize production factors internationally, with the accompanying risk of plant closure or rationalization, will have an impact on management–labor negotiations at a national level. However, technical and economic investments would reduce a multinational's propensity to relocate facilities.
- *A remote locus of authority* (i.e., the corporate head-office management of a multinational firm). While many multinationals report decentralization and local responsiveness of HRM and industrial relations, trade unions and works councils have reported that the multinational decision-making structure is opaque and the division of authority obscured. Further, employee representatives may not be adequately aware of the overall MNE organizational strategy and activities.[45]
- *Production facilities in many industries.* As Vernon[46] has noted, most multinationals operate in many product lines.

- *Superior knowledge and expertise in labor relations.*
- *The capacity to stage an "investment strike,"* whereby the multinational refuses to invest any additional funds in a plant, thus ensuring that the plant will become obsolete and economically noncompetitive.

Another issue reported by labor unions is their claim that they have difficulty accessing decision makers located outside the host country and obtaining financial information. For example, according to Martinez Lucio and Weston:

> Misinformation has been central to the management strategy of using potential investment or disinvestment in seeking changes in certain organizations... For example, in companies such as Heinz, Ford, Gillette, and General Motors, workers have established that they had on occasions been misinformed by management as to the nature of working practices in other plants.[47]

The response of labor unions to multinationals has been threefold: to form international trade secretariats (ITSs), to lobby for restrictive national legislation, and finally, to try and achieve regulation of multinationals by international organizations.

International Trade Secretariats (ITSs). There are 15 ITSs, which function as loose confederations to provide worldwide links for the national unions in a particular trade or industry (e.g., metals, transport, and chemicals). The secretariats have mainly operated to facilitate the exchange of information.[48] One of the fastest growing of the ITSs is the International Federation of Commercial, Clerical, Professional, and Technical Employees (generally known by its French initials, FIET), which is focused on the service sector.[49] The long-term goal of each ITS is to achieve transnational bargaining with each of the multinationals in its industry. Each ITS has followed a similar program to achieve the goal of transnational bargaining.[50] The elements of this program are (1) research and information, (2) calling company conferences, (3) establishing company councils, (4) companywide union-management discussions, and (5) coordinated bargaining. Overall, the ITSs have met with limited success, the reasons for which Northrup[51] attributes to (1) the generally good wages and working conditions offered by multinationals, (2) strong resistance from multinational firm management, (3) conflicts within the labor movement, and (4) differing laws and customs in the labor relations area.

Lobbying for Restrictive National Legislation. On a political level, labor unions have for many years lobbied for restrictive national legislation in the United States and Europe. The motivation for labor unions to pursue restrictive national legislation is based on a desire to prevent the export of jobs via multinational investment policies. For example, in the United States, the AFL-CIO has lobbied strongly in this area.[52] A major difficulty for unions when pursuing this strategy is the reality of conflicting national economic interests. In times of economic downturn, this factor may become an insurmountable barrier for trade union officials. To date, these attempts have been largely unsuccessful and, with the increasing internationalization of business, it is difficult to see how governments will be persuaded to legislate in this area.

Regulation of Multinationals by International Organizations. Attempts by labor unions to exert influence over multinationals via international organizations have met with some success. Through trade union federations such as the European Trade Union Confederation (ETUC) and the International Confederation of Free Trade Unions (ICFTU), the labor movement has been able to lobby the International Labor Organization (ILO), the United Nations Conference on Trade and Development (UNCTAD),[53] the Organization for Economic Cooperation and Development (OECD), and the European Union (EU). The ILO has identified a number of workplace-related principles that should be respected by all nations: freedom of association, the right to organize and collectively bargain, abolition of forced labor, and nondiscrimination in employment. In 1977 the ILO adopted a code of conduct for multinationals (Tripartite Declaration of Principles Concerning MNEs and Social Policy).[54] The ILO code of conduct, which was originally proposed in 1975, was influential in the drafting of the OECD guidelines for multinationals, which were approved in 1976. These voluntary guidelines cover disclosure of information, competition, financing, taxation, employment and industrial relations, and science and technology.[55]

A key section of these guidelines is the *umbrella* or *chapeau clause*, (the latter is the more common term in the literature) that precedes the guidelines themselves. This clause states that multinationals should adhere to the guidelines "within the framework of law, regulations and prevailing labor relations and employment practices, in each of the countries in which they operate." Campbell and Rowan[56] state that employers have understood the chapeau clause to mean compliance with local law supersedes the guidelines, while labor unions have interpreted this clause to mean that the guidelines are a "supplement" to national law. The implication of this latter interpretation is significant: a firm could still be in violation of the OECD guidelines even though its activities have complied with national law and practice. Given the ambiguity of the chapeau clause and the fact that the OECD guidelines are voluntary, it is likely that this issue will remain controversial.

There is also some controversy in the literature as to the effectiveness of the OECD guidelines in regulating multinational behavior.[57] This lack of agreement centers on assessments of the various challenges to the guidelines. The best-known of these challenges is the *Badger* case. The Badger Company is a subsidiary of Raytheon, a U.S.-based multinational. In 1976 the Badger Company decided to close its Belgian subsidiary, and a dispute arose concerning termination payments.[58] Since Badger (Belgium) NV had filed for bankruptcy, the Belgian labor unions argued that Raytheon should assume the subsidiary's financial obligations. Raytheon refused, and the case was brought before the OECD by the Belgian government and the International Federation of Commercial, Clerical, Professional, and Technical Employees (FIET), an international trade secretariat. The Committee on International Investments and MNEs (CIIME) of the OECD indicated that paragraph six of the guidelines (concerned with plant closures) implied a "shared responsibility" by the subsidiary and the parent in the event of a plant closing. Following this clarification by the CIIME and a scaling down of initial demands, Badger executives and Belgian government officials negotiated a settlement of this case.

Blanpain[59] concludes that the *Badger* case made clear the responsibility of the parent company for the financial liability of its subsidiary, but that this responsibility is not unqualified. As to whether the *Badger* case proved the "effectiveness" of the OECD guidelines, Jain[60] and Campbell and Rowan[61] point out that the Belgian unions devoted considerable resources to make this a test case and had assistance from both American unions (which, through the AFL-CIO, lobbied the U.S. Department of State) and the Belgian government in their negotiations with the OECD and Badger executives. Liebhaberg[62] is more specific in his assessment:

Despite an outcome which those in favor of supervision consider to be positive, the Badger Case is a clear demonstration of one of the weaknesses in the OECD's instrument, namely that it does not represent any sort of formal undertaking on the part of the twenty-four member states which are signatories to it. The social forces of each separate country must apply pressure on their respective governments if they want the guidelines applied.

Recognizing the limitations of voluntary codes of conduct, European labor unions have also lobbied the Commission of the European Union to regulate the activities of multinationals.[63] Unlike the OECD, The Commission of the EU can translate guidelines into law, and has developed a number of proposals concerning disclosure of information to make multinationals more "transparent."[64] These are discussed in more detail in the next section.

REGIONAL INTEGRATION: THE EUROPEAN UNION (EU)

Regional integration such as the development of the European Union (EU) has brought significant implications for international labor relations.[65] In the Treaty of Rome (1957), some consideration was given to social policy issues related to the creation of the European Community. In the EU, the terms "social policy," or "social dimension," are used to cover a number of issues including, in particular, labor law and working conditions, aspects of employment and vocational training, and social security. There have been a number of significant developments in EU social policy over the past four decades. The Social Charter of the Council of Europe came into effect in 1965. In 1987, the major objective of the implementation of the Single European Act was to establish the Single European Market (SEM) on December 31, 1992, in order to enhance the free movement of goods, money, and people within the SEM.[66] Hence, the social dimension aims to achieve a large labor market by eliminating the barriers that restrict the freedom of movement and the right of domicile within the SEM. The European Community Charter of the Fundamental Social Rights of Workers (often referred to simply as the Social Charter) was introduced in 1989, and has guided the development of social policy in the 1990s.[67] Naturally, the social dimension has been the subject of much debate—proponents defend the social dimension as a means of achieving social justice and equal treatment for EU citizens, while critics see it as a kind of social engineering.[68]

At the signing of the Treaty on European Union in Maastricht in February 1992, Britain was allowed to opt out of the social policy agreements. The other eleven member states were party to a protocol (The

Social Policy Protocol), which allows them to agree their own directives without Britain's participation.[69] With the election of the Blair Labor government in Britain in 1997, this anomaly was resolved when all members of the EU signed the Treaty of Amsterdam on June 17, 1997. This means that there now exists a single coherent legal basis for action by the EU Member States with regard to social policy.

The Social Chapter in the Treaty of Amsterdam opens with a general statement of objectives.[70] Its first Article (Article 117 of the EC Treaty), drawn largely from Article 1 of the Maastricht Social Agreement, begins with a reference to fundamental social rights such as those in the European Social Charter of 1961 and the Social Charter of 1989. It then sets out the objectives for the EU: to support and complement the activities of the Member States in a number of listed areas. These include improvement of working conditions and of the working environment in the interest of workers' health and safety, information and consultation of workers, integration of persons excluded from the labor market, and equality of opportunity, and at work, between men and women. However, the Treaty excludes matters of pay, the right of association, and the right to strike or to lock out.

The European Commission department responsible for social policy is known as Directorate-General V (often abbreviated to 'DG V'). Exhibit 8–4 summarizes the six directorates of DG V and the different areas of social policy covered by each directorate.

Disclosure of Information and European Works Councils

The EU has introduced a range of directives related to the social dimension. Of the directives concerned with multinationals, the most contentious has been the Vredeling directive (associated with Henk Vredeling, a former Dutch member of the EU Commission).[71] The Seventh (Vredeling) Directive's requirement of disclosure of company information to unions faced strong opposition led by the British government and employer representatives. They argued that employee involvement in consultation and decision making should be voluntary.

More recently, the European Works Councils (EWC) Directive was approved on September 22, 1994, and implemented two years later. Under the terms of the Treaty of Amsterdam, this directive applies to all EU member states. This is the first pan-European legislation that regulates collective relationships between multinationals and employees.

EXHIBIT 8-4   *The Six Directorates*

Introduction
Based in Brussels and Luxembourg DG V is the European Commission department responsible for social policy. It is made up of six directorates responsible for different areas of social policy.

Directorate General
Directorate A: is responsible for employment policies, labour market policies, employment services (EURES), and local development and readaption.

Directorate B: is responsible for policy development of the European Social Fund, information on the Fund, assessment of the political impact of the Fund, the Community Initiatives, technical assistance and innovation studies, and adaptation to industrial change.

Directorate C: is responsible for the operation of the European Social Fund in the Member States.

Directorate D: is responsible for relations with the social partners and organisation of the social dialogue, industrial relations and labour law, coordination of social security for migrant workers, migration policy and promotion of free movement for workers, equal opportunities for women and men, and family policy.

Directorate E: is responsible for analysis of and research on the social situation, social security and actions in the social field, and integration of disabled people. It also deals with external relations, international organisations, information and publications on behalf of the whole Directorate-General.

Directorate F: (based in Luxembourg) is responsible for analysis, coordination and development of policies and programmes in the field of public health, implementation of action programmes targeted on diseases, health promotion and disease surveillance, and health and safety at work. It also provides the permanent secretariat for the Advisory Committee of Safety, Hygiene and Health Protection at the Workplace.

Directorate G: is responsible for the management of human and financial resources for the Directorate-General, for audit and inspection, and evaluation.

Source: http://europa.eu.int/en/comm/dg05/staffgui/cover.htm

The directive requires EWCs to be established in multinationals with at least 1,000 employees, having 100 or more employees in each of two member states. According to Chesters, more than 1,000 multinationals, including around 200 U.S.-based firms, are affected by the

EWC directive.[72] The directive is designed to provide coverage to all employees, whether unionized or not. The EWC directive aims to enhance employees' rights to information and consultation in general, and provide rights to information regarding international corporate decisions that would significantly affect workers' interests.[73] Partly in response to the EWC directive, firms such as General Motors and Heinz have subsidized visits of worker representatives to other plants and provided information and forums for discussion at the European level.[74]

Obviously all firms will need to become familiar with EU directives and keep abreast of changes. While harmonization of labor laws can be seen as the ultimate objective, Michon[75] argues that the notion of a European social community does not mean a unification of all social conditions and benefits or, for that matter, of all social systems. However, the EU does aim to establish minimal standards for social conditions that will safeguard the fundamental rights of workers.

Social "Dumping"

One of the concerns related to the formation of the SEM was its impact on jobs. There was alarm that those member states that have relatively low social security costs would have a competitive edge and that firms would locate in those member states that have lower labor costs. The counter-alarm was that states with low-cost labor would have to increase their labor costs, to the detriment of their competitiveness.[76] There are two industrial relations issues here: the movement of work from one region to another and its effect on employment levels; and the need for trade union solidarity to prevent workers in one region from accepting pay cuts to attract investment at the expense of workers in another region. There is some, although not as much as was expected, evidence of "social dumping" in the EU.[77] It is likely that this issue will be a contentious one in Europe for some time and multinationals need to be aware of this debate when doing business in Europe.

REGIONAL INTEGRATION: THE NORTH AMERICAN FREE TRADE AGREEMENT (NAFTA)

Another important regional economic integration involves the formation of a free trade zone between the United States, Canada, and Mexico. The Canada–United States Free Trade Agreement (FTA) went into effect on January 1989, and a draft accord to create NAFTA, which brought

Mexico into the trading bloc, was announced in August 1992. The NAFTA agreement was signed by the governments of the United States, Mexico, and Canada in December 1992, ratified by the U.S. Congress in November 1993, and came into force in January 1994.[78] It is important to stress here that NAFTA differs from the Single European Market in that it is a free trade zone and not a common market. NAFTA deals only with the flow of goods, services, and investments among the three trading partners; it does not address labor mobility or other common policies of the SEM.[79] However, in an effort to manage the social dimension of NAFTA, the North American Agreement on Labor Cooperation (NAALC) came into effect in 1993. Although it has been criticized as weak and ineffective, this accord has introduced new institutions to process complaints of violations of labor laws, and committed each of the three nations to introduce a set of 11 labor rights principles.[80]

There are significant HR implications in NAFTA that must be considered by HR managers in North American firms. While NAFTA does not include workplace laws and their enforcement, as was discussed in the context of the SEM, the country with the least restrictive workplace laws will have a competitive advantage.

Organized labor in the United States and Canada responded to the passage of NAFTA with substantial opposition, based on fear of job losses due to the transfer of production to Mexico to take advantage of lower wage rates and lax enforcement of social and labor legislation.[81] In other words, the concern about social dumping is similar to the concern at the formation of the SEM, but there is a difference. In the case of NAFTA, jobs are able to cross borders, but workers are not.[82] Although there has been a general lack of coordination between labor organizations of the NAFTA countries, examples in telecommunications, trucking, and electrical industries show that NAFTA has stimulated some strategic crossborder collaboration among individual labor unions and their allies.[83]

The EU and NAFTA provide examples of regional integration, which present many issues for international labor relations. As regional integration, and interregional integration, develop in other parts of the world, issues will continue to emerge for international labor relations.[84]

SUMMARY

The literature reviewed in this chapter and the discussion surrounding the formation of regional economic zones such as the European Union and the North American Free Trade Agreement, supports the conclusion that transnational collective bargaining has yet to be attained by labor unions.[85] As Enderwick[86] has stated:

> The international operations of MNCs do create considerable impediments in effectively segmenting labor groups by national boundaries and stratifying groups within and between nations. Combining recognition of the overt segmentation effects of international business with an understanding of the dynamics of direct investment yields the conclusion that general multinational collective bargaining is likely to remain a remote possibility.

Enderwick argues that labor unions should opt for less ambitious strategies in dealing with multinationals, such as strengthening national union involvement in plant-based and company-based bargaining, supporting research on the vulnerability of selective multinationals, and consolidating the activities of company-based ITSs. Despite setbacks, especially with the regional economic integration issues discussed in this chapter, it is likely that labor unions and the ILO will pursue these strategies and continue to lobby for the regulation of multinationals via the European Commission and the United Nations.

Recent research on multinationals and labor relations has provided useful information on the issues and challenges related to this aspect of international HRM.[87] Further research is needed on how multinationals view developments in international labor relations and whether these developments will influence the overall business strategy of the firm. Research is also needed on how global firms implement labor relations policy in various countries.

QUESTIONS

1. Why is it important to understand the historical origins of national industrial relations systems?
2. In what ways can labor unions constrain the strategic choices of multinationals?
3. Identify four characteristics of multinationals that give labor unions cause for concern.
4. How have labor unions responded to multinationals? Have these responses been successful?
5. What is "social dumping," and why should unions be concerned about it?

FURTHER READING

1. Bamber, G., and R. Lansbury, eds. 1998. *International and Comparative Employment Relations*, London: Sage.
2. Kochan, T.A., R. Batt, and L. Dyer. 1992. International human resource studies: A framework for future research, in *Research Frontiers in Industrial Relations and Human Resources*, D. Lewin, O.S. Mitchell, and P.D. Sherer, eds. Madison, WI: Industrial Relations Research Association.
3. Kuruvilla, S., 1996. National industrialisation strategies and their influence on patterns of HR practices, *Human Resource Management Journal*, vol. 6, no. 3, pp. 22–41.
4. Locke, R., T. Kochan, and M. Piore, 1995. Reconceptualizing comparative industrial relations: Lessons from international research, *International Labour Review*, vol. 134, no. 2, pp. 139–161.
5. Marginson, P., P. Armstrong, P.K. Edwards, and J. Purcell, 1995. Extending beyond borders: Multinational companies and the international management of labour, *International Journal of Human Resource Management*, vol. 6, no. 3, pp. 702–719.
6. Pincus, L., and J. Belohlav, 1996. Legal issues in multinational business strategy: To play the game, you have to know the rules, *Academy of Management Executive*, vol. 10, no. 3, pp. 52–61.
7. Rothman, M., D. Briscoe, and R. Nacamulli, eds. 1993. *Industrial Relations Around the World: Labor Relations for Multinational Companies*, Berlin: de Gruyter.
8. *World Labour Report 1997–98*, 1997. Geneva: International Labour Office.

ENDNOTES

1. These introductory comments are drawn from J. Schregle, 1981. Comparative industrial relations: Pitfalls and potential, *International Labour Review*, vol. 120, no. 1, pp. 15–30.
2. This point is also referred to as the *emic–etic* problem. See Chapter 1 for a detailed discussion of this point.
3. O. Kahn-Freund, 1979. *Labor Relations: Heritage and Adjustment*, Oxford: Oxford University Press. Also see R.B. Peterson, and J. Sargent, 1997. Union and employer confederation views on current

labour relations in 21 industrialized nations, *Relations Industrielles*, vol. 52, no. 1, pp. 39–59.

4. Schregle, Comparative industrial relations, p. 28.

5. M. Poole, 1986. *Industrial Relations: Origins and Patterns of National Diversity*, London: Routledge.

6. See, for example, J. Jeong, 1995. Enterprise unionism from a Korean perspective, *Economic and Industrial Democracy*, vol. 16, no. 2, pp. 253–273; S. Kuruvilla, and C.S. Venkataratnam, 1996. Economic development and industrial relations: The case of South and Southeast Asia, *Industrial Relations Journal*, vol. 27, no. 1, pp. 9–23.

7. C.K. Prahalad, and Y.L. Doz, 1987. *The Multinational Mission: Balancing Local Demands and Global Vision*, New York: The Free Press.

8. We noted in Chapter 3 that many U.S. multinational firms are reducing the number of expatriates on overseas assignment (see S.J. Kobrin, 1988. Expatriate reduction and strategic control in American multinational corporations, *Human Resource Management*, vol. 27, no. 1, pp. 63–75). With regard to labor relations, this reduction has the effect of reducing the opportunities of U.S. managers to gain firsthand experience of labor relations in various countries.

9. For general reviews of the comparative labor relations literature, see T. Kennedy, 1980. *European Labor Relations*, Lexington. MA: Lexington Books. R. Bean, 1985. *Comparative Industrial Relations: An Introduction to Cross-National Perspectives*, New York: St. Martin's Press. M. Poole, 1987. *Industrial Relations; International and Comparative Industrial Relations*, G.J. Bamber, and R.D. Lansbury, eds. Sydney: Allen & Unwin.

10. P. Marginson, P. Armstrong, P.K. Edwards, and J. Purcell, 1995. Extending beyond borders: Multinational companies and the international management of labour, *International Journal of Human Resource Management*, vol. 6, no. 3, pp. 702–719; also see M. Martinez Lucio, and S. Weston, 1994. New management practices in a multinational corporation: The restructuring of worker representation and rights, *Industrial Relations Journal*, vol. 25, pp. 110–121.

11. J. Hamill, 1983. The labor relations practices of foreign-owned and indigenous firms, *Employee Relations*, vol. 5, no. 1, pp. 14–16; J. Hamill, 1984. Multinational corporations and industrial relations in the U.K., *Employee Relations*, vol. 6, no. 5; J. Hamill, 1984. Labor

relations decision-making within multinational corporations, *Industrial Relations Journal*, vol. 15, no. 2, pp. 30–34.

12. Marginson, Armstrong, Edwards, and Purcell, Extending beyond borders.

13. Hamill, Labor relations decision-making.

14. S.H. Robock, and K. Simmonds, 1989. *International Business and Multinational Enterprises*, 4th ed. Homewood, IL: Irwin; Marginson, Armstrong, Edwards, and Purcell, Extending beyond borders.

15. D.F. Hefler, 1981. Global sourcing: Offshore investment strategy for the 1980's, *Journal of Business Strategy*, vol. 2, no. 1, pp. 7–12.

16. K. Starkey, K. and A. McKinlay, 1993. *Strategy and the Human Resource. Ford and the Search for Competitive Advantage*, Oxford, U.K.: Blackwell.

17. B.C. Roberts, and J. May, 1974. The response of multinational enterprises to international trade union pressures, *British Journal of Industrial Relations*, vol. 12, pp. 403–416; Hamill, The labor relations practices, multinational corporations, and labor relations decision-making; R. Hyman, and A. Ferner, 1992, cited in Bean, *Comparative Industrial Relations*.

18. See J. La Palombara, and S. Blank, 1976. *Multinational Corporations and National Elites: A Study of Tensions*, New York: The Conference Board; A.B. Sim, 1977. Decentralized management of subsidiaries and their performance: A comparative study of American, British and Japanese subsidiaries in Malaysia, *Management International Review*, vol. 17, no. 2, pp. 45–51; and Y.K. Shetty, 1979. Managing the multinational corporation: European and American styles, *Management International Review*, vol. 19, no. 3, pp. 39–48.

19. Bean, *Comparative Industrial Relations*.

20. Hamill, Labor relations decision-making.

21. See P. Marginson, 1992. European integration and transnational management-union relations in the enterprise, *British Journal of Industrial Relations*, vol. 30, no. 4, pp. 529–545.

22. Martinez Lucio, and Weston, New management practices in a multinational corporation.

23. See Bean, *Comparative Industrial Relations*; D. Bok, 1971. Reflections on the distinctive character of American labor law, *Harvard Law Review*, vol. 84, pp. 1394–1463; and 1984. *Employers Associations and Industrial Relations: A Comparative Study*, J.P. Windmuller, and A. Gladstone, eds. Oxford: Clarendon Press.

24. Hamill, Labor relations decision-making.

25. P. Enderwick, 1984. The labor utilization practices of multinationals and obstacles to multinational collective bargaining, *Journal of Industrial Relations*, vol. 26, no. 3, pp. 354–364.

26. P.M. Rosenzweig, and N. Nohria, 1994. Influences on human resource management practices in multinational corporations, *Journal of International Business Studies*, vol. 25, no. 2, pp. 229–251.

27. Hamill, Labor relations decision-making.

28. Also see Bean, *Comparative Industrial Relations*.

29. P. Marginson, A. Buitendam, C. Deutschmann, and P. Perulli, 1993. The emergence of the Euro-Company: Towards a European industrial relations? *Industrial Relations Journal*, vol. 24, no. 3, pp. 182–190; P. Marginson, and K. Sisson, 1994. The structure of transnational capital in Europe: The emerging Euro-Company and its implications for industrial relations, in R. Hyman, and A. Ferner, eds. *New Frontiers in European Industrial Relations*, Oxford: Blackwell.

30. For a lucid discussion of the importance of understanding ideology, see G.C. Lodge, 1985. Ideological implications of changes in human resource management, in *HRM Trends and Challenges*, D.R.E. Walton, and P.R. Lawrence, Boston: Harvard Business School Press.

31. T.A. Kochan, R.B. McKersie, and P. Cappelli, 1984. Strategic choice and industrial relations theory, *Industrial Relations*, vol. 23, no. 1, pp. 16–39.

32. See V. Frazee, 1998. Trade union membership is declining globally, *Workforce*, vol. 3, no. 2, p. 8; 1997. *World Labour Report 1997–98. Industrial Relations, Democracy and Social Stability*, Geneva: ILO; W. Groot, W. and A. van den Berg, 1994. Why union density has declined, *European Journal of Political Economy*, vol. 10, no. 4, pp. 749–763.

33. See Bean, *Comparative Industrial Relations*; Poole, *Industrial Relations*; and J. Visser, 1988. Trade unionism in Western Europe: Present situation and prospects, *Labour and Society*, vol. 13, no. 2, pp. 125–182.

34. Hamill, Multinational corporations.

35. Hamill, Labor relations decision-making, p. 34.

36. This section is based in part on Chapter 5, "The impact of organized labor," in Prahalad and Doz, *The Multinational Mission*.

37. For example, the decision by Hoover to shift some of its production from France to Scotland in the early 1990s appeared to be influenced by the ease with which the employer could implement layoffs. See D. Goodhart, 1993. Ground rules for the firing squad, *Financial Times*, February 15, p. 8.

38. Prahalad and Doz, *The Multinational Mission*.

39. Ibid., p. 102.

40. M. Allen, 1993. Worldly wisdom, *New Statesman and Society*, vol. 6, pp. xii.

41. Kennedy, *European Labor Relations*.

42. Bean, *Comparative Industrial Relations*, p. 191.

43. Bean, *Comparative Industrial Relations*.

44. Marginson, Armstrong, Edwards, and Purcell, Extending beyond borders.

45. B. Mahnkopf, and E. Altvater, 1995. Transmission belts of transnational competition? Trade unions and collective bargaining in the context of European integration, *European Journal of Industrial Relations*, vol. 1, no. 1, pp. 101–117.

46. R. Vernon, 1977. *Storm over the Multinationals: The Real Issues*. Cambridge, MA: Harvard University Press.

47. M. Martinez Lucio, and S. Weston, 1995. Trade unions and networking in the context of change: Evaluating the outcomes of decentralization in industrial relations, *Economic and Industrial Democracy*, vol. 16, p. 244.

48. For a detailed analysis of ITSs, see R. Neuhaus, 1982. *International Trade Secretariats: Objectives, Organization, Activities*, 2d ed. Bonn: Friedrich-EbertStiftung. For an overview of international labor politics and organizations, see T. Boswell, and D. Stevis, 1997. Globalization and international labor organizing: A world-system perspective, *Work and Occupations*, vol. 24, no. 3, pp. 288–308.

49. For further information on the FIET, see their web page at www.fiet.org/fietdoc1.html

50. N. Willatt, 1974. *Multinational Unions*, London: Financial Times.

51. H.R. Northrup, 1978. Why multinational bargaining neither exists nor is desirable, *Labor Law Journal*, vol. 29, no. 6, pp. 330–342. Also see J. Gallagher, 1997. Solidarity forever, *New Statesman & Society*, p. 10.

52. See Kennedy, *European Labor Relations*; and R.B. Helfgott, 1983. American unions and multinational enterprises: A case of

misplaced emphasis, *Columbia Journal of World Business*, vol. 18, no. 2, pp. 81–86.

53. Up to 1993 there was a specialized UN agency known as the United Nations Centre on Transnational Corporations (UNCTC), which had published a number of reports on MNEs (see for example, *Trans-border Data Flows: Transnational Corporations and Remote-sensing Data*, New York, 1984; and *Transnational Corporations and International Trade: Selected Issues*, New York, 1985). Since 1993, the responsibilities of the UNCTC have been assigned to UNCTAD. For further information, see the UNCTAD web site at www.unicc.org/unctad/en/aboutorg/inbrief.htm. See Boswell, and Stevis, Globalization and international labor organizing, for more information on these international organizations.

54. See B. Leonard, 1997. An interview with Anthony Freeman of the ILO, *HRMagazine*, vol. 42, no. 8, pp. 104–109. For coverage of the ongoing debate on international labor standards and globalization, see E. Lee, 1997. Globalization and labour standards: A review of issues, *Management International Review*, vol. 136, no. 2, pp. 173–189.

55. For a detailed description and analysis of the OECD Guidelines for Multinational Enterprises, see D.C. Campbell, and R.L. Rowan, 1983. *Multinational Enterprises and the OECD Industrial Relations Guidelines*, Industrial Research Unit Philadelphia: The Wharton School, University of Pennsylvania; and R. Blanpain, 1985. *The OECD Guidelines for Multinational Enterprises and Labour Relations, 1982-1984: Experiences and Review*, Deventer, The Netherlands: Kluwer.

56. Campbell, and Rowan, *Multinational Enterprises and OECD.*

57. J. Rojot, 1985. The 1984 revision of the OECD guidelines for multinational enterprises, *British Journal of Industrial Relations*, vol. 23, no. 3, pp. 379–397.

58. For a detailed account of this case see R. Blanpain, 1977. *The Badger Case and the OECD Guidelines for Multinational Enterprises*, Deventer, The Netherlands: Kluwer.

59. R. Blanpain, 1979. *The OECD Guidelines for Multinational Enterprises and Labour Relations, 1976-1979: Experience and Review*, Deventer, The Netherlands: Kluwer.

60. H.C. Jain, 1980. Disinvestment and the multinational employer— A case history from Belgium, *Personnel Journal*, vol. 59, no. 3, pp. 201–205.

61. Campbell, and Rowan, *Multinational Enterprises and OECD.*
62. B. Liebhaberg, 1980. *Industrial Relations and Multinational Corporations in Europe*, London: Cower.
63. C.S. Jensen, J.S. Madsen, and J. Due, 1995. A role for a Pan-European trade union movement? Possibilities in european IR-regulation, *Industrial Relations Journal*, vol. 26, no. 1, pp. 4–18; Mahnkopf, and Altvater, Transmission belts of transnational competition?
64. G.W. Latta, and J.R. Bellace, 1983. Making the corporation transparent: Prelude to multinational bargaining, *Columbia Journal of World Business*, vol. 18, no. 2, pp. 73–80; J.T. Addison, and W.S. Siebert, 1994. Recent developments in social policy in the new European Union, *Industrial and Labor Relations Review*, vol. 48, no. 1, pp. 5–27; and N. Donnelly, and C. Rees, 1995. *Industrial Relations and Multinational Companies in the European Community: The Work of the International Companies Network*, Warwick Papers in Industrial Relations no. 54, Warwick Business School, United Kingdom.
65. See, for example, P. Teague, 1994. EC social policy and European human resource management, in C. Brewster, and A. Hegewisch, eds. *Policy and Practice in European Human Resource Management*, London: Routledge, and L. Ulman, B. Eichengreen, and W.T. Dickens, eds. *Labor and an Integrated Europe*, Washington, D.C.: The Brookings Institution.
66. H. De Cieri, and P.J. Dowling, 1991. An examination of the implications of the social dimension for entry of Australian firms to the Single European Market, Paper presented at the 17th Annual Meeting of the European International Business Association, Copenhagen, December 15–17, p. 2.
67. Commission of the European Communities, 1990. *Community Charter of the Fundamental Social Rights of Workers*, Luxembourg: Office for Official Publications of the European Communities.
68. See, for example, J. Lodge, 1989. Social Europe: Fostering a people's Europe?, in *European Community and the Challenge of the Future*, J. Lodge, ed. London: Pinter. J. Addison, and S. Siebert, 1991. The social charter of the European community: Evolution and controversies, *Industrial and Labor Relations Review*, vol. 44, no. 4, pp. 597–625; and M. Hall, 1994. Industrial relations and the social dimension of European integration: Before and after Maastricht, in

New Frontiers in European Industrial Relations, R. Hyman, and A. Ferner, eds. Oxford, U.K.: Blackwell.

69. J. Pickard, 1992. Maastricht deal worries the multinationals, *PM Plus*, January, p. 4; B. Fitzpatrick, 1992. Community social law after Maastricht, *Industrial Law Journal*, vol. 21, no. 3, pp. 199–213; and B. Bercusson, and J.J. Van Dijk, 1995. The implementation of the protocol and agreement on social policy of the treaty on European Union, *The International Journal of Comparative Labour Law and Industrial Relations*, vol. 11, no. 1, pp. 3–30.

70. The Treaty of Amsterdam revised the Treaties on which the European Union was founded. For further information see http://europa.eu.int/abc/obj/amst/en/index.htm and http://www.europarl.eu.int/basicdoc/en/default.htm.

71. For a detailed analysis of the Vredeling Directive, see D. Van Den Bulcke, 1984. Decision making in multinational enterprises and the information and consultation of employees: The proposed Vredeling Directive of the EC commission, *International Studies of Management and Organization*, vol. 14, no. 1, pp. 36–60.

72. See A. Chesters, 1997. What you need to know about works councils, *Workforce*, July, pp. 22–23. Also see Anonymous, 1996. New legislation on EWCs and collective bargaining, *European Industrial Relations Review*, December, pp. 15–16; M. Gold, and M. Hall, 1994. Statutory European works councils: The final countdown?, *Industrial Relations Journal*, vol. 25, no. 3, pp. 177–186; and Marginson, European integration and transnational management-union relations in the enterprise.

73. Addison, and Siebert, Recent developments in social policy; P. Knutsen, 1997. Corporatist tendencies in the Euro-Polity: The EU Directive of 22 September 1994, on European works councils, *Economic and Industrial Democracy*, vol. 18, no. 2, pp. 289–323.

74. Martinez Lucio, and Weston, Trade unions and networking in the context of change.

75. F. Michon, 1990. The 'European Social Community': A common model and its national variations? Segmentation effects, societal effects, *Labour and Society*, vol. 15, no. 2, pp. 215–236. Also see E. Szyszczak, 1995. Future directions in European Union social policy law, *Industrial Law Journal*, vol. 24, no. 1, pp. 19–32.

76. W. Nicoll, and T.C. Salmon, 1990. *Understanding the European Community*, Hertfordshire, U.K.: Philip Allan.

77. C.L. Erickson, and S. Kuruvilla, 1994. Labor costs and the social dumping debate in the European Union, *Industrial and Labor Relations Review*, vol. 48, no. 1, pp. 28–47.
78. For more detail on the FTA and NAFTA, see R. Adams, 1997. The impact of the movement towards hemispheric free trade on industrial relations, *Work and Occupations*, vol. 24, no. 3, pp. 364–380; and, M. Cook, and H. Katz, eds. 1994. *Regional Integration and Industrial Relations in North America*. Ithaca, NY: ILR Press; http://iepnt1. itaiep.doc.gov/nafta/nafta2.htm; http://www.nafta.net/
79. Society for Human Resource Management, 1993. *Briefing Paper on the North American Free Trade Agreement*, International Division, Institute of International Human Resources, Washington, D.C., January, p. 1.
80. Adams, The impact of the movement.
81. Adams, The impact of the movement; D. Daniels, and L.H. Radebaugh, 1992. *International Business: Environments and Operations*, 6th ed. Reading, MA: Addison-Wesley.
82. Society for Human Resource Management, *Briefing Paper*.
83. See Boswell, and Stevis, Globalization and international labor organizing; M.L. Cook, 1997. Cross-border labor solidarity, *Dissent*, vol. 44, no. 1, p. 49; and Adams, The impact of the movement.
84. For example, see, A. Verma, T.A. Kochan, and R.D. Lansbury, 1995. *Employment Relations in the Growing Asian Economies*, London: Routledge; D. Turner, 1996. Investment is key to EU-Asia future, *Europe Business Review*, vol. 1, no. 4, pp. 6–7.
85. See H. Ramsey, 1997. Solidarity at last? International trade unionism approaching the millenium, *Economic and Industrial Democracy*, vol. 18, no. 4, pp. 503–537; and Jensen, Madsen, and Due, A role for a Pan-European trade union movement?
86. Enderwick, The labor utilization practices of multinationals, p. 357.
87. For example, Hamill, The labor relations practices and Multinational corporations; Marginson, Armstrong, Edwards, and Purcell, Extending beyond borders.

C H A P T E R *9*

Issues, Challenges, and Theoretical Developments in IHRM

I n this book we have explored the international HRM issues relating to managing people in a multinational context. To that end, we have focused on the implications that the process of internationalization has for the activities and policies of HRM. Where possible and appropriate, we have endeavored to broaden the discussion of the various topics so that we take account of the fact that there is more to IHRM than expatriation. Despite this objective, there remains an imbalance towards expatriation issues at the expense of the subsidiary perspective. This is mainly due to the increasing volume of expatriate-related literature. As a way of redressing the balance, in this chapter we explore some of the issues and challenges related to host-country staffing through an examination of the HR implications of operating in China and India. These two countries represent huge growth markets, and also are good examples of contrasting societies in which foreign firms attempt to operate. A focus on expatriation also precludes broader strategic issues. We, therefore, include in this chapter a short discussion of key concerns related to ethics and social responsibility—topics, such as bribery, that are receiving increased attention and are somewhat controversial.

While some scholars and practitioners would still regard IHRM as a scientific field in its infancy, there has been considerable progress toward developing theoretical bases. The remainder of this chapter identifies such developments, particularly those that attempt to place specific IHRM activities into the organizational and strategic contexts.

MANAGING PEOPLE IN AN INTERNATIONAL CONTEXT

This section looks at key HRM aspects of operating in two different countries as a way of illustrating the situations that may confront multinationals attempting to penetrate developing markets. We will trace the impact that recent economic reforms in China and India have had in terms of staffing foreign operations in these two markets. As the more common mode of operation in both cases has been the international joint venture (IJV), it allows us to elaborate on the HRM challenges posed by IJV operations, which were briefly outlined in Chapter 2.

CHINA*

In late 1978, the Chinese government announced an open-door policy and began economic reforms aimed at moving the country from a centrally planned economy to a market economy. Under its centrally planned economy, industries "were owned and run by the state, and their growth was regulated by planning targets rather than by the profit-maximizing decisions of independent entrepreneurs."[1] Thus, planning was the dominant control mechanism, with the market mechanism in a supplementary role. Industrial enterprises (the Western term *firm* is inappropriate in the communist context) were under the control of relevant government departments.

The past two decades of economic reforms have seen foreign multinationals expand their operations into China—many attracted by the sheer size of its potential market. By the end of 1996, China had absorbed a total foreign direct investment (FDI) of U.S.$171.8 billion with 281,298 projects, and was ranked second to the United States as a global destination for FDI. Of particular interest is the enthusiasm for establishing *foreign invested enterprises (FIEs)*, including foreign joint ventures and

---

* The authors wish to acknowledge Cherrie Zhu, Monash University, for her contribution to this section.

wholly foreign-owned ventures (FIEs is commonly used as the umbrella term to describe FDI in China). Consequently, employment in FIEs has increased from 550,000 employees in 1986 to 8,820,000 in 1995.[2] FDI has tended to take the form of an international joint venture (IJV) with a state-owned enterprise (SOE) as the local partner, or as a fully owned subsidiary. To a certain extent, foreign ownership is instrumental in protecting FIEs from the various pressures of localization.[3] However, many FIEs in China are either under-performing or failing. As we discuss later in this chapter, the management of people is a critical factor in determining success or failure in international joint ventures. Chinese HRM policies and practices are quite different from those used in developed and market-economy developing countries, and careful consideration of local idiosyncratic practices is required to operate successfully.[4] "The legacy of management 'with Chinese characteristics' still weighs heavily on all firms operating in China."[5] Knowledge of how employees have been managed in the past may help multinationals to understand local managers' difficulty or inertia in accepting nontraditional or Western-style HRM practices. Therefore, we include prior as well as current practices to provide a better appreciation of the effect that the transition to a market economy is having on the four major functions of HRM.[6]

Staffing[7]

Prior to the reforms, Chinese employees were classified into two groups:

- *Workers:* all blue-collar employees, who were administered by the Ministry of Labor.
- *Cadres:* white-collar staff, managed by the Ministry of Personnel. The broad definition of cadres is "state institution and military 'civil servants' and [its] narrow meaning is persons engaged in 'certain specified leadership work or management work' (e.g., organization cadres and enterprise cadres)."[8]

Since the reforms, the distinction between cadres and workers has gradually become blurred, particularly in foreign-invested and privately owned enterprises. Employees belong to either managerial or nonmanagerial groups. However, the Ministry of Labor and the Ministry of Personnel are still two separate government departments in China.

A centralized labor allocation system determined the staffing levels in Chinese enterprises. Established in the early 1950s, this system was based on the Maoist theory that labor was not a commodity but a national resource, and that the government had a monopoly control of urban jobs. The Ministry of Labor and Ministry of Personnel maintained a tight control over labor allocation by setting quotas for employment at individual enterprises, including annual quotas for new recruits. Local bureaus of labor and personnel assigned workers and staff to a particular job in a work unit–called *danwei* in Chinese. Centralized allocation effectively deprived enterprises of their autonomy to select employees, denied the individual the right to choose his or her employment,[9] and ignored changes in labor supply and demand. However, the centralized allocation system did achieve a high employment rate in urban areas.

Accompanying the centralized labor allocation was the belief in lifelong employment: "the worker's inalienable right to his job and other related benefits."[10] Therefore, over 80 percent of employees in stateowned enterprises (approximately 80 million) enjoyed job security, especially those employed in heavy industries such as mining.[11] The guaranteed continuation of employment, along with various welfare and benefits offered to employees, such as accommodation, medical treatment, child care, and pensions, has been referred to as the *iron rice bowl*. In exchange for job security, employees had little freedom to move to another work unit—that is, they were unable to quit or transfer jobs and were locked into a dependency relationship with their enterprises. Managers were deprived of their right to fire or layoff unqualified employees.[12]

From October 1986, all newly employed workers in the state sector were hired on a contract basis rather than effectively being given permanent employment.[13] By the end of 1996, a labor contract system had become compulsory in both public and private sectors, including the managerial level, thus revoking the long-standing tradition of lifetime employment. In theory, both workers and managers had the freedom to select each other.[14] The new labor contract system has facilitated decentralization of employment practices. Governmental influence has gradually diminished. Enterprises have more autonomy to select their employees, and "two-way selection"—that is, free selection of occupation by individuals and free selection of employees by enterprises—is more common. Two-way selection has been facilitated by the emergence of a labor market with personnel exchange and service centers established by the government to provide job information and relevant services.[15] Western recruitment methods, such as job advertisement and employment tests, are now used, especially by FIEs and privately owned enterprises. As enterprises now have to match production to market demands and be responsible for their own survival, they need to attract and retain competent and motivated employees.

Performance Appraisal[16]

Prior to the current reforms, performance appraisal for *cadres* was mainly for promotion or transfer, with the main criteria being political loyalty and seniority;[17] the appraisal was usually conducted annually by the personnel department of the cadre's organization. Each cadre was given an appraisal form divided into three parts: self-evaluation, peer-group opinions, and an assessment written by the head of the department in which the cadre worked. Thus, the appraisal method relied heavily on "superior rating subordinate," and lacked specified criteria and other performance measures commonly used in Western market economies.[18]

Performance appraisal for blue-collar *workers* was used less frequently. It was an informal and subjective process, reflected in the emphasis placed on one's *biao-xian*. The term *biao-xian* refers to the "broad and vaguely defined realm of behavior and attitudes subject to leadership evaluation—behavior that indicates underlying attitudes, orientations, and loyalties worthy of reward."[19] A worker's *biao-xian* was usually judged on the basis of subjective impressions of day-to-day job performance and demonstrated cooperation. Consequently, personal relationships with colleagues, especially with the leaders, became the key to getting a good *biao-xian*.[20] Such appraisals were characterized by vagueness, open to individual interpretation, and dominated by political ideology.

As part of the economic reforms, aimed at breaking the iron rice bowl, the government issued a document: "Suggestion for Implementing the Cadre Performance Appraisal System" outlining a performance appraisal scheme for cadres. The new scheme was based on the socialist principle of distribution (i.e., from each according to one's ability and to each according to one's work). It aimed at identifying training needs, as well as distinguishing between high and low performers. More importantly, it held cadres accountable to, as well as for, their subordinates via subordinates' evaluation.[21] New appraisal criteria focused on four broad areas:

- Good moral practice (*de*)—virtue or moral integrity. The cadre is evaluated on whether he or she is in step politically with the Party, and carries out government orders and regulations.

- Adequate competence (*neng*). This covers three main aspects: educational background; ability in leadership, organization, negotiation, planning, forecasting, and decision making; and physical status, which also includes age.
- Positive working attitude (*qing*) refers to diligence and usually assesses attendance at work, discipline, initiative, and sense of responsibility.
- Strong performance record (*jie*) measures the cadre's work effectiveness, including quality and quantity, as well as other contributions made to the organization.[22]

While these criteria have been in practice since the 1980s, some new methods for assessing cadres have been introduced, such as computer-aided panel assessment (*ceping kaohe*) and position-related yearly assessment (*gangwei niandu kaohe*).[23] These methods require both quantitative and qualitative measurement to reduce the subjectivity and informality inherent in the traditional performance appraisal approach.

Performance appraisal has also become more widely used in enterprises at the worker level since 1978. In mid-1990 "The Regulation on Workers' Performance Appraisal" was issued by the Ministry of Labor, which specified the type, content, method, and management of appraisals.[24] Some new approaches have been developed, such as position specification, management by objectives, and internal subcontracting.[25] All aim to break the iron rice bowl by distinguishing high and low performers and linking performance to rewards. For example, position specification usually includes quality control, technical requirements, quantified work loads, tools and machine maintenance, labor discipline, caring for the working environment, team-work cooperation, and safety of production methods.

In their study of performance appraisal in China, Zhu and Dowling[26] found that over 78 percent of employees surveyed (*n* = 440) confirmed that performance appraisal was conducted by their enterprises; however, only 53 percent indicated that a job description existed. Also, whereas the majority of the enterprises surveyed conducted performance appraisal on a yearly basis, the bonus was usually distributed more frequently (either monthly or quarterly). This raises doubt as to whether performance was really being linked to rewards. In addition, other researchers have noted problems with performance assessment in China because of the emphasis given to political considerations, and problems with inconsistent measurement, subjectivity, static rather than forward-looking attitudes, and a lack of communication.[27] Although performance appraisal is primarily used for determining bonus and wages rather than for developmental or communication purposes, it is being used by many Chinese enterprises to weaken the old practice of egalitarianism and to facilitate the abolition of the iron rice bowl.

Compensation[28]

The compensation system before the reforms was characterized by egalitarianism at both enterprise and individual levels regardless of performance. Enterprises had no right to set up or change any wage scale, let alone to increase (or decrease) their total payroll. A nationally unified wage system was structured by the state in 1956 for both blue- and white-collar employees. Under this system, there were 8 grades for workers, 15 grades for technical personnel, and 25 grades for cadres such as managers and administrative personnel. Usually the highest pay received in an enterprise was only two to three time more than one in the lowest, and the entry level was very low. These minimal wage differentials reflected the strong ideological and political influence upon work enterprises. Wage increases were infrequent, occurring at intervals of several years, and commonly took the form of national unified grade promotions for all employees. Not only was the wage system egalitarian, it also provided numerous benefits to employees, such as insurance, medical coverage, public welfare, nonstaple food, winter heating subsidy, and a home leave travelling allowance. These benefits helped to maintain the iron rice bowl and made the enterprises mini-welfare states.[29]

Reform of the compensation system began at the enterprise level. Enterprises were treated as relatively independent business units, and compensation was linked to performance. The enterprise reform launched in 1984, the Enterprise Law issued in 1988, and related regulations during the 1990s aimed at separating the ownership of an enterprise from its controlling authority so each enterprise had autonomy and incentives.[30] The state-regulated wage system has now been replaced by diversified wage packages with more emphasis on enterprise profitability and individual performance. Since 1985, different systems of wage determination have been introduced, such as floating and structural wage systems.[31] In 1992, the Minister of Labor introduced a new position-and-skills wage system based on the four major working factors emphasized by the International Labor Organization in 1950 (i.e., knowledge and skills required, responsibility assumed, work intensity (load) involved, and working conditions).[32] Enterprises were required to include these four components in their wage packages to override the egalitarianism of the old wage scales. These reforms have tried to quantify each worker's performance and link performance to pay. However, in the absence of job descriptions and performance appraisal, the degree to which performance-related pay was fairly distributed could vary across enterprises.

No matter how diversified wage packages might be, all packages had a bonus as an important part (since the restoration of the bonus after the reforms).[33] As enterprise reform has become more widespread, the distribution of bonuses has been more closely tied to individual performance.[34] How to match compensation with the contributions made by individuals remains a difficult issue and the bonus system is still at an experimental stage. Nonetheless, performance-based compensation has become the trend, and egalitarianism is being replaced by wage differentiation based on individual and enterprise performance.

Training and Development[35]

Pre-reform employee training was generally divided into two parts:

- *Training for blue-collar workers:* This was primarily in the form of apprenticeships and technical school education that were the major sources of skilled workers.[36] Technical school students would be assigned to an enterprise by the state after completing two to three years of study.
- *Training for cadres:* Training for managers, especially managers who were also members of the Communist Party, was mainly offered by schools run by the Party at central, provincial, and municipal levels, or colleges for cadre education and training. Training priority was usually given to political studies, and this focus is regarded as a major cause of the current shortage of qualified managers in industry. Many cadres, especially managerial staff, lack the knowledge and skills required to change their roles from merely carrying out government orders to assuming full responsibility for the enterprise's performance or deciding on management matters.[37] This shortage has hampered the move to a market economy.

At the *workers'* level, lack of education and training is widespread. A survey covering 20 million industrial employees in 26 provinces and cities was conducted in 1980. It revealed that 8.2 percent of employees were literate or semiliterate, 32 percent had less than 9 years of education, 40.8 percent had completed year 9, 15.9 percent had finished year 12, and only 3.1 percent had a university education.[38] In mid-1980, the state re-introduced apprenticeship programs, which had been abolished during the Cultural Revolution (1966–1976). The traditional post-employment apprenticeships were gradually replaced by pre-employment traineeships and this practice was legitimized in the Labor Law, which became effective in 1995. Reforms introduced in 1990 sought to connect training, examination, job arrangement, and compensation to encourage employees to learn technical skills.[39] These have since been replaced gradually by a vocational qualification verification system. This latest system reflects, to some extent, the government's recognition of the German model of a dual-education system (i.e., liberal education and vocational training). The practice of double certificate (i.e., education certificate and vocational qualification certificate) aims to achieve an outcome similar to the situation in Germany, with young people attaining vocational knowledge and skills. This system has now been widely implemented and has enabled workers to take the training course of their choice and to be more flexible in job selection,[40] and is consistent with the two-way selection system and the position-and-skills wage system discussed above.

Because the lack of adequately trained management had been identified as a major impediment to its reforms, the government established institutions for adult further education for professional and management training.[41] A nationwide program of management training has supported these institutions and the government has collaborated with institutions from several countries, including the United States, United Kingdom, Australia, Canada, Japan, and the European Union nations, to conduct courses, including MBA programs.

In spite of the progress achieved in employee and management training and development many inadequacies and limitations remain. The results from a 1994 survey disclosed that 34 percent of 1,508 respondents had not received any training opportunities in enterprises.[42] Researchers have also found that Chinese enterprises usually only emphasize technical training rather than behavioral training.[43] Many foreign managers may regard training as costly and risky, because they may not receive immediate returns and employees may leave the enterprise after training.[44]

Implications for Multinationals

By way of conclusion, and to assist in understanding the impact of the transition on HR practices, we pose and answer three questions in relation to managing HCNs in FIEs:

1. *How can foreign firms develop effective HRM strategies to improve the productivity of their workforce in China?* Multinationals need to know the current HRM practices in China. Many practices commonly used in the West are now employed in China. However, foreign firms need to be aware that in China, "the shift from the older practices has only been partial, especially in larger enterprises, whether state-owned enterprises or even Sino-foreign joint ventures."[45] This is mainly because multinationals have a stronger association with government partners in China than in other developing countries, and thus tend to be somewhat locked into maintaining management practices that are a legacy of pre-reform days.[46] Researchers have noted that in some FIEs, the egalitarian pay system is still in practice even though the eight-grade wage structure has been abandoned.[47]

2. *To what extent can foreign multinationals transfer their home-country's HR practices to their subsidiaries in China?* Multinational managers should not assume that identical HR practices can be applied to their Chinese enterprises. Some researchers claim that Western-style HRM practices should be introduced only when a Chinese perspective, and Chinese values and methods, have been incorporated.[48] Take performance appraisal as an example. It has been argued that to increase the effectiveness of appraisal in China, the Western appraisal system, which encourages individual economic performance, should incorporate the Chinese values of satisfying performance, such as harmonious functioning in a work group and fulfillment of individual obligations towards the work unit and colleagues.[49]

3. *What are the future HRM issues for China due to its ongoing economic reforms?*

    Developing and retaining quality staff. Chan has noted that "both Western and Chinese management find HRM appropriate as a nonadversarial and consensual management style that succeeds in co-opting the workforce."[50] However, a particular term may have a different connotation or orientation. For example, while the training and development function does exist in China, it is still passive and narrowly defined "in contrast to the Western HRM notion of planning for long-term staff development."[51] Training is more focused on improving current performance deficiencies. There is a lack of career development, particularly as employees tend to change jobs frequently in pursuit of higher wages rather than skills development.[52] The absence of career development plus a high emphasis on material incentives have partly contributed to the problems of high turnover and "disloyalty" observed in many enterprises, including FIEs.[53]

Compensation. The change in employee attitudes toward the distribution of bonuses is another identified trend. Traditionally, China has been a collective-oriented society,[54] however, Chinese employees now prefer reward differentials "determined primarily according to individual contributions"[55] and there is greater acceptance of wider reward disparities based on individual performance.[56] With further reforms inevitable in China, a compensation system based on individual performance will become more common and more entrenched.[57]

Localizing Staffing. As more foreign multinationals expand their businesses into China, they have sought local management for their operations in order to develop a large corporate presence in China.[58] When hiring Chinese nationals for executive jobs (because of their communication skills, local contacts, and understanding of the domestic market)[59] many multinationals have found that Chinese managers lack decision-making skills and are wary of taking personal initiatives. Along with job-related skills, corporate management training programs are required that provide HRM skills appropriate to the Chinese context and skills for problem-solving in high-pressure situations.[60]

To conclude, it is necessary to remember that China is still undergoing a transition stage, and will continue its economic restructuring and reforms into the next century. The government expects enterprises to become corporate entities and competitors adaptable to the market,[61] so effective HRM practices are needed to develop a competitive workforce.

INDIA*

With an estimated population of 973.5 million, India is the world's fifth largest economy.[62] It is a heterogeneous country characterized by diverse cultural groups (or subcultures) and a strong social class system (known as the caste system).[63] While the official languages are Hindi and English, there are 14 recognized regional languages. The main religions, as a proportion of the total population, are Hindu (84 percent), Muslim (11 percent), Sikh (2 percent), and Christian (2 percent).[64] In 1997, the country celebrated 50 years of independence from British colonial rule.

Post independence, India pursued a protectionist, import-substitution policy to promote local industries, and this involved restrictions on foreign investment and imports. Foreign firms were "encouraged" to localize, by taking Indian partners and adopting Indian, or hybrid, brand names (such as Lehar-Pepsi or Hero-Honda).[65] However, since 1991, the Indian government has been progressively liberalizing its economy. Foreign firms may now own 100 percent of Indian companies in some sectors, and as much as 74 percent in others. Its large market potential has attracted interest from multinationals from various countries, exposing once protected local firms to foreign competition.

For foreign firms, part of the attraction has been the low cost of Indian labor.[66] However, the competitiveness of India in terms of the availability, qualifications, and skills of its human resources is considered to be one of the lowest in the world.[67] Geissbauer and Siemsen argue that the cost advantage derived from the availability of cheap labor tends to be neutralized by lower productivity.[68] According to the Australian Department of Foreign Affairs and Trade, the low investment of capital employed per worker, combined with a work culture that does not encourage high performance work practices, are mainly responsible for the low level of productivity of the Indian labor force.[69] This adds another dimension to the "expense of cheap labor" paradox we discussed in Chapter 5. However, it is important not to make generalizations. For example, the Indian software industry is highly competitive—Indian firms do not just compete on price, but on the basis of quality, innovation, and technical expertise, and draw on a huge pool of relatively

* The authors would like to acknowledge Sharif As-Saber, Massey University, for his contribution to this section.

low-cost, technically-qualified, English-speaking software profession-als.[70] In 1996, 104 firms out of the Fortune 500 outsourced their soft-ware development to India. About 10 percent of Microsoft's 20,000 worldwide workforce is Indian.[71]

The complexity of the Indian business environment has impacted on the method that foreign firms have tended to use to enter and service the Indian market. Even though there is less restriction on the form of opera-tion mode since 1991, when it comes to equity arrangements, foreign multinationals have shown a preference for international joint ventures (IJVs). For those foreign firms not able or willing to invest in equity arrangements, licensing has been a heavily used alternative (see the dis-cussion on mode of operation in Chapter 2).

We discussed briefly the IJV as an example of a strategic alliance in Chapter 2. The motives for entering into an IJV arrangement are many and varied, but a major reason is to spread risks. However, as many firms soon discover, forming an IJV creates a risk in itself and the relevant lit-erature reports a high failure rate.[72] Success seems to depend on an abil-ity to balance "the desire and need to control the venture on the one hand, and the need to maintain harmonious relations with the partner(s) on the other hand."[73] Likewise, the factors attributed to the failure of a joint venture are most frequently human-related—poor decisions, be-havioral errors, or unanticipated staffing events. Interests may be incon-gruent, particularly when one of the parents is the host government. Therefore, an IJV presents a major management challenge, particularly so when a foreign firm has been forced into the IJV by necessity rather than choice—as is often the case in both China and India. It is evident that selecting the right people for key management positions is criti-cal to success, and the harmonization of management styles is also essential.[74]

Of the many reasons for establishing an IJV, two seem particularly relevant for India—dealing with bureaucracy and unfamiliarity and cul-tural distance.

Dealing with Bureaucracy. The pervasive corruption encountered by Western firms is attributed to excessive controls and unfulfilled demand for goods and services, leading to India being ranked as the ninth most corrupt country in the world. Indian bureaucracy is said to be parochial and obstructionist—"red tape" is considered one of the most significant problems in conducting business in India.[75] Widespread tax evasion is another feature of the Indian economy.[76]

In the face of such reports, many foreign firms do not want to confront these issues directly. A recent study of Australian firms operating in India found that a major reason for forming IJVs was to entrust the local partner to deal with government officials, other agencies, and the "bureaucracy."[77] Likewise, a study of 26 Norwegian firms in India found that 11 had established IJVs, and only one had a wholly owned subsidiary. The overriding reason for the Norwegian preference for the IJV was to reduce risks by having the local partner deal with "things Indian." As one Norwegian executive commented: "The Indian market is difficult and complex. It's good to have a partner who knows the business and the bureaucracy. A partner who has the right connections."[78]

Unfamiliarity and Cultural Distance. Generally speaking, most Westerners perceive India to be culturally distant and this can lead to a preference for an IJV with a local partner. Hofstede[79] classified India as high on his power-distance dimension (i.e., a society where less powerful members accept the unequal distribution of power). He also ranked India as weak on the uncertainty-avoidance dimension (tolerance for future uncertainty and risk), dominant on the collectivism dimension (emphasis on group orientation), and dominant on the masculine dimension (characterized by, for example, its high level of bureaucracy and the social caste system). One could suggest that high-power distance is one of the major features of the Indian management style. According to Sharma,[80] an average Indian manager represents:

> a plausible picture of the average Indian's resistance for change, his willingness to delegate but unwillingness to accept authority, his fear of taking an independent decision, his possessive attitude towards his inferiors and his abject surrender to his superiors, his strict observance of rituals and his disregard of them in practice, his preaching of high morals against personal immorality, and his near-desperate efforts at maintaining the status quo while talking of change.

The extent of power distance may have a negative correlation with the level of trustworthiness—that is, the higher the power distance, the lower the trust.[81] Ratnam regards perceived trustworthiness as a key HRM problem in the Indian context. He described the scenario as follows:

> Workers consider employers as *Paisa chor* (they swindle and appropriate surpluses from the enterprise). Balance sheets are generally considered to be

excellent pieces of fiction. Employers consider workers as *Kam chor* (mean, lazy people who shun work).[82]

Labor unrest is a related feature of the Indian environment that may make an IJV attractive. Two major areas of industrial disputation are wages and working hours.[83] Due to the constant pressure from trade unions, it is often difficult to maintain a part-time and contractual work-force, even though there has been an increase in the number of such arrangements. It has been suggested that, because of the antagonistic nature of trade unions, it is often very difficult to organize an Indian work-force into teams.[84] State intervention is the norm in industrial matters. However, as most trade unions have strong links with political parties and many politicians are current or former union leaders, such interventions tend to be biased towards labor.[85] As a consequence, most multinationals find a local partner very helpful in dealing with situations involving trade unions and labor legislation.

However, the advantages of the local partner can be offset by some of the problems inherent in the IJV as a form of international operation. As we will now explore, HRM plays an important role in assisting foreign firms to achieve their goals for their Indian IJVs.

Staffing

In a complex cultural context like India, it may be more advantageous to use local managers. A study by As-Saber, Dowling, and Liesch[86] found that there was a clear preference for using HCNs in key positions by multinationals operating in India. The authors suggest that a major reason for HCN preference is the belief that the right Indian will know more than an expatriate manager could learn in years on the job. Additional reasons given by the multinationals in their study were:

- Avoids extra costs associated with relocating expatriates;
- Reluctance of many Western managers to live in India;
- Ensures continuity of management as HCNs are likely to stay longer in the position; and
- Creates higher morale among HCNs due to a perceived career path.

Thus, the motives identified in this study for adopting a polycentric approach to staffing Indian IJVs are consistent with those discussed in general terms in Chapter 3. However, the question of control over the IJV remains a concern for multinational firms. In situations of minority equity, control can be obtained through the use of managers who are loyal to the parent company and its organizational ethos. The success of some foreign firms in India may be attributed to effective integration of the local IJV managers into the "global family" as illustrated in the case of Hindustan Lever presented in Exhibit 9–1.

EXHIBIT 9–1   *Unilever's Indian Experience*[87]

Unilever, the consumer goods multinational (food, and home and personal care products), was created through the merger in 1929 of the British firm, Lever Brothers, and The Netherlands firm, Margarine Unie. In 1998, it was operating in 90 countries worldwide. It is controlled by two holding companies: Unilever PLC (English) and Unilever N.V. (Netherlands). Its two Chairmen head the seven-member Executive Committee—which includes the Personnel Director—the top decision-making body. Reporting to the Executive Committee is the Executive Council, which includes the heads (Presidents) of the 12 Business Groups based essentially on geographical markets. The Business Groups establish regional strategies and policies. Individual companies in each country report to a business group. Unilever has over 1,000 brands and 13 product categories. It describes itself as an international, multi-focal firm rather than a global multinational—half the products are foods, aimed at local tastes, and it tries to localize as much as possible. The firm currently has an expatriate workforce of 7 percent of total employees, drawn from many countries, including India.

Unilever has been operating in India for over 60 years through a 51 percent local entity, Hindustan Lever. Unilever endeavors to establish a strong sense of corporate identity, referred to as "Unileverization." It has been rather successful in India—to the extent that there is a popular saying: You can take the person out of Hindustan Lever, but you can't take Hindustan Lever out of the person. Values such as thrift and simplicity are advocated from the top. Its current team of 1,200 managers have been drawn from graduates of India's top business schools and developed through its in-house training program. Cultivating its own talent that is familiar with the Indian way of doing business, combined with loyalty to Unilever's worldwide approach to managing, has made Hindustan Lever staff attractive to foreign and local competitors. There has been active poaching of its management staff. In a newspaper interview last year, the Hindustan Lever Chairman was asked about the effects of the arrival of more foreign multinationals in India. He commented that Hindiustan Lever has had to make adjustments: "We have significantly increased our salaries at various levels." Management costs have doubled over the previous four to five years as a percentage of turnover.

Recruitment and Selection of HCNs

Once hired, it is not easy to dismiss employees under Indian labor law.[88] The Industrial Dispute Act provides strict rules for layoffs and dismissals. Consequently, dismissals and layoffs are difficult, and such actions can be contested through a petition to the government and can lead to a time-consuming process of negotiation.[89] The prolonged dismissal process may be avoided through appropriate selection of staff. One of the attractions of the IJV is the assumption that a more experienced local partner can assist in identifying a suitable workforce. The IJV may perhaps even use the existing human resources (its internal labor market) of the local partner, if this pool of labor is considered to be sufficient in terms of skill and productivity levels.

Compensation

Since the economic liberalization in the early 1990s, it has become more difficult for foreign multinationals to find and retain high-quality local staff, as the rapid rise in the level of foreign and local investments in India has lead to a shortage of skilled people.[90] This, in turn, is placing pressure on the compensation packages of qualified managers. According to a recent survey, an average Indian manager's annual real-salary increase is one of the highest in the world.[91] Consistent with this report, a recent study found that continuous pay increases, along with a commitment to improve working conditions, are two preconditions to retain experienced staff,[92] particularly in high-growth industries such as telecommunications and computer software development. Pressure is also being brought to bear on the minimum wage level, and this will increase the cost of labor over the longer term. The case of Unilever, outlined in Exhibit 9–1, illustrates how competition for key people can affect even an established subsidiary operation.

Training and Development

As was discussed in Chapter 5, international business operations places specific demands on effective training and development of PCN, TCN, and HCN staff. The IJV complicates this issue due to potential conflicts in managerial styles and expectations. Training expatriates in negotiation and conflict-resolution skills is advocated to enable them to cope with, and resolve, the unexpected issues and problems inherent in both the Indian context and operating in the joint venture situation.[93]

Despite the availability of cheap labor, as mentioned earlier in this section, low labor productivity is a common complaint among existing manufacturers in India. As a consequence, a multinational may have to provide extensive training programs for its local staff. The introduction of new production equipment and concepts such as just-in-time, quality management, and so on, require additional training. Developing and retaining the workforce so that the multinational has a pool of managerial talent to draw on is also a challenge, as illustrated by the competitive situation now confronting Unilever's Indian operations (Exhibit 9–1).

Implications for Multinationals

Considering the cultural differences outlined above, it would appear that including local staff and practices is essential in building a performance-based work culture in Indian operations. A skill-based approach may contribute to improved labor productivity and better performance.[94] It is also evident that, as FDI expands, foreign firms are being forced to pay a premium price for quality people. Despite wage and salary increases, it is still cheaper to hire quality HCNs than employing expatriates, with the added advantage that locals are more familiar with the complexities of Indian business culture. However, staff training and development remain as important considerations.

Through this brief overview of two countries undergoing market reforms and liberalization, it has been possible to illustrate the critical role that competent and trained staff play in partly determining the multinational's ability to achieve its strategic goals in these markets. It also reminds us that, as discussed in Chapter 1, having the right people in the right place remains the perennial challenge for firms operating internationally.

HUMAN RESOURCE ISSUES IN MULTINATIONAL CORPORATE SOCIAL RESPONSIBILITY*

Ethics and the question of corporate social responsibility are complex and the source of much controversy. In this section, we briefly discuss questions often raised about the existence of transcultural standards of moral behavior and the implications for IHR and international managers. Our intention is not to review the literature in international business ethics, but to demonstrate the complexity that surrounds

---

*The authors would like to acknowledge Lorraine Carey, University of Tasmania, for her contribution to this section.

international business conduct, for the multinational, and for expatriates and local staff in subsidiary operations.

In the domestic context, debates about corporate social responsibility have focused on whether a firm should adopt noneconomic goals. Those who argue for a narrow view of corporate social responsibility believe that a firm's only responsibility is to maximize profits for shareholders within the law.[95] Proponents of a broader view of corporate social responsibility argue that firms should adopt the role of a "good citizen" and balance the interests of shareholders with the best interests of society.[96] When business is conducted across national and cultural borders, the debate about corporate social responsibility takes on added layers of complexity.[97] In particular, perplexing questions about the existence of universal ethical standards are raised. This is especially problematic when multinationals operate in host countries with different standards of business practice.[98] The questions of ethical relativity and corporate social responsibility arise not only in the context of different home- and host-country employment practices but also in the central operations and policies of multinationals.

To appreciate the dilemma, take the situation of a multinational assigning a PCN to manage its operations in a host country. Whose standards should prevail? Those of the multinational's parent country or the host country? (This question also arose in Chapter 8 when discussing labor relations.) There are three main responses to this question. The first involves ethical relativism, the second ethical absolutism, and the third, ethical universalism.

For the *ethical relativist*, there are no universal or international rights and wrongs: it all depends on a particular culture's values and beliefs. Thus, if the people of Indonesia tolerate the bribery of their public officials, this is morally no better or worse than the people of Singapore or Denmark who refuse to accept bribery. For the ethical relativist, when in Rome, one should do as the Romans do. While relativism may be appealing to those who fear cultural imperialism, it is a logically and ethically incoherent theory.[99]

Unlike the relativist, the *ethical absolutist* (or imperialist) believes that when in Rome, one should do what one would do at home, regardless of what the Romans do. This view of ethics gives primacy to one's own cultural values. Opponents of this view argue that ethical absolutists are intolerant individuals who confuse respect for local traditions with ethical relativism. It must be noted that while some behaviors are wrong wherever they are practiced (e.g., bribery of government officials), other behaviors may be tolerated in their cultural context (e.g., the practice of routine gift giving between Japanese business people). When PCNs discover too late that the political–legal environment in which their home-country policies were formulated is significantly different from that of the host countries in which they operate, the results can be extreme. Donaldson cites an example of a U.S. expatriate manager in China who followed her firm's policy on employee theft. On catching an employee stealing, she fired the employee and notified the relevant authorities. She was horrified to later learn that the employee had been executed.[100]

In contrast to the ethical relativist, the *ethical universalist* believes there are fundamental principles of right and wrong, which transcend cultural boundaries, and that multinationals must adhere to these fundamental principles. However, unlike the absolutist, the universalist is careful to distinguish between practices that are simply culturally different and those that are morally wrong. The difficulty for managers operating in diverse cultural environments is to identify moral norms, which transcend cultural boundaries, and then, without compromising those norms, recognize and respect diversity where it is morally appropriate to do so.[101] One useful way to determine the ethical dimensions of a proposed project, policy, or behavior is to consider consequences, as well as rights and justice claims, for all stakeholders.

The Multinational as a Global Citizen

A global world is an interconnected world. It presents a critical challenge to identify common ethical values that underlie cultural, religious, and philosophical differences. While there are important differences between Western and Eastern philosophical traditions, they share four fundamental core human values: good citizenship, respect for human dignity, respect for basic rights, and equity.[102] For example, Donaldson links the Western values of individual liberty and human rights to the Japanese value of living and working together for the common good (*kyosei*) and the Muslim value of the duty to give alms to the poor (*Zakat*).[103] Applications of core human values to specific duties of multinationals include the adoption of adequate workplace and environmental health and safety standards, the payment of basic living wages, equal employment opportunity, refraining from the use of child labor, providing basic employee training and education, and allowing workers to organize and form unions. Many multinationals now place considerable importance on being regarded as good global citizens and have initiated action to address public concerns about the environment and human rights.[104]

However, translating general ethical principles and core values into practice in the international business domain, even allowing for some limited consensus within the international community, is an enormous task in the absence of a supranational legislative authority. A number of mechanisms to facilitate the incorporation of ethical principles into international business behavior have been suggested. Predictably, these have centered on regulation, both self-imposed and government-decreed, the development of international accords, and the use of education and training programs.

International Accords and Corporate Codes of Conduct

One of the most interesting initiatives in international business self-regulation is the Caux Roundtable Principles for Business Conduct, developed in 1994 by Japanese, European, and North American business leaders meeting in Caux, Switzerland. This is the first international ethics code for business and aims to set a global benchmark against which individual firms can write their own codes and measure the behavior of their executives. The Caux Principles are grounded in two basic ethical ideals: *kyosei* and human dignity. The preamble to the Caux Principles states that:

> The Japanese concept of *kyosei* means living and working together for the common good—enabling cooperation and mutual prosperity to coexist with healthy and fair competition. Human dignity relates to the sacredness or value of each person as an end, not simply as the means to the fulfillment of other's purposes or even majority prescription.[105]

The Caux Principles aim to further the twin values of living and working together and human dignity by promoting free trade, environmental and cultural integrity, and the prevention of bribery and corruption. The Principles have their origin in the Minnesota principles developed by the Minnesota Center for Corporate Responsibility in the United States. Following their adoption in 1994, worldwide endorsements have been sought.

There are a number of international agreements and treaties in place which provide guidelines for managing corporate social responsibility across a wide range of problems in the multinational context. Some of these multilateral compacts were discussed in Chapter 8.[106] Of particular interest to multinationals are the OECD Guidelines for Multinational Enterprises (1976) and the International Labor Office Tripartite Declaration of Principles Concerning Multinational Enterprises and Social Policy (1977). Based on their study of the international codes of conduct of the Organization for Economic Cooperation and Development (OECD), the International Chamber of Commerce (ICC), the International Labor Organization (ILO), and the United Nations, Payne, Raiborn, and Askvik[107] suggest that international standards of ethics should address six major issues:

1. *Organizational relations*—including competition, strategic alliances, and local sourcing;
2. *Economic relations*—including financing, taxation, transfer prices, local reinvestment, equity participation, and fiscal policies;
3. *Employee relations*—including compensation, safety, human rights, nondiscrimination, collective bargaining, whistle blowing, training, and sexual harassment;
4. *Customer relations*—including pricing, quality, and advertising;
5. *Industrial relations*—including technology transfer, research and development, infrastructure development, and organizational stability/ longevity; and
6. *Political relations*—including legal compliance, bribery and other corrupt activities, subsidies, tax incentives, environmental protection, and political involvement.[108]

Industries or individual firms can also develop self-regulatory codes. A corporate code of conduct is a public statement of the firm's values and guiding principles. The need for comprehensive and cohesive codes of conduct for firms involved in international business is widely recognized as an important issue. Donaldson reports that 90 percent of all Fortune 500 firms have codes of conduct and 70 percent have statements of vision and values. The percentages in Europe and Asia are lower but increasing rapidly.[109] An example of a U.S. multinational's code of ethics, which is comprehensive in recognizing relationships between the company and its many stakeholders, is Johnson & Johnson's Credo, which, in part, states:

> We are responsible to our employees, the men and women who work with us throughout the world. Everyone must be considered as an individual. We must respect their dignity and recognize their merit. They must have a sense

of security in their jobs. Compensation must be fair and adequate, and work-ing conditions clean, orderly, and safe. We must be mindful of ways to help our employees fulfill their family responsibilities. Employees must feel free to make suggestions and complaints. There must be equal opportunity for employment, development and advancement for those qualified. We must provide competent management, and their actions must be just and ethical. We are responsible to the communities in which we will live and work and to the world community as well. We must be good citizens—support good works and charities and bear our fair share of taxes. We must encourage civic im-provements and better health and education. We must maintain in good order the property we are privileged to use, protecting the environment and natural resources.[110]

A common difficulty with codes of conduct is their enforcement. The attitudes of senior management play a crucial role in developing, imple-menting, and sustaining high ethical standards. Expatriates, line mana-gers, and HR professionals may also play a role in institutionalizing adherence to ethics codes through a range of HR-related activities, in-cluding training and the performance–reward system. If self-regulatory mechanisms fail to shape the level of socially responsible behavior re-quired of multinationals by society, then firms can expect legislative measures will be called for to resolve conflicts between themselves and host and home countries. Such is the case with bribery.

Bribery: A Recurring Problem in International Business

Bribery and corruption top the list of the most frequent ethical problems encountered by international managers.[111] Macken estimates that about U.S.$85 billion is involved in bribes from industrialized countries to de-veloping nations.[112] Bribery involves the payment of agents to do things that are inconsistent with the purpose of their position or office in order to gain an unfair advantage. Bribery can be distinguished from so-called gifts and "facilitating" or "grease," payments. The latter are payments to motivate agents to complete a task they would routinely do in the normal course of their duties. While most people do not openly condone bribery, many argue for a lenient approach based on the view that bribery is necessary to do business. However, it is now generally agreed that bribery undermines public confidence in markets, adds to the cost of products, and may affect the safety and economic well-being of the gen-eral public.[113]

For these reasons, there is increased interest in the regulation of bribery. In 1977 the United States enacted the Foreign Corrupt Practices Act (FCPA) to prohibit U.S.-based firms from making bribery payments to foreign government officials. The FCPA also applies to individual U.S. citizens, nationals, and residents. The Act was amended in 1988 to permit "facilitating" payments. In addition, payments to agents violate the Act if it is known that the agent will use those payments to bribe a government official. Sanctions under the Act are severe. Corporate fines can go up to U.S.$2 million and individual penalties to U.S.$100,000 and five years imprisonment. The FCPA mandates record-keeping provisions to help ensure that illegal payments are not disguised as entertainment or business expenses.

The FCPA has been criticized because it places U.S. firms at a competitive disadvantage since European and Japanese firms do not face criminal prosecution for paying bribes to foreign officials.[114] Moreover, nine European countries, as well as Australia and New Zealand, have allowed firms to deduct bribery payments as "business expenses" from their taxable income; on this latter point, it should be noted that most countries require a receipt for such an expense, and receipts for bribes are relatively uncommon. The evidence on the effect of the FCPA is mixed. While some studies report that the Act has had adverse effects, other studies have shown that even though some business may have been lost, the Act has not made U.S. firms less competitive, nor has it caused U.S. exports to decline.[115]

In the absence of adequate international self-regulation to control bribery and corruption, the OECD countries have looked to uniform domestic government regulation to provide a level playing field. At the end of 1997, 34 member countries of the OECD reached formal agreement on an international convention that criminalizes corporate bribery of foreign officials. The *Convention on Combating Bribery of Foreign Public Officials in International Business Transactions* was signed on December 17, 1997. According to the Convention, each member country must introduce and enact its own legislation criminalizing bribery by the end of 1998. Thus it would seem that by the turn of the century the United States will not be alone in legislating against corruption and bribery in the international arena. At the instigation of the United States, the OECD Convention signatories have also been asked to adopt a resolution that prohibits the tax deductibility of bribes, and to rewrite their legislation to bring it into line with the Convention.

Some non-OECD countries have also moved to curtail bribery and corruption. For example, in Malaysia and Singapore several foreign firms caught bribing public officials have been declared ineligible to bid on future government contracts. The debate over payment to foreign officials is likely to continue well into the twenty-first century.

Implications for the HR Function of the Multinational Firm

Ethical issues are also people issues and thus the issues raised above have direct implications for the HR function. It is recognized that the HR function is responsible for many of the activities that build a sense of corporate identity,[116] such as staff selection and training. As we discussed in Chapter 2 (see Exhibit 2–10), corporate culture is one of the soft control mechanisms, and ethical codes of conduct—along with public statements regarding corporate values—are an important element of such normative control.

To achieve the goal of corporate social responsibility, HR professionals in multinationals may be required to:

- Minimize the exposure of employees to corrupt conduct by assisting in the development, publication, and implementation of appropriate codes of conduct;
- Ensure training programs cover areas of ethical concern—such as bribery, human rights, justice, and the common good—in a manner consistent with the multinational's objectives in this regard;
- Align performance appraisal and compensation systems so that they support the ethical stance taken;
- Be conversant with the type of requests that may be made of staff operating internationally—not just expatriates but also those who visit foreign markets in various capacities—and provide the necessary training so that they have the requisite negotiating skills to handle problem situations that may arise; and
- Ensure that employees understand the difference between corrupt bribery payments, gifts, and allowable facilitation payments. Given the strong positions taken by governments on ethical behavior, it is important that all staff are fully briefed on their responsibilities in this regard.

In conclusion, while people involved in international business activities face many of the same ethical issues as those in domestic business, the issues are made more complex because of the different social, economic, political, cultural, and legal environments in which multinationals operate. Some firms do prepare expatriate managers for the ethical choices they will face in relation to bribery and corruption. However, in their study of 31 U.S. firms, Carlson and Blodgett found that few provided their employees with information about the firm's stand on issues such as child labor, unfair trade practices, pirating of copyrights, and environmental protection.[117] This study indicates that many firms may need to place more emphasis on predeparture training and in-country orientation of expatriates that includes an ethics component covering such basic information. To not do so is likely to increase the risk that difficulties will arise in the operationalization of ethical responsibilities for multinationals.

Theoretical Developments in International HRM

Various researchers in the IHRM field have been endeavoring to develop a theoretical body of knowledge to provide the necessary robust frameworks and models pertaining to a more mature scientific field of inquiry. Many of these developments have been incorporated into the relevant chapters of this text where appropriate. Reviewing these theoretical contributions, it is possible to identify two streams of inquiry: the micro-level, which has concentrated on HRM activities particularly expatriate management, and the macro-level, which has a more strategic focus. Both streams of research are appropriate and critical to theory development.

Early work in the IHRM field has been dominated by large-scale quantitative studies by U.S. researchers on expatriate management issues in U.S. firms. These have a common approach in using HR managers as the respondents. The work by Tung, Black, Oddou, Mendenhall, Gregersen, and Harvey (reviewed in Chapters 3, 4, 5, and 7) are good examples of such contributions. These studies are important in that the empirical findings identified key issues and challenges in the use of expatriates in staffing subsidiary operations. More significantly, these researchers raised the profile of IHRM as an area of scientific inquiry.

Surveying HR managers is a logical and useful contribution to research and theory building, but it became somewhat inevitable that IHRM, as a scientific field, would need to consider other IHRM phenomena than expatriation management activities. It was also desirous for research to move beyond description—broadening methodological approaches to include inductive as well as deductive research. Some researchers, therefore, are using an inductive, exploratory approach. For example, Welch (see Chapter 2), Monks (Chapter 3), and Tahvanainen (Chapter 4) utilize qualitative case studies. Also, utilizing research methods that allow HR managers' perspectives to be supported by others such as expatriates and partners, as well as archival material and documentation, has yielded additional insights into IHRM activities and issues, and consideration of broader organizational factors. Other researchers have used quantitative methodology to determine linkages between a specific HRM activity and broader organizational strategies. For example, the investigation of Spanish multinationals' expatriate compensation approaches and subsidiary strategies by Bonache and Fernandez; and the study linking the HR function to firm performance by Stroh and Caligiuri.[118]

In a recent review of IHRM research trends, De Cieri and Dowling[119] identify a line of research that has come to be termed *strategic international human resource management (SIHRM)*. It considers the HRM issues and activities that result from, and impact on, the strategic activities and international concerns of multinationals.[120] This line of inquiry parallels that of strategic HRM, which focuses on the link between organizational strategy and performance, and HRM. Its strength, in terms of theory development, is that it draws on various schools in strategic management, rather than solely on domestic human resource management. Thus, institutional theory, resource dependence theory, transaction cost, the behavioral school, and the resource-based view have been drawn on in order to develop a more informed perspective of SIHRM. The theoretical framework derived by Schuler, Dowling, and De Cieri[121] is a good example of such work.

Commenting on the emerging body of research into SIHRM, De Cieri and Dowling remark that, while SIHRM as a distinct area of research has been a useful step, it may be more appropriate to speak of *strategic HRM in multinationals*. This allows a more balanced view to be taken of the similarities and differences between international and domestic HRM. To this end, De Cieri and Dowling propose a revised framework of SHRM in multinational firms, which is shown in Exhibit 9–2.

As depicted in Exhibit 9–2, multinationals operate in the context of worldwide conditions, including the exogenous contexts of industry, nation, region, and interorganizational networks and alliances. The

EXHIBIT 9–2   *Integrative Framework of Strategic HRM in Multinational Enterprises*

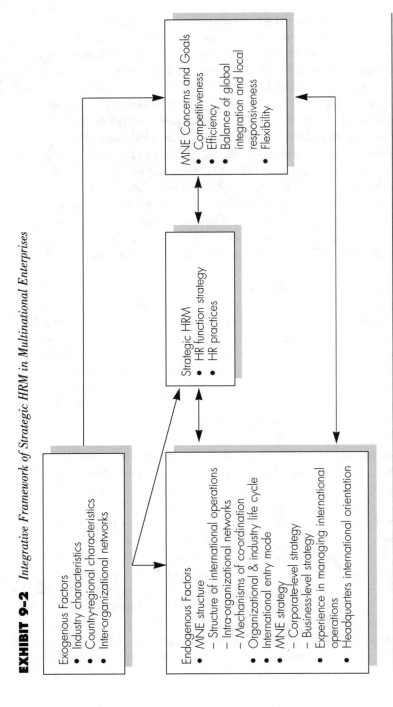

Source: H. De Cieri, and P.J. Dowling, 1998. Strategic human resource management in multinational enterprises: Theoretical and empirical developments, unpublished paper. Adapted from: R.S. Schuler, P.J. Dowling, and H. De Cieri, 1993. An integrative framework of strategic international human resource management, *Journal of Management*, vol. 19, pp. 419–459.

economic reforms in China and India, as discussed earlier in this chapter, are strong examples of the impact that the exogenous context has on HR practices. Likewise, the removal of internal trade barriers and integration of national markets in the European Union has brought a new range of interorganizational relationships. The introduction of the European Monetary Union from January 1999 has the potential to hold significant implications for interorganizational relationships. As indicated in their above figure, De Cieri and Dowling, therefore, argue that exogenous factors exert a direct influence on endogenous factors, SHRM strategy and practices, and multinational concerns and goals.

In the above exhibit, endogenous factors are shown in order of most "tangible" to most "intangible." Multinational structure is used as an umbrella term to cover structure of international operations, intraorganizational networks, and mechanisms of co-ordination (such as those outlined in Chapter 2). The life-cycle stage of the firm and the industry in which it operates are important influences for SHRM in multinationals as are international operation modes (although De Cieri and Dowling term these as international entry modes) and levels of firm strategy. Intangible endogenous factors include the multinational's experience in international business and its headquarters' international orientation.

Following developments in the literature, particularly that integrating resource dependence and resource-based perspectives,[122] the authors develop an argument for reciprocal relationships between endogenous factors, SHRM, and multinational concerns and goals, as indicated in Exhibit 9–2. It is also possible to identify reciprocal relationships between strategic issues and SHRM strategy and practices. De Cieri and Dowling refer to several studies that have shown that HR activities such as expatriate management are influenced by both endogenous and exogenous factors. One can see, for example, a similarity between these authors' endogenous factors and the firm-specific variables in the model developed by Welch, reviewed in Chapter 2. Effective SHRM is expected to assist the firm in achieving its goals and objectives. In supporting this position, De Cieri and Dowling refer to the emerging body of SHRM literature that examines the relationships between endogenous characteristics, SHRM strategy and practices, and firm performance or competitive advantage.[123] These authors, however, recognize that some research has suggested that multinationals will gain by utilizing and integrating appropriate SHRM strategy and practices to enhance firm performance,[124] but point out that important questions about the nature of this relationship remain.[125]

Thus, it appears that IHRM research is entering the second phase of theory building. Based on multiple-theory and multiple-method approaches, further work should move the level of analysis from the micro to the more strategic level. Further, the field is increasingly being driven by research outside of the United States. This is evident from the number of studies from scholars from Europe (including the Nordic countries and the United Kingdom), Asia, and the Pacific included in this book. While most research is still single-country, these various studies have identified common IHRM concerns facing firms as they internationalize, regardless of their country of origin. The real challenge is to develop innovative and effective research approaches including the conduct of multi-team, multi-country research that would support the repeated calls for multi-discipline, multi-level, and multi-method theory development. In so doing, scholars may answer some of the methodological criticisms we briefly discuss in the Appendix to this book.

CONCLUDING REMARKS

Throughout this book, we have endeavored to highlight the challenges faced by firms as they confront human resource management concerns related to international business operations. In the discussion of key aspects pertaining to the management of people in a multinational context, staffing foreign operations remains the critical issue. As we identified, dual-career couples and repatriation are emerging as constraints to the use of expatriates. However, simply switching to host-country nationals is not necessarily the answer. In markets characterized by an acute shortage of skilled staff, it may not be a viable option. More importantly, staff transfers are an important control mechanism. The movement of staff between subsidiaries and into parent-country operations remains an important part of informal control, through the establishment of personal networks and information channels, as well as assisting in knowledge and skills transfer, and the appreciation of global concerns. Thus, despite their cost and other reported disadvantages of their use, staff transfers remain a key mechanism for informal control, and thus expatriate management concerns remain of strategic importance.

However, as we have also stressed throughout this book, IHRM does not equal expatriate management. We pointed out in Chapter 2, for example, that a lot of activity—such as visits to foreign markets for negotiations, foreign intermediary management, and the like—occurs before, and alongside, that of expatriation. Managing people in a multinational context, we argue, is the essence of international human resource management. This requires a broader perspective of what operating internationally involves, and a clear recognition of the range of issues pertaining to all categories of staff operating in different functional, task, and managerial capacities is essential.

QUESTIONS

1. What are some of the common problems faced by multinationals operating in China and India?
2. Do you agree with the idea of universal ethical principles that transcend national and cultural boundaries or do you wish to develop an argument to defend ethical relativism? Explain your answer and provide examples.
3. What is your view of the recent international initiatives to criminalize foreign bribery? Justify your answer.
4. In what ways might the core ethical values and proposed guidelines for MNEs, identified in this chapter, apply to the HRM problems identified in both India and China?
5. In what way do exogenous and endogenous factors impact on the strategic HR strategy and practices of a multinational firm?

FURTHER READING

1. Budhwar, P.S., and P.R. Sparrow, 1997. Evaluating levels of strategic integration and devolvement of human resource management in India, *International Journal of Human Resource Management*, vol. 8, no. 4, pp. 476–494.
2. DeGeorge, R.T., 1993. *Competing with Integrity in International Business*, New York: Oxford.
3. Donaldson, T., 1989. *The Ethics of International Business*, New York: Oxford.
4. Lindholm, N., M. Tahvanainen, and I. Björkman, 1998 (forthcoming). Performance appraisal of host country employees: Western MNCs in China, in *International HRM: Contemporary Issues in Europe*, C. Brewster, and H. Harris, eds. London: Routledge.

5. Stroh, L.H., and P.M. Caligiuri, 1998. Strategic human resources: A new source for competitive advantage in the global arena, *International Journal of Human Resource Management*, vol. 9, no. 1, pp. 1–17.
6. Tung, R.L., and V. Worm, 1997. East meets West: Northern European expatriates in China, *Business and the Contemporary World*, vol. 9, no. 1, pp. 137–148.
7. Zhu, C.J., and P.J. Dowling, 1994. The impact of the economic system upon human resource management practices in China, *Human Resource Planning*, vol. 17, no. 4, pp. 1–21.

ENDNOTES

1. L. Putterman, 1992. Dualism and reform in China, *Economic Development and Cultural Change*, vol. 40, no. 3, p. 468.
2. 1996. *People's Daily*, December 19; T. Walker, and J.Ridding, 1996. Far less of an easy ride, *Financial Times*, May 10, p. 21; and 1996. *China Labor Statistical Yearbook*, Beijing, China: Statistical Publishing House.
3. See Y. Lu, and I. Björkman, 1997. MNC standardization versus localization: HRM practices in China-Western joint ventures. *The International Journal of Human Resource Management*, vol. 8, no. 5, pp. 614–628.
4. P.W. Beamish, 1993. The characteristics of joint ventures in the People's Republic of China. *Journal of International Marketing*, vol. 1, no. 2, pp. 29–48; J. Child, 1994. *Management in China during the Age of Reform*, London: Cambridge University Press; D. Ding, D. Fields, and S. Akhtar, 1997. An empirical study of human resource management policies and practices in foreign-invested enterprises in China: The case of Shenzen Special Economic Zone. *The International Journal of Human Resource Management*, vol. 8, no. 5, pp. 595–613. K. Goodall, and M. Warner, 1997. Human resources in Sino-foreign joint ventures: Selected case studies in Shanghai, compared with Beijing, *The International Journal of Human Resource Management*, vol. 8, no. 5, pp. 567–594; Y. Paik, C.M. Vance, and H.D. Stage, 1996. The extent of divergence in human resource practice across three Chinese national cultures: Hong Kong, Taiwan and Singapore. *Human Resource Management Journal*, vol. 6, no. 2, pp. 20–31.

5. M. Warner, 1996. Management of joint ventures in China, Paper presented at the conference on Cross-cultural Management in China, Baptist University, Hong Kong, August 26–28, p. 5.

6. Although the term *human resource management* has been commonly used in the relevant literature about Chinese management, the Western connotation does not readily apply. Before the reforms, personnel managers administering both workers and cadres at the enterprise level were policy implementers rather than strategic decision makers. In contrast, HRM in the Western context often focuses more on managing organizations than administrative activities. However, the term *human resource management* has become more common in China to show a move away from its traditional personnel and labor administration, and is used in this paper in this broader sense. See for example, J. Child, *Management in China During the Age of Reform*; T.A. Mahoney, and J.R. Deckop, 1986. Evolution of concept and practice in personnel administration/human resource management (PA/HRM), *Yearly Review of Management in the Journal of Management*, vol. 12, no. 2, pp. 223–241.

7. This section is partly based on C.J. Zhu, and P.J. Dowling, 1998. Employment systems and practices in China's industrial sector during and after Mao's regime, Paper presented at the 1998 Annual Meeting of the Academy of Management, San Diego, California.

8. S. Yabuki, 1995. *China's New Political Economy: The Giant Awakes*, S.M. Harner, trans. Oxford: Westview Press.

9. Y.J. Bian, 1994. Guanxi and the allocation of urban jobs in China. *The China Quarterly*, pp. 971–999; M.K. Nyaw, 1995. Human resource management in the People's Republic of China, in *Human Resource Management in the Pacific Rim*, L.F. Moore, and P.D. Jennings, eds. Berlin: Walter de Gruyter.

10. P.N. Lee, 1987. *Industrial Management and Economic Reform in China, 1949–1984*. New York: Oxford University Press.

11. L.J. Yu, and Z.X. Xin, eds. 1994. *Qiye laodong guanlixue jichu (Introduction to enterprise labour management)*, Beijing: China Labor Press. Z.J. Zhang, ed. 1991. *Laodongli guanli yu jiuye (Laborforce management and employment)*, Beijing: China Labour Press. See also, C. Tausky, 1991. Perestroika in the U.S.S.R. and China: Motivational lessons, *Work and Occupations*, vol. 18, no. 1, pp. 94–108.

12. A.G. Walder, 1986. *Communist Neo-traditionalism: Work and Authority in Chinese Industry*. Berkeley: University of California Press; M. Maurer-Fazio, 1995. Labor reform in China: Crossing the river by feeling the stones, *Comparative Economic Studies*, vol. 37, no. 4, pp. 111–123. See also A.H. Chan, 1990. Managerial reforms in Chinese enterprises, in *Advances in Chinese Industrial Studies*, J. Child, and M. Lockett, eds. vol. 1, part A, London: JAI press, pp. 167–177; S. Jackson, 1992. *Chinese Enterprise Management: Reforms in Economic Perspective*, Berlin, New York: Walter de Gruyter; S. Shi, 1995. A new system for utilising human resources. *Laodong Jinji yu Renli Ziyuan Guanli (Labour Economy and Human Resource Management)*, vol. 9, Beijing: China People University Press, pp. 8–10.

13. P. Howard, 1991. Rice bowls and job security: The urban contract labour system. *The Australian Journal of Chinese Affairs*, vol. 25, pp. 93–114; M. Korzec, 1988. Contract labor, the 'right to work' and new labor laws in the People's Republic of China. *Comparative Economic Studies (ASE)*, vol. 30, no. 2, pp. 117–149; C. Riskin, 1987. *China's Political Economy: The Quest for Development Since 1949*. Oxford: Oxford University Press.

14. M. Branine, 1997. Change and continuity in Chinese employment relationships, *New Zealand Journal of Industrial Relations*, vol. 22, no. 1, pp. 77–94; Howard, Rice bowls and job security; M. Warner, 1995. *The Management of Human Resources in Chinese Industry*, London: St. Martin's Press.

15. S.M. Zhao, 1994. Human resource management in China, *Asia Pacific Journal of Human Resources*, vol. 32, no. 2, Winter, pp. 3–12.

16. This part is based on C.J. Zhu, and P.J. Dowling, 1998. Performance appraisal in China, in *International Management in China*, J. Selmer, ed. London: Routledge, in press.

17. T.L. Su, and Q.F. Zhu, eds. 1992. *Ren shi xue dao lun (Fundamentals of personnel)*, Beijing: Beijing Normal College Press; G. Young, 1989. Party reforms, in *China: Modernization in the 1980s*, Cheng, ed. Hong Kong: The Chinese University Press, pp. 61–93.

18. J.P. Burns, 1989. Civil service reform in contemporary China, in *China: Modernisation in the 1980s*, Cheng, ed. Hong Kong: The Chinese University Press, pp. 95–130.

19. Walder, *Communist Neo-traditionalism: Work and Authority in Chinese Industry*, p. 132.

20. D.H. Brown, and M. Branine, 1995. Managing people in China's foreign trade corporations: Some evidence of change, *The International Journal of Human Resource Management*, vol. 6, no. 1, February, pp. 159–175; Walder, *Communist Neo-traditionalism: Work and Authority in Chinese Industry.*

21. Su, and Zhu, *Ren shi xue dao lun (Fundamentals of personnel).*

22. Child, *Management in China During the Age of Reform*; Brown, and Branine, Managing people in China's foreign trade corporations: Some evidence of change; J.P. Burns, 1989. Civil service reform in contemporary China, in *China: Modernisation in the 1980s*, Cheng, ed. Hong Kong: The Chinese University Press, pp. 95–130; S.J. Han, 1992. *Renshi Guanli Xue (Personnel Management)*, Anhui, China: Anhui People's Press; 1986. *Renshi Guanlixue Gaiyao (Introduction to Personnel Management)*, L.K. Zhao, ed. Beijing: China Labor Press.

23. S. Chen, ed. 1990. *Contemporary Labour and Personnel Administration Handbook*, Shanghai, China: People Publishing House; Su, and Zhu, *Ren shi xue dao lun (Fundamentals of personnel).*

24. H.J. Lu, and H.Z. An, 1991. *Xiandai qiye laodong renshi guanli (Personnel and labor administration in contemporary enterprises)*, Beijing: China Labor Press; 1992. *Laodong xinzheng guanli zhishi daquan (Encyclopedia of labor administration)*, J.Z. Xia, ed. Beijing: China Labor Press.

25. S.M. Zhao, 1995. *Zhongguo qiye renli ziyuan guanli (Human resource management in China's enterprises)*, Nanjing, China: Nanjing University Press.

26. Zhu, and Dowling, Performance appraisal in China.

27. Brown, and Branine, Managing people in China's foreign trade corporations: Some evidence of change; J.F. Huang, 1994. *Xiandai qiye zuzhi yu renli ziyuan guanli (Modern enterprise organisation and human resource management)*, Beijing: People's Daily Press; Nyaw, Human resource management in the People's Republic of China.

28. 1998. This section is based on C.J. Zhu, H. De Cieri, and P.J. Dowling, The reform of employee compensation in China's industrial enterprises, Paper presented at the Sixth Conference on International Human Resource Management, June 22–25, Paderborn: Germany.

29. W.H. Li, 1991. *Zhongguo gongzi zhidu (China's wage system)*, Beijing: China Labor Press. See also, L.M. Shore, B.W. Eagle, and M.J.

Jedel, 1993. China-United States joint ventures: A typological model of goal congruence and cultural understanding and their importance for effective human resource management, *International Journal of Human Resource Management*, vol. 4, no. 1, pp. 67–84; 1997. *Gongzi yu gongzi zhengyi chuli shiwu (Wage and wage arbitration)*, X.L. Wang, ed. Beijing: People's Court Press; S.M. Zhao, 1995. *Zhongguo qiye renli ziyuan guanli (Human resource management in China's enterprises)*, Nanjing, China: Nanjing University Press; and Y. Zhu, and I. Campbell, 1996. Economic reform and the challenge of transforming labor regulation in China, *Labour and Industry*, vol. 7, no. 1, p. 33.

30. K. Chen, 1995. *The Chinese Economy in Transition: Micro Changes and Macro Implications*, Singapore: Singapore University Press; Y.C. Xu, 1996. Deepening and widening the economic reform in China: From enterprise reform to macroeconomic stability, *The Journal of Developing Areas*, vol. 30, April, pp. 361–384.

31. S. Jackson, 1988. Management and labour in Chinese industry: A review of the literature, *Labour and Industry*, vol. 1, no. 2, pp. 335–363; A. Takahara, 1992. *The Politics of Wage Policy in Post-Revolutionary China*, London: The Macmillan Press Ltd. The floating wage aimed to link individual wages to enterprise and/or individual performance, and the range of wage fluctuation was usually half or less of the total income. The structural wage was usually composed of four parts: basic pay, post (or job-related) pay, seniority pay (based on the length of service), and bonus. See also, Child, *Management in China During the Age of Reform*; Nyaw, Human resource management in the People's Republic of China.

32. 1992. *Gangwei jineng gongzi shishi wenda (The implementation of post-plus-skills wage system)*, X.Y. Hu, and P. He, eds. Beijing: Wage Research Institute of the Ministry of Labor of China.

33. J.S. Henley, and M.K. Nyaw, 1987. The development of work incentives in Chinese industrial enterprises—material versus nonmaterial incentives, in *Management Reform in China*, M. Warner, ed. London: France Pinter; O. Laaksonen, 1988. *Management in China During and After Mao*, Berlin, New York: Walter de Gruyter; J. Nelson, and J. Reeder, 1985. Labor relations in China, *California Management Review*, vol. 27, no. 4, pp. 13–32; H.S. Tu, and C.A. Jones, 1991. Human resource management issues in Sino-U.S. business ventures, *Akron Business and Economic Review*, vol. 22, no. 4, Winter, pp. 18–28.

34. Ding, Fields, and Akhtar, An empirical study of human resource management policies and practices in foreign-invested enterprises in China: The case of Shenzen Special Economic Zone; Goodall, and Warner, Human resources in Sino-foreign joint ventures: Selected case studies in Shanghai, compared with Beijing; M.H. Zhao, and T. Nichols, 1996. Management control of labor in state-owned enterprises: Cases from the textile industry, *The China Journal*, vol. 36, July, pp. 1–21.

35. This section is based in part on C.J. Zhu, 1997. Human resource development in China during the transition to a new economic system, *Asia Pacific Journal of Human Resources*, vol. 35, no. 3, pp. 19–44.

36. Y.T. Guan, ed. 1990. *Zhiye peixun gailun (An introduction to vocational training)*, Beijing: China's Labor Press; Zhao, Human resource management in China; and Yu, and Xin, *Qiye laodong guanlixue jichu (Introduction to enterprise labour management)*.

37. Su, and Zhu, *Ren shi xue dao lun (Fundamentals of personnel)*; J. Borgonjon, and W.R. Vanhonacker, 1992. Modernizing China's managers, *The China Business Review*, September–October, Special Report, p. 12; A.H. Chan, 1990. Managerial reforms in Chinese enterprises, in *Advances in Chinese Industrial Studies*, J. Child, and M. Lockett, eds. vol. 1, part A, London: JAI Press, pp. 167–177; and Y. Sha, 1987. The role of China's managing directors in the current economic reform, *International Labor Review*, vol. 26, no. 6, pp. 691–701.

38. Yu, and Xin, *Qiye laodong guanlixue jichu (Introduction to enterprise labour management)*.

39. Guan, *Zhiye peixun gailun (An introduction to vocational training)*; Zhao, Human resource management in China.

40. CVQDV (China Vocational Qualification Development and Verification), 1994. *Enhancing China's Vocational Qualification Verification System*, vol. 7, Beijing: Vocational Qualification Verification Centre of the Ministry of Labor.

41. Child, *Management in China During the Age of Reform*; M. Warner, 1993. Human resource management 'with Chinese characteristics,' *International Journal of Human Resource Management*, vol. 4, no. 1, pp. 45–65.

42. Y. Lu, 1994. Cross-century human resource development, *Laodong Jingji yu Renli Ziyuan Guanli (Labor Economy and Human*

Resource Management), vol, 12, Beijing: China People's University, pp. 66–73.

43. M.A. Von Glinow, and M.B. Teagarden, 1990. Contextual determinants of human resource management effectiveness in international cooperative alliances: Evidence from the People's Republic of China, in *International Human Resource Management Review*, A. Nedd, ed. vol. 1, pp. 75–93; C.J. Zhu, 1997. Human resource development in China during the transition to a new economic system, *Asia Pacific Journal of Human Resources*, vol. 35, no. 3, pp. 19–44.

44. Yu, and Xin, *Qiye laodong guanlixue jichu (Introduction to enterprise labour management)*; Zhao, *Zhongguo qiye renli ziyuan guanli (Human resource management in China's enterprises)*.

45. M. Warner, 1997. Management-labour relations in the new Chinese economy, *Human Resource Management Journal*, vol. 7, no. 4, pp. 30–43: 40.

46. Beamish, The characteristics of joint ventures in the People's Republic of China.

47. Goodall, and Warner, 1997. Human resources in Sino-foreign joint ventures: Selected case studies in Shanghai, compared with Beijing.

48. J. Child, 1993. A foreign perspective on the management of people in China, in *Readings in Management, Organisation and Culture in East and Southeast Asia*, P. Blunt, and D. Richards, eds. Darwin: Northern Territory University Press, pp. 213–225; R.J. Fung, 1995. *Organizational Strategies for Cross-Cultural Cooperation: Management of Personnel in International Joint Ventures in Hong Kong and China*, The Netherlands: Eburon Publishers.

49. Fung, ibid.

50. A. Chan, 1995. The emerging patterns of industrial relations in China and the rise of two new labor movements, *China Information*, vol. IX, no. 4, pp. 36–59: 48.

51. Warner, Human resource management 'with Chinese characteristics,' p. 460.

52. Zhu, Human resource development in China.

53. R. Tomlinson, 1997. You get what you pay for, corporate recruiters in China find, *Fortune*, April 28, pp. 218–219.

54. G. Hofstede, 1993. Cultural constraints in management theories, *Academy of Management Executive*, vol. 7, no. 1, pp. 81–94.

55. Y. Zhao, 1995. 'Chinese' motivation theory and application in China: An overview, in *Effective Organizations and Social Values*, H.S.R. Kao, D. Sinha, and S.H. Ng, eds. New Delhi: Sage, p. 127.

56. P. Aiello, 1991. Building a joint venture in China: The case of Chrysler and the Beijing Jeep Corporation, *Journal of General Management*, vol. 17, no. 2, pp. 47–64; Ding, Fields, and Akhtar, An empirical study of human resource management policies and practices in foreign-invested enterprises in China: The case of Shenzen Special Economic Zone; A.G. Walder, 1991. Workers, managers and the state: The reform era and the political crisis of 1989, *China Quarterly*, vol. 127, pp. 247–492.

57. Zhu, De Cieri, and Dowling, The reform of employee compensation in China's industrial enterprises.

58. 1996. *The China Business Review*, July–August, p. 46; S. Melvin, and K. Sylvester, 1997. Shipping out, *The China Business Review*, May–June, pp. 30–34.

59. T.L. Kamis, 1996. Education for the PRC executive, *The China Business Review*, July–August, pp. 36–39.

60. S. Melvin, 1996. Training the troops, *The China Business Review*, March–April, pp. 22–28.

61. *Documents* 1997. Jiang Zemin's report—Hold high the great banner of Deng Xiaoping theory for an all-round advancement of the cause of building socialism with Chinese characteristics into the 21st century, *Beijing Review*, October 6–12, p. 20.

62. According to ranking in terms of purchasing power parity (PPP). See International Institute for Management Development (IMD), 1997. *The World Competitiveness Yearbook 1997*, Lausanne: IMD. The *Financial Times* gave a 1997 estimate of India's population in its June 24, 1997 Supplement on India. The 1991 Census records 846 million. Further statistical information about India can be accessed from the following website: http://www.meadv.gov.in/info/profile/intro.htm.

63. M. Tayeb, 1996. India: A non-tiger of Asia, *International Business Review*, vol. 5, no. 5, pp. 425–445.

64. 1997. *Financial Times*, Supplement on India, June 24, p. 26.

65. 1992. Rao's new dowry, *Far Eastern Economic Review*, February 20, p. 40.

66. Price Waterhouse, 1993. *Doing Business in India*, Calcutta: Price Waterhouse.

67. International Institute for Management Development (IMD), 1997. *The World Competitiveness Yearbook 1997*, Lausanne: IMD.

68. R. Geissbauer, and H. Siemsen, 1996. *Strategies for the Indian Market: Experiences of Indo-German Joint Ventures*, Bombay: Indo-German Chamber of Commerce.

69. Australian Department of Foreign Affairs and Trade, 1995. *Country Economic Brief: India*, Canberra: Department of Foreign Affairs and Trade.

70. 1996. Review of Information Technology, Part II, *Financial Times*, November.

71. 1997. India's software industry, *Financial Times*, Special Report, December.

72. Some U.S. studies, for example, record 50 percent of IJVs failing, while others put the figure as high as 70 percent. Consequently, writers in this area stress the importance of building up a relationship between the partners that will encourage cooperation and trust. See for example, S. Schuler, S.E. Jackson, P.J. Dowling, D.E. Welch, and H. De Cieri, 1991. Formation of an international joint venture: Davidson instrument panel, *Human Resource Planning*, vol. 14, no. 1, pp. 51–60. R.S. Schuler, P.J. Dowling, and H. De Cieri, 1992. The formation of an international joint venture: Marley automotive components, *European Management Journal*, vol. 10, no. 3, pp. 304–309.

73. J-L Schaun, 1988. How to control a joint venture even as a minority partner, *Journal of General Management*, vol. 14, no. 1, p. 5. For a summary of the literature on success factors, see P. Lorange, and G.J.B. Probst, 1987. Joint ventures as self-organizing systems: A key to successful joint venture design and implementation, *Columbia Journal of World Business*, vol. 22, no. 2, pp. 71–77.

74. M.A. Lyles, 1987. Common mistakes of joint venture experienced firms, *Columbia Journal of World Business*, vol. 22, no. 2, p. 80. See also, D. Lei, and J.W. Slocum, 1991. Global strategic alliances: Payoffs and pitfalls, *Organizational Dynamics*, Winter, pp. 44–62; W.F. Cascio, and M.G. Serapio, 1991. Human resource systems in an international alliance: The undoing of a done deal?, *Organizational Dynamics*, Winter, pp. 63–74.

75. 1994. East Asia Analytical Unit, *India's economy at the Midnight Hour: Australia's India Strategy*, Canberra: Department of Foreign Affairs. See also, S. Sen, 1996. Fettered by corruption, *Business India*, November 18–December 1, p. 186; H.B. Rajshekar, and

T. Raman, 1994. Awaiting the deluge, *Business India*, November 7–20, pp. 141–143.

76. D. Khambata, and R. Ajami, 1992. *International Business: Theory and Practice*, New York: Macmillan Publishing Company.

77. S.N. As-Saber, P.J. Dowling, and P.W. Liesch, (forthcoming). The role of human resource management in international joint ventures: A study of Australian-Indian joint ventures, *International Journal of Human Resource Management*.

78. S. Tomassen, L.S. Welch, and G. Benito, 1997. Norwegian companies in India: Operation mode choice, Paper presented at the 23rd Annual Meeting of the European International Business Academy, Stuttgart, December.

79. G. Hofstede, 1980. *Culture's Consequences*, Beverly Hills, CA: Sage Publications.

80. I.J. Sharma, 1994. The culture context of Indian managers, *Management and Labour Studies*, vol. 9, no. 2, pp. 72–80.

81. S. Shane, 1994. The effect of national culture on the choice between licensing and direct foreign investment, *Strategic Management Journal*, vol. 15, no. 8, pp. 627–642.

82. C.S.V. Ratnam, 1995. Economic liberalization and the transformation of industrial relations policies in India, in *Employment Relations in the Growing Asian Economies*, A. Verma, T.A. Kochan, and R.D. Lansbury, eds. London: Routledge.

83. The labor force in India has a reputation for being "militant and obstructionist." See R. Thakur, Restoring India's economic health, *Third World Quarterly*, vol. 14, no. 1, pp. 137–157. See also Ratnam, Economic liberalization and the transformation of industrial relations policies in India; P. Joshi, 1995. Liberalisation ushered problems for workers, *The Pioneer* (Delhi), December 30, p. 3; and Tayeb, India: A non-tiger of Asia.

84. H.C. Jain, and C.S.V. Ratnam, 1994. Affirmative action in employment for the scheduled castes and the scheduled tribes in India, *International Journal of Manpower*, vol. 15, pp. 6–25; and Sharma, The culture context of Indian managers.

85. See Tayeb, India: A non-tiger of Asia; and Ratnam, Economic liberalization and the transformation of industrial relations policies in India; and L. Clarke, and M.A. Von Glinow, 1996. From India to China: A cross-cultural comparative assessment of management practices in Asia, Paper presented at the 13th Pan-Pacific Conference, Chiba, Japan.

86. S.N. As-Saber, P.J. Dowling, and P.W. Liesch, 1997. The role of human resource management in international joint ventures: A study of Australian-Indian joint ventures, *Enhancing Global Business Knowledge Through Business, Government and Academic Community Interface: Surviving Change in the International Business Environment by Developing Dynamic Business Strategies and Policies*, Proceedings of Sixth World Business Congress, International Management Development Association, pp. 21–29. This trend is also observed by R. Jacob, 1992. India: Open for business, *Fortune*, August 10, pp. 20–24; and M. Vicziany, 1993. Australian companies in India: The ingredients for successful entry into the Indian market, in *Australia-India Economic Links: Past, Present and Future*, M. Vicziany, ed. Nedlands, Western Australia: Indian Ocean Centre for Peace Studies, pp. 24–83.

87. This case was prepared by D. Welch and is based on information obtained from Unilever's website, and a report by Miriam Jordan, 1997. Role model for the new multi-nationals, *Financial Times*, India Survey, June 24, *India Business*, p. 19.

88. *The Economist*, 1994. An Indian tiger, April 9, p. 15; and 1994. India's businesses: Blinking in the sunlight, April 9, pp. 76–78.

89. Price Waterhouse, *Doing Business in India*.

90. 1995. On the threshold of a take-off into high economic growth, *Asian Business Review*, June, pp. 22–24.

91. G. Koretz, 1996. Asia's getting the big raises, *Business Week*, November 4, p. 16.

92. S.N. As-Saber, P.W. Liesch, and P.J. Dowling, 1997. Human resource practices in international joint ventures: Preliminary evidence from Australian-Indian joint ventures, *International Business Strategies for Asia-Pacific at the Dawn of the 21st Century*, Asia-Pacific Area Conference Proceedings, Academy of International Business, pp. 121–126.

93. D. Lei, and J.W. Slocum, 1991. Global strategic alliances: Payoffs and pitfalls, *Organizational Dynamics*, Winter, pp. 44–62.

94. P.J. Dowling, S.N. As-Saber, and P.W. Liesch, 1996. International joint ventures as a mechanism for accessing skills sets in culturally different societies: A case for Indo-Australian joint ventures in India, Paper presented at the 16th Annual International Strategic Management Society Conference, Phoenix, U.S.A., November 10–13.

95. Milton Friedman, a Nobel Prize winning economist, strongly endorses this view. See, for example, M. Friedman, 1970. The social responsibility of business is to increase its profits, *New York Times Magazine*, September 13, pp. 32–33, 122, 126.

96. See, for example, R.E. Freeman, 1997. A stakeholder theory of the modern corporation, in *Ethical Theory and Business*, T.L. Beauchamp, and N.E. Bowie, eds. 5th ed. Upper Saddle River, NJ: Prentice Hall, pp. 66–75.

97. The July 1997 special issue of *Business Ethics Quarterly* addresses the growing interconnectedness of ethical issues between international and domestic business. It also reports the proceedings of the First World Congress of Business, Economics and Ethics (1996).

98 For a more complete discussion of the factors impacting upon complexity in international business ethics, see R.T. De George, 1995. *Business Ethics*, 4th ed. Englewood Cliffs, NJ: Prentice Hall, pp. 475–485.

99. For a discussion of ethical relativism, see De George, ibid.

100. T. Donaldson, 1996. Values in tension: Ethics away from home, *Harvard Business Review*, September–October, pp. 48–62.

101. R.M. Green, 1994. *The Ethical Manager*, New York: Macillan, p. 62.

102. A number of comparative studies have found little variation from culture to culture in fundamental ethical beliefs. What differences existed between members of the various cultural groups, appeared to be more a function of differences in their reasoning and decision-making processes rather than core ethical values. See, for example, R. Abrat, D. Nel, and N.S. Higgs, 1992. An examination of the ethical beliefs of managers using selected scenarios in a cross-cultural environment, *Journal of Business Ethics*, vol. 11, pp. 29–35; D. Izraeli, 1988. Ethical beliefs and behavior among managers: A cross-cultural perspective, *Journal of Business Ethics*, vol. 7, pp. 263–271; M. Nyaw, and I. Ng, 1994. A comparative analysis of ethical beliefs: A four country study, *Journal of Business Ethics*, vol. 13, no. 7, pp. 543–556; M.W. Small, 1992. Attitudes towards business ethics held by Western Australian students: A comparative study, *Journal of Business Ethics*, vol. 11, pp. 745–752; J. Tsalikis, and D.J. Fritzsche, 1989. Business ethics: A literature review with a focus on marketing ethics, *Journal of Business Ethics*, vol. 8, pp. 695–743; J. Tsalikis, and O. Nwachukwu, 1989. An in-

vestigation on the ethical beliefs: Differences between Greeks and Americans, *Journal of International Consumer Marketing*, Spring, vol. 1; J. Tsalikis, and O. Nwachukwu, 1991. A comparison of Nigerian to American views of bribery and extortion in international commerce, *Journal of Business Ethics*, vol. 10, pp. 85–98.

103. Donaldson, Values in tension: Ethics away from home.

104. Ironically, the market mechanism itself may yet provide a potent mechanism for multinationals to be good corporate citizens as investors as well as the broader communities of many countries demand greater corporate responsibility than was generally evident during the profligate 1980s. See, for example, D. Spar, 1998. The spotlight and the bottom line, *Foreign Affairs*, vol. 77, no. 2, pp. 7–12.

105. Preamble to the Caux Round Table Principles. Available from *Business Ethics*, 52 S. 10th St., Suite 110, Minneapolis, MN 55403. Reprinted in L.P. Hartman, 1998. *Perspectives in Business Ethics*, Chicago: McGraw-Hill, pp. 723–726. See also web site: www.bath. ac.uk/Centres/Ethical/Papers/caux.htm.

106. A useful description and discussion of multilateral compacts is given by R.A. Buchholz, 1995. *Business Environment and Public Policy Implications for Management*, Upper Saddle River, NJ: Prentice Hall, Chapter 16.

107. D. Payne, C. Raiborn, and J. Askvik, 1997. A global code of business ethics, *Journal of Business Ethics*, vol. 16, no. 16, pp. 1727–1735.

108. For a comprehensive set of guidelines derived from international codes, see W.C. Frederick, 1991. The moral authority of transnational corporate codes, in *Ethical Theory and Business*, T.L. Beauchamp, and N.E. Bowie, eds. pp. 576–588.

109. Donaldson, Values in tension: Ethics away from home.

110. J.R. Boatright, 1997. *Ethics and the Conduct of Business*, 2d ed. Upper Saddle River, NJ: Prentice Hall.

111. See Green, *The Ethical Manager*, p. 290 for a list of practices that pose the most frequent problems for international managers.

112. J. Macken, 1998. Dirty money, *The Australian Financial Review*, March 31, p. 13.

113. An interesting nongovernment lobby group in this field is the Berlin-based *Transparency International (TI)* group, which publishes an annual Corruption Perception Index. For an up-to-

date TI Corruption Index consult the Internet at http://www/gwdg.de/~uwvw/icr.htm.

114. T.L. Carson, 1984. Bribery, extortion, and the foreign corrupt practices act, *Philosophy and Public Affairs*, pp. 66–90.

115. De George, *Business Ethics*.

116. M. Alvesson, and P.O. Berg, 1992. *Corporate Culture and Organizational Symbolism*, Berlin: Walter de Gruyter.

117. Cited in Hartman, *Perspectives in Business Ethics*.

118. J. Bonache, and Z. Fernandez, 1997. Expatriate compensation and its link to the subsidiary strategic role: A theoretical analysis, *Journal of International Human Resource Management*, vol. 8, no. 4, pp. 457–475; L.K. Stroh, and P.M. Caligiuri, 1998. Strategic human resources: A new source for competitive advantage in the global arena, *International Journal of Human Resource Management*, vol. 9, no. 1, pp. 1–17.

119. H. De Cieri, and P.J. Dowling, 1998 (forthcoming). Strategic human resource management in multinational enterprises: Theoretical and empirical developments, in *Research and Theory in SHRM: An Agenda for the 21st Century*, Wright et. al., eds. Greenwich, CT: JAI Press. This section of the chapter draws from the material in this article.

120. R.S. Schuler, P.J. Dowling, and H. De Cieri, 1993. An integrative framework of strategic international human resource management, *Journal of Management*, vol. 19, pp. 419–459.

121. Ibid.

122. S. Taylor, S. Beechler, and N. Napier, 1996. Towards an integrative model of strategic international human resource management, *Academy of Management Review*, vol. 21, pp. 959–985; K. Kamoche, 1997. Knowledge creation and learning in international HRM, *International Journal of Human Resource Management*, vol. 8, pp. 213–222.

123. B. Becker, and B. Gerhart, 1996. The impact of human resource management on organizational performance: Progress and prospects, *Academy of Management Journal*, vol. 39, no. 4, pp. 779–801; L. Dyer, and T. Reeves, 1995. Human resource strategies and firm performance: What do we know and where do we need to go?, *International Journal of Human Resource Management*, vol. 6, pp. 656–670.

124. M. Festing, 1997. International human resource management strategies in multinational corporations: Theoretical assumptions and empirical evidence from German firms, *Management International Review*, vol. 37, no. 1, special issue, pp. 43–63; S.J. Kobrin, 1994. Is there a relationship between a geocentric mind-set and multinational strategy?, *Journal of International Business Studies*, vol. 25, pp. 493–511.

125. P.M. Caligiuri, and L.K. Stroh, 1995. Multinational corporate management strategies and international human resource practices: Bringing IHRM to the bottom line, *International Journal of Human Resource Management*, vol. 6, pp. 494–507; R.B. Peterson, J. Sargent, N.K. Napier, and W.S. Shim, 1996. Corporate expatriate HRM policies, internationalization, and performance in the world's largest MNCs, *Management International Review*, vol. 36, pp. 215–230; P. Sparrow, R.S. Schuler, and S.E. Jackson, 1994. Convergence or divergence: Human resource practices and policies for competitive advantage worldwide, *International Journal of Human Resource Management*, vol. 5, pp. 267–299.

A P P E N D I X

PART A: RESEARCH ISSUES

The field of international HRM, like that of international management, has yet to build a rigorous body of theory. For example, Schollhammer[1] noted that much of the field of international management was criticized as being descriptive and lacking in analytical rigor, ad hoc and expedient in research design and planning, self-centered in the sense that existing research literature is frequently ignored, and lacking a sustained research effort to develop case material.

To a certain extent, these criticisms remain valid some 23 years later. There are several reasons for this. First, until recently, the field has tended to be regarded by many management and HRM researchers as a marginal academic area. This attitude is reflected in the relatively small number of stand-alone courses in IHRM on the teaching side, and the lack of visibility of IHRM researchers at international business conferences. One could add that the dominance of economics in the international business field to date, with its focus on foreign direct investment, is a contributing factor here.

A second reason for the lack of international research is cost. International studies are invariably more expensive than domestic studies, and this is a liability for international researchers in a competitive research funding environment.[2] In addition, international research takes more time, involves more travel, and frequently requires the cooperation of host-country organizations, government officials, and researchers. Development of a stream of research is consequently much more difficult.

Third, there are major methodological problems involved in the area of international management and HRM. These problems greatly increase

307

the complexity of doing international research and, as Adler[3] has noted, frequently are impossible to solve with the rigor usually required of within-culture studies by journal editors and reviewers. The major methodological problems in this area are:

- Defining culture;
- The emic–etic distinction;
- Static group comparisons; and
- Translation and stimulus equivalence.

The problems of defining culture and the emic–etic distinction were discussed in Chapter 1. In this appendix, we briefly explore the remaining two problem areas.

Static Group Comparisons

An enduring issue in international research is that virtually all crosscultural comparisons are based on "static group designs."[4] The difficulty with static group comparisons in international research is that subjects are not randomly assigned from a superordinate population to different levels of a treatment variable. In practice, it is impossible for crosscultural researchers to avoid this methodological problem. Ill-defined notions of culture as an independent variable further compound this difficulty. As Malpass[5] has observed,

> No matter what attribute of culture the investigator prefers to focus upon or to interpret as the causative variable, any other variable correlated with the alleged causative variable could potentially serve in an alternative explanation of a mean difference between two or more local populations.

As a practical solution to this problem, Malpass recommends that investigators attempt to obtain data on as many rival explanations as possible and then demonstrate that they are less plausible (by conducting post hoc statistical analyses, for example) than the investigator's favored interpretation.[6]

Translation and Stimulus Equivalence

Another issue in international research is that of translation and stimulus equivalence. Researchers need to be aware that problems may arise when translating concepts central to one culture into the language of another culture. Triandis and Brislin[7] note that the problem of translation has received a great deal of attention in the literature[8] and that translation problems should be "a starting point for research rather than a frustrating end to one's aspirations for data collection." Using methods such as the decentering technique,[9] which involves translating from the original to the target language and back again through several iterations, a researcher can test to see if there is any emic coloring of the concepts under investigation. If there are few differences between the original and target translation, then stimulus equivalence has been demonstrated.

Stimulus equivalence problems may also arise on a more subtle level when the researcher and target population speak the same language and national differences are less obvious (in the case, for example, of a U.S. researcher studying Australian managers).

A related point is the need for non-native speakers to translate research findings into English for publication in English language journals. Again, techniques such as decentering are important because the language used during the data collection stage differs from that used at the reporting stage. This applies to within-country as well as across-country studies. It is particularly critical for qualitative data such as that obtained through open-ended items on mail questionnaires and interviews. As with the emic–etic distinction, awareness of possible problems is a precondition for dealing with translation and stimulus equivalence problems.

Different cultures have different attitudes towards mail questionnaires and this may influence a poor response rate. Commenting on the difficulties of conducting large scale, crossnational surveys, Harzing[10] bemoans the paucity of articles that an international business researcher can consult for assistance. She compares this with the wealth of information available about, and congruency of opinion on, conducting mail surveys in a domestic setting. Harzing found, in her study of multinationals operating in 22 countries, that the higher the cultural distance between the country of the researcher (the sender) and the targeted country (the receiver), the lower the response rate. She admits that using English as the language of the questionnaire was probably a contributing factor and speculates that the international orientation of the respondent may have a positive influence on the response rate.

PART B: RESOURCES IN INTERNATIONAL HRM

This section contains a short review of major resources that may be helpful for additional material for teaching and research purposes. It is meant only as a starting point and as a way of illustrating the diverse nature of resources now available through electronic databases. We leave it up to the individual to "surf the Net" and explore firms' home pages.

IHRM-Related Web Sites

http://www.shrm.org/hrlinks/intl.htm
This is the (U.S.) Society for Human Resource Management (SHRM) home page list of International HR web sites.

http://www.shrm.org/docs/IIHR.html
Homepage of the Institute for International HR, a division of the Society for Human Resource Management (SHRM).

This home page is valuable in its details of the *International Human Resource Management Reference Guide*, mentioned later in this Appendix.

http://www.the-hrnet.com/
This is the Web site for Human Resource Professionals worldwide.

http://www.cba.hawaii.edu/aib/
The Academy of International Business home page.

http://www.arthurandersen.com/hcs/globalhr/linkhr.htm
Arthur Andersen–International Executive Services: IHRM Link. A list of Arthur Andersen services related to global HRM and expatriation, and links to other web sites relevant to IHRM. For example, one can obtain details of the results of the R.L Tung–Arthur Andersen survey entitled, A study of the expatriation/repatriation process, referred to in this text, particularly Chapters 3 and 7.

http://www.mcb.co.uk/apmforum/nethome.htm
Produced by MCB publishers, this has more general Asia-Pacific management information.

http://www.ihrim.org/
Home page of the International Association for Human Resource Information Management.

http://www.hrhq.com/index.html
Includes access to a searchable database of 194 articles from *Personnel Journal*.

http://www.ipma-hr.org/
Home page of the International Personnel Management Association (IPMA), a professional association for public personnel professionals, primarily those who work in federal, state, or local government.

The page includes a list of useful HRM sites around the world.

http://www.ipd.co.uk/
Home page of the Institute of Personnel and Development, UK.

http://www.workindex.com/
A search engine (based at Cornell University) targeting work and HR-related web sites.

http://www.euen.co.uk/
The EU Employers' Network and the Personnel Policy Research Unit.

http://www.library.yale.edu/govdocs/euinfor.html
This has links to European Institutions, journal and official European Union texts.

http://www.eurunion.org/
The U.S. site of the European Union.

http://www.ibrc.bschool.ukans.edu/index.htm
The Kansas University International Business Resource Center home page. Aimed at small and medium-sized companies, this web site includes a good list of other web sites.

http://ciber.bus.msu.edu/
The World Wide Web server of the Center for International Business Education and Research (CIBER) at Michigan State University.

http://ciber.centers.purdue.edu/
CIBERWeb, the Internet Hub of the USA's Centers for International Business Education and Research.

http://dylee.keel.econ.ship.edu/intntl/int_home.htm
A list of internet resources for international economics and business.

http://www.webcom.com/one/world/
International business kiosk includes basic information, for example, time zones, voltage, accommodation, car rentals, visa information.

http://www.ita.doc.gov/
This site is produced and maintained by the International Trade Administration, U.S. Department of Commerce.

http://www.windhamint.com/
Windham International's web site provides information about international relocation and expatriate management.

http://www.erc.org/
Employee Relocation Council's web site provides information about international relocation and expatriate management.

http://www.fedworld.gov/
Fedworld information network.

http://www.expatworld.com/
Magazine for expatriates.

http://www.livingabroad.com/
Magazine for expatriates.

http://www.expatforum.com/
Another site aimed at expatriates, with a chat line.

http://www.hbsp.harvard.edu
CD-Rom interactive program on managing across cultures.

http://www.travalang.com/
Online language lessons.

http://www.unicc.org/unctad/en/aboutorg/inbrief.htm
United Nations Centre on Transnational Corporations and International Trade.

http://www.gwdg.de/-uwvw/icr.htm
Transparency International's Corruption Index—ranks over 50 countries on perceived level of corruption.

Other Resources

The Institute for International Human Resources, a division of the Society for Human Resource Management, produces a *Reference Guide* that is updated regularly. It lists resource organizations, expatriate policies, embassy listings, and web sites. It contains a glossary of terms used in IHRM, classified and alphabetically grouped into six major HRM functional areas: Management Practices, Employment, Training and Development, Employee and External Relations, Compensation and Benefits, and other HRM (such as travel).

The 1997–98 International Human Resource Management Reference Guide can be obtained from the SHRM Store, P.O. Box 930, Atlanta, GA 31193. The cost is U.S.$75 per copy (overseas rate U.S.$85 per copy U.S.$/U.S. Bank). Further details can be obtained by visiting the home page listed above.

ENDNOTES

1. H. Schollhammer, 1975. Current research in international and comparative management issues, *Management International Review*, vol. 15, no. 2–3, pp. 29–40.
2. See N. Adler, 1983. Cross-cultural management research: The ostrich and the trend, *Academy of Management Review*, vol. 8, pp. 226–232.
3. Ibid.
4. See R.S. Bhagat, and S.J. McQuaid, 1982. Role of subjective culture in organizations: A review and directions for future research, *Journal of Applied Psychology*, vol. 67, pp. 653–685; D.T. Campbell, and J. Stanley, 1966. *Experimental and Quasi-Experimental Design for Research*, Chicago: Rand-McNally; and R.S. Malpass, 1977. Theory and method in cross-cultural psychology, *American Psychologist*, vol. 32, pp. 1069–1079.
5. Malpass, Theory and method, p. 1071.
6. See L. Kelly, and R. Worthley, 1981. The role of culture in comparative management: A cross-cultural perspective, *Academy of Management Journal*, vol. 24, pp. 164–173; and P.J. Dowling, and T.W. Nagel, 1986. Nationality and work attitudes: A study of Australian and American business majors, *Journal of Management*, vol. 12, pp. 121–128, for further discussion on this point.
7. H.C. Triandis, and R.W. Brislin, 1984. Cross-cultural psychology, *American Psychologist*, vol. 39, pp. 1006–1016.
8. See R. Brislin, 1976. *Translation: Applications and Research*, New York: Gardner Press, for a review of this literature.
9. O. Werner, and D. Campbell, 1970. Translating, working through interpreters, and the problem of decentering, in *A Handbook of*

Method in Cultural Anthropology, R. Naroll, and R. Cohen, eds. New York: Natural History Press.

10. A-V. Harzing, 1997. Response rates in international mail surveys: Results of a 22-country study, *International Business Review*, vol. 6, no. 6, pp. 641–665.

I N D E X